TW

# Teacher Power —
# Professionalization
# and
# Collective Bargaining

# Teacher Power — Professionalization and Collective Bargaining

Donald A. Myers
State University of New York, Albany

**Lexington Books**
D.C. Heath and Company
Lexington, Massachusetts
Toronto          London

**Library of Congress Cataloging in Publication Data**

Myers, Donald A
    Teacher power.

    Bibliography: p.
    1. Teaching as a profession. 2. Collective
bargaining – Teachers – United States. I. Title.
LB1775.M9        371.1'0023        72-6946
ISBN 0-669-84558-2

Third Printing June 1974

Published simultaneously in Canada.

Printed in the United States of America.

International Standard Book Number: 0-669-84558-2

Library of Congress Catalog Card Number: 72-6946

To My Mother and Father

209642

# CONTENTS

# LIST OF ILLUSTRATIONS

# LIST OF TABLES

# PREFACE

Teachers are becoming a discipline problem. They are no longer waiting passively for others to seek their advice. They are offering their advice whether it is wanted or not. They are demanding the right to make decisions concerning their personal welfare, the educational program for students, and the governance of their profession. They are no longer willing to remain silent or engage in collective begging — advising legislatures, boards of education, and administrators who then make decisions for them. They are demanding autonomy — the right of all professionals to govern their own affairs. Teachers, in other words, are becoming professionals.[a]

I became interested in teacher professionalization the first year I was a teacher. At that time, an atrocious textbook was imposed upon me and my students by the department chairman. I was not permitted to substitute another textbook; however, I did not require my students to read it. My colleagues did not hire me, evaluate my teaching, or determine my tenure. I had no welfare benefit provisions other than ten days sick leave. I had no control over such questions as class size, and the principal looked startled when I refused to serve lunchroom duty or patrol the corridors between classes.

As I continued to think about teacher decision making, I wrote a monograph in 1970 concerned with who should make what decisions in curriculum and instruction. The monograph spoke to an ideal, but my concept of a theoretical ideal began to conflict with the world of reality facing teachers. This conflict became more evident with the increase in collective bargaining and teacher professionalization. In reading this book, it is hoped that teachers will become alert to the arduous task ahead, since the professionalization of an occupation is not achieved without a struggle.

While the book is intended primarily for teachers, it should be extremely useful for prospective teachers who are being thrust into an environment demanding peer and administrative adjustments that may be as difficult to achieve as their adjustments to students. This suggests that the teacher not begin teaching without a minimal knowledge of what constitutes a profession, the characteristics of the school as a bureaucracy, the rationale for collective bargaining, as well as some knowledge of concepts such as power, authority, and autonomy.

Administrators, too, should benefit by reading the book. The role of the administrator is being altered dramatically by the rising power of teachers. The administrator who survives the coming decade will be one who understands the shift in the authority structure of the school and who develops a leadership style

---

a. Profession, professionalization, professionalism, professional group, and professionals are defined at the beginning of Chapter 2.

complementary to that structure. Those who fail will do so because they persist unknowingly in using leadership techniques that were successful in an age that is now history — an age when teachers were obedient, compliant, and powerless.

# ACKNOWLEDGMENTS

Several persons have assisted me in the preparation of this book. In its initial development, I benefited by reading several unpublished manuscripts by Richard Williams, assistant dean for student affairs, Graduate School of Education, University of California, Los Angeles. He was also kind enough to read a late draft of the manuscript and offer suggestions. Bruce Joyce, professor of education, Teachers College, Columbia University (and his wife, Betsy), read the manuscript and suggested publishers. Robert Bhaerman, director of educational research, American Federation of Teachers, wrote a candid but enormously helpful appraisal of an early draft. David Darland, coordinator, Instruction and Professional Development, National Education Association, also read an early draft and offered suggestions that resulted in several substantive changes in the manuscript.

Girard Hottleman, director of educational services, Massachusetts Teachers Association, was suggested as a worthy reviewer. Indeed so! His biting criticism covered several pages, but I was encouraged by his closing comment, "I want you to know that this is the most functional and valuable book in the education market that I have ever read, and I have read quite a few of them."

In addition to these reviewers, several other persons offered suggestions on the manuscript: Dominick DeCecco, an insightful teacher at Bethlehem Central Senior High School, Central District No. 6, Delmar, New York; Ellwood R. Erickson, staff associate, National Education Association; J. Howard Moore, Capitol Hill Educator; and Lilian Myers.

Several persons read and made suggestions on specific chapters of the book: Donald Walker, chief, Negotiation Research Unit, National Education Association; and Daniel Duke, graduate fellow, School of Education, State University of New York at Albany. I also benefited by discussions with Mary Hruby, formerly research assistant, Institute for Development of Educational Activities, Inc.; Joel Burden, director, and Joost Yff, associate director, ERIC Clearinghouse; and Alvin P. Lierheimer, assistant commissioner for higher education, New York State Department of Education.

I would be remiss if I did not acknowledge the pioneering work in the area of teacher professionalization by Myron Lieberman. His *Education as a Profession*, published in 1956, is still relevant today. Lieberman's book was prophetic, preceding the teacher professionalization movement by more than a decade.

Finally, I would like to acknowledge my appreciation to two outstanding educators who were responsible for the organizations of which I was a member while writing this book: John Goodlad, director, Institute for Development of Educational Activities, Research Division, Los Angeles; and Joseph Leese, chairman, Department of Curriculum and Instruction, School of Education, State University of New York at Albany. Both believe that persons should contribute to the attainment of the goals of the organization, but feel just as strongly that the organization should assist all persons meet their own needs — even at the expense of organizational goals.

# INTRODUCTION

The purpose of this book is to provide teachers and students contemplating entering teaching as a career with further insight into the process of teacher professionalization. It analyzes the role of collective bargaining in teacher professionalization and suggests structures and tactics for continuing teachers' struggle for professional status. Teachers' knowledge of areas such as the characteristics of a profession, the authority structure in schools as bureaucracies, collective bargaining and strikes, and the attitudes of fellow teachers is seriously lacking. Many teachers believe a professional teacher is a dedicated soul who works sixty hours a week teaching, correcting English themes, and volunteering to serve on curriculum committees. This is simply inaccurate. This type of behavior has little to do with the professionalization of teachers. Similarly, a majority of teachers has a limited knowledge of the stresses that often result when professionals work in a bureaucracy and are thus unable to cope with their day-to-day frustrations in the classroom. In addition, while many teachers have engaged in strikes, few have considered the advantages and disadvantages of such actions. Finally, most teachers know very little about teachers as an occupational group—their socioeconomic background, their attitudes toward authority, their aspirations, or their prestige compared to other occupations.

During the coming decade, teachers will need to improve their personal welfare (salaries, working conditions, etc.), gain an improved educational program for students, and gain the right to govern their profession. If the decade of the sixties accomplished nothing else, it buried permanently the myth that teachers are self-sacrificing missionaries content to work for whatever wages and under whatever conditions the patrons in a local community thought appropriate for such "service-minded folk."

Teachers now stand eye-to-eye with members of boards of education and demand salaries and fringe benefits, some of which have been commonplace in blue collar occupations for thirty years. Teachers will continue to concentrate on welfare objectives until improved working conditions prevail. They need not apologize to citizens or students for doing so.

Teachers will not experience genuine satisfaction in obtaining higher salaries and improved working conditions, however, if they do not succeed also in gaining improvements in the educational programs. Teachers need more than a thirty-minute, duty-free lunch period and an improved salary schedule. This does not mean that teachers should advance educational objectives for students at the expense of their own welfare objectives. That would be tantamount to teachers financing the programs themselves; a practice that has been all too prevalent in the past. Rather, both teacher welfare objectives and educational objectives should be advanced simultaneously, the emphasis depending upon prevailing local conditions.

Some persons believe all teacher welfare objectives are detrimental to students because they result in the use of funds that could be used for students' instructional materials and supplies. This is a parochial view. In the first place, unless teachers' working conditions improve, competent teachers will not remain in the field, and it will be difficult to recruit capable persons. Second, competent teachers, attracted by high salaries and favorable working conditions, are likely to do more for students than almost any amount of materials and supplies. Third, some teacher welfare objectives do not require additional funds.

While teachers have used their collective power to improve educational programs, these efforts have been eclipsed, justifiably, by teacher welfare issues. In the future, however, teachers will increasingly direct their efforts to gain not only unlimited sick leave but also the establishment of federally-supported day care centers. They will support not only improved sabbatical leave policies but also an increase in instructional materials and supplies for students. They will support not only free group health and accident insurance but also an adequate library in each school. Strikes or sanctions will be imposed on those states and school districts that do not provide, for example, adequate financial support, needed redistricting, or pre-school programs. Collective bargaining may be legitimately advanced solely as a means for improving the welfare of employees, but teachers will likely demand that it be used also as a means for improving the educational program for students.

Each issue that teachers advance should be studied carefully to determine whether it assists them in their quest for the governance of their profession. Teachers are striving for professional status and will not be content until considerable progress is made in that direction.

There is much confusion concerning the terms profession, professional, professionalism, and professionalization. Teachers are often suspicious of anyone who uses the terms. Some teachers have been unjustly and inaccurately labeled nonprofessional because they joined a teachers' union or participated in a strike. There is no evidence, however, that one teacher association is more professional than the other. Shanker is one of many who has expressed his concern with the term professionalism. "The word itself is becoming more and more a dirty word for teachers."[a] His statement is understandable considering the gross misuse of the word in the sixties. While the term has become emotion-laden and thus lost some of its value in educational discourse, it should not be abandoned because collective bargaining without teacher professionalization is self-defeating in the long run.

In addition to the confusion concerning professionalism, there is also the belief among some persons that there is a conflict between teacher professionali-

---

a. Albert Shanker, *Teachers and School Committees: Negotiations in Good Faith* (Cambridge, Mass.: The New England School Development Council, September, 1967), reprinted in *The Collective Dilemma: Negotiations in Education*, ed. Patrick W. Carlton and Harold I. Goodwin (Worthington, Ohio: Charles A. Jones Publishing Company, 1969), p. 78. Used by permission of Albert Shanker.

zation and collective bargaining. This is a divisive myth that needs a decent but immediate burial. It is understandable that editorial writers in many newspapers support this view; it is no longer acceptable for teachers to support it. Teacher professionalization and collective bargaining are not antithetical; they are complementary. It may be argued that the degree of teacher professionalization enjoyed today is the result of collective bargaining of teachers in the sixties. It can be further argued that collective bargaining, while of considerable importance in the past and in the future, is not sufficient to ensure teachers' increased professionalization. What is needed is not more polemics about professionalism versus collective bargaining, but more serious study of areas in which collective bargaining and teacher professionalization go hand-in-hand while advancing the profession and improving the education of students.

There is a widespread belief that an occupation will use power solely for its own self-interest. The truth, however, is that it takes a powerful occupation to assist both the members of the occupation and the society. Lieberman said it clearly in 1964:

A group which is too weak to protect its immediate welfare interests will usually be too weak to protect the public interest as well. Teachers need power to protect academic freedom, to eradicate racial segregation in education, to secure more and better instructional materials, and to do many other things that have little or no relationship to teacher welfare. If teachers are weak, they cannot protect the public interest in education. This is why the weakness of teachers as an organized group is one of the most important problems in American education today.[b]

Teachers are becoming professionalized, but this does not guarantee that the actions of teachers will always serve to advance professionalization. Professionalization is not merely an opportunity to gain autonomy from laymen and administrators. Professionalization is amoral rather than moral. It can be used for good or evil, depending upon the wisdom of the leadership, the membership, and the issues involved. Professionalization does not ensure the public or teachers that wise decisions will always be made. It does not even ensure that wise decisions will be made a majority of the time.

An increase in the power of teachers could lead to disenchanted teachers, angry parents, a weakened educational program, and a decrease in authority for teachers. There is reason to believe, however, that collective bargaining and teacher governance, working in concert, will provide teachers with competitive salaries and comfortable working conditions, an improved educational program for students, and an occupational group that is truly professionalized.

Teacher professionalization will not be advanced until a larger percentage of teachers draw upon a scientific body of knowledge rather than their own intuition when teaching in a classroom. It will not be advanced until teachers determine the courses and programs required at colleges and universities that

---

b. Myron Lieberman, "Power and Policy in Education: Power and Professionalism in Teaching," *Bulletin of the School of Education*, ed. Lewis A. Bayles, Indiana University, 40 (September, 1964), p. 22.

prepare them for teaching; until teachers complete at least a five-year training program and a one-year internship in a classroom; and until certification boards are manned by teachers. It will not be advanced until teachers gain considerably in income, power, and prestige; until teachers are free to govern their own profession without interference from citizens and parents; until teachers are strongly identified with teaching as a career and remain in teaching without interruption for a lifetime. It will not be advanced until all teachers belong to a united teacher association; until teachers select, evaluate, and confer tenure on fellow teachers; until teachers develop their own in-service programs; until teachers understand the necessity for theory and research in education. It will not be advanced until teachers select all supervisors who have authority over "educational," in contrast to management, decisions in schools. Most important of all, teacher professionalization will not be advanced without a concerted effort on the part of every teacher in America to gain professional status.

A united teacher association is imminent. It will serve to advance teacher professionalization because it will possess considerable power. This power is needed, but power per se is complementary rather than synonymous with professionalization. For professionalization, power must be legitimized by demonstrating to citizens and teachers as well that teacher governance of the profession rather than lay or administrator governance will result in improved education for students.

Teacher professionalization will not be realized until new organizational structures are created, roles and responsibilities for each structure established and understood, and viable communication linkage created from the individual teacher working in his classroom to a national teacher association. Such a structure is presented in the final chapter.

Analogies to "established" professions have been used several times in the book. Analogies frequently provoke controversy because their intention is to show a likeness or resemblance between two phenomena. Differences can always be found. Analogies are often useful, nonetheless, because they have a way of shedding light on areas that were formerly vague. It seems more useful to search for the central intent of an analogy than to demonstrate defensively the obvious point that no two phenomena are alike. Most of the analogies cited are about physicians. The medical profession was not selected as a model for teachers to emulate; rather, it was selected because virtually everyone is familiar with medical practice as a result of visits to physicians and hospitals. Analogies to nuclear scientists could have been used if the author and the readers were as familiar with that profession.

Chapter One describes teacher authority with particular attention to the political factors that cause teachers to seek more authority. Chapter Two presents the characteristics of a profession. Chapters Three, Four, and Five offer three different statuses for teachers—professional, functionary, and semi-professional. Chapter Six describes the existing structure in education, the sociological factors contributing to the perpetuation of that structure, and the school as a bureaucracy; particularly the strain that exists between the needs of teachers and the demands of the school as a bureaucracy. Chapter Seven discusses collective bargaining of teachers, the process most frequently used at present to increase and improve the extent of teacher participation in decision making. Chapter Eight explores the implications that increased teacher decision making has on administrators. Chapter Nine discusses problems and issues that may be obstacles to teacher professionalization. Chapter Ten proposes a structure for advancing teacher professionalization at the local, regional, state, and national levels, and offers twenty-eight recommendations.

# ONE
# TEACHER AUTHORITY

*"Teachers cannot be trusted with responsibility for educational policies in curriculum or discipline or promotion standards; nor can they be trusted with professional controls, such as entry requirements or judgment of one another's competence; nor can they be trusted with a voice in the terms of employment; nor, most emphatically, can they be trusted with the power of independent and cohesive professional organization. No, teachers cannot be trusted—except in the classroom with our children."\**

*"Power is never given to anyone. Power is taken, and it is taken from someone. Teachers, as one of society's powerless groups, are now starting to take power from supervisors and school boards. This is causing and will continue to cause a realignment of power relationships."\*\**

*"Teachers have simply become irritated beyond the point of tolerance with the failure of the American people to demand the right of teachers to share equitably in the fruits of an affluent society."\*\*\**

*"When a profession starts to govern itself, then it is in a position to negotiate; it is in a position to get responsibility; and then it can be held accountable. But under the existing circumstances, any teacher who would accept accountability is a damn fool!"\*\*\*\**

*"Anyone who has ever taught knows that teaching is a demanding task. People who measure the difficulty of a job by the amount of sweat on the worker's brow may find this fact hard to accept, but those of us who have been in charge of twenty-five or thirty children from 8:45 in the morning until 3:15 in the afternoon know how comforting it can be to see the last yellow bus pull out of the school driveway."\*\*\*\*\**

A revolution of major importance is taking place in education—not voucher systems, not computer-aided instruction, and not performance contracting, but one that dwarfs them in terms of its ultimate impact on the education of students—the professionalization of teachers.

Teachers are told to be professionals. Indeed, they are told they are professionals,[a] but they are not treated as professionals by many citizens, legislators, board members, or administrators. Teachers are no longer willing to live in the midst of such hypocrisy. Once a passive and obedient group of so-called do-gooders, they are becoming an outspoken and, at times, rude group of self-centered professionals

---

a. Some persons view teaching as a profession while others do not. In fact, all occupations are at some stage of professionalization. This point of view is discussed thoroughly in Chapter Two.

dedicated to improving their lot and, at the same time, improving the education of students. Teachers are no longer pawns of the state, willing to sit by idly regardless of the educational policies instituted by the state legislature, the state board of education, and the local board of education. Above all, they are no longer blindly obedient.

Teachers are now demanding "revolutionary" things—the right to decide themselves how students should be grouped for instruction; the right to decide how to work most effectively with colleagues (in teams, self-contained, etc.); the right to be represented, not by one member but by a majority of members at local school district committees in charge of developing courses of study; the right to evaluate colleagues and to determine which of their colleagues gain tenure; the right to select department chairmen and supervisors; the right to accredit and approve courses of study for colleges and universities that prepare teachers.

It would be simple for boards of education and administrators if teachers were demanding only more representation on committees. It is easy to add a few teachers to a committee, the majority of whose members are administrators and citizens. It would be simple also to grant teachers a majority of the membership of district-wide committees, provided that all decisions reached by the committees were subject to review by the board of education, the superintendent of schools, or the district administrative staff. In other words, boards of education and administrators would have no problems with teachers as long as it is clearly understood that teachers continue to have limited authority, are told what to teach, the sequence in which to teach it, the students they will teach, the materials they will use, the persons with whom they will teach, and the principals to whom they will report; so long as it is clearly understood by everyone that teachers have no authority and are subject to the dictates of superiors.

The practice of persons other than teachers making instructional decisions concerning teaching in the classroom has become so widespread in America today that when teachers are allowed, indeed encouraged, to make decisions, they are often not competent to fulfill the role of decision maker and tend to resist what is considered by some to be an inappropriate role. Decisions such as which reading program to use, which mathematics program to adopt, how to organize most effectively the students and teachers, and which instructional materials to use, are often made by higher authorities, often the principal or district personnel, and occasionally by higher officers such as the members of the local board of education or the state department of education.

Decisions concerning the governance of the profession outside of the classroom, such as teacher certification, accreditation of teacher preparation institutions, employment and according of tenure, and the type of training program for new teachers are invariably made by higher officials and agencies, normally without even seeking teachers' opinions.

A teacher goes to a school (often assigned by an administrator) the number of days prescribed by the state legislature. He arrives daily at a time prescribed by the superintendent and his staff. In most schools, students are assigned to him without prior consultation. The subjects offered are often prescribed by the state legislature and always by the local board of education. The textbooks used in classrooms are approved by the local school district, and, in many states, by the state department of education. The textbooks allocated are generally on one grade level and the teacher is too often expected by superiors to proceed methodically through the books.

The method of reporting student progress to parents is determined by the district administration or the principals. The standard practice is to send report cards home. Teachers cannot deviate from this practice even though many disagree with it. Students who misbehave seriously in class are sent to the principal's office, but only if the principal approves such a procedure.

When the school bell rings at 3:15, the teacher is often not permitted to leave the school; instead, in many districts he is required to remain after school for thirty minutes. This is a petty, irritating, yet blatantly accurate reminder of how "professional" the board, the superintendent, and the principal consider teachers.

At the end of the school day, the teacher is frustrated not so much because of the difficult and complex decisions that were made during the day, but from having to follow a prescribed time schedule, a prescribed curriculum, and a prescribed set of policies and rules in which he has little or no say. If medicine were a profession like teaching, the surgeon would be told by the state legislature the number of minutes permitted to perform surgery; the hospital administrator would suggest surgical instruments; and friends of the patient would stand around the periphery of the operating room offering unsolicited advice from information they and their friends had gained from previous operations. Teachers are resisting this wholesale interference in their work. They are seeking less authority by others and more authority for themselves.

The amount of authority granted to persons in an organization depends upon several factors. No one advocates the same model of authority for the Department of Defense, Harvard University, and Central Grade Elementary School. Most persons are willing to grant more authority to a lawyer than a service station attendant.

Authority may be centralized or decentralized. Centralization is thought useful to guarantee responsible action of subordinates, to coordinate activities to help accomplish overall goals, and to utilize the superior decision-making talents of the few at the top of an organization. Decentralization is thought useful because decisions are best made at the level where they are implemented, it is more efficient, there is greater subordinate motivation and commitment, and there is flexibility for the individuals involved in making the decisions.

Authority is not the exclusive right of administrators to wield over subordinates whenever it is thought necessary; authority, paradoxically, resides to a great extent in subordinates, since the superior has no authority unless the subordinate responds.[1] The orders of a superior must usually "conform" to the norms of the group or organization if they are to be accepted and obeyed.

Many teachers accept administrative authority as unalterable. In this respect, they are much like nurses who spend so much of their time doing work planned for them by administrators, doctors, therapists, etc., that they do not have the time for the quantity and quality of nursing care which they themselves consider necessary.[2]

This situation could easily be applied to teachers. Over and over again, teachers complain that they do not have time to work with students. Is this because teachers are busy working with other students? In most cases, no. It is because they are doing work that others (PTAs and other community groups, administrators, and even custodians) have loaded upon them.

Teachers are not likely to gain significantly increased authority through the efforts of administrators or anyone else. Teachers themselves must lead their own way by determining areas over which they need authority. If they take no action, it will be viewed as approval of the status quo by parents, boards of education, administrators, and students.

Teachers lack authority, in part, because of the hierarchical authority pattern that exists in bureaucratically-oriented school districts. Bureaucracies demand a vertical structure of authority whereas professions tend to follow a horizontal structure.

Hierarchical, vertical authority patterns are not a recent development. They have been the prevailing pattern from antiquity. Table 1-1 shows the formal, hierarchical authority pattern in five organizations. In this model, persons can be viewed as being at one of various levels in the hierarchy with power, wealth, and status at the top, and a lack of these at the bottom.

No organization has exactly six levels. In education, one could add the governor, district superintendents, county boards of education, assistant principals, department chairmen, para-professionals, and students. Nevertheless, organizations can profitably be conceptualized in this way highlighting the hierarchy that exists in almost all formal organizations.

A vertical structure of authority results in a power pyramid whereby an order given by one official at the top influences a much larger number of persons below. The higher a person in the power pyramid, the more persons he controls. The Pope and his immediate staff, for example, in eliminating the disciplinary law that Roman Catholics abstain from eating meat on Friday, influenced over 500 million persons. Figure 1-1 shows a power pyramid in education. A law passed by the state legislature can influence directly all teachers in a state. Local boards of education, superintendents, and principals have similar power, but their power influences a smaller group of persons.

The superior in a vertical organization often uses much of his energy to maintain his position. He may seek to keep subordinates subordinate. If subordinates look too good, they can be a threat to his position. If subordinates come up with ideas, it implies that the superior does not have ideas. Any change is a threat to his position. Often, then, superiors suppress good ideas. The superior tends to hire persons who are less capable than he. Communication becomes distorted as it goes up. Persons at the top ranks are older; at the bottom, younger. Thus, there is a good possibility of a generation gap.

**Table 1-1.** Formal Hierarchical Authority Pattern in Five Organizations

| Classes | Ancient Egypt | Early 18th Century America | Roman Catholic Church | Military | American Education Today |
|---------|---------------|---------------------------|-----------------------|----------|--------------------------|
| Class 1 | Pharaoh | King George | Pope | Generals | State Legislature |
| Class 2 | Chief Priest | Lords | Cardinals | Majors | State Board of Education |
| Class 3 | Temple Priest | Colony Governor | Archbishops | Captains | Local Board of Education |
| Class 4 | Village Officials | Town Officials | Bishops | Lieutenants | Superintendent of Schools |
| Class 5 | Farmers, Peasants | Farmers | Monsignors | Sergeants | Principals |
| Class 6 | Slaves | Indentured Slaves and Servants | Priests | Privates | Teachers |

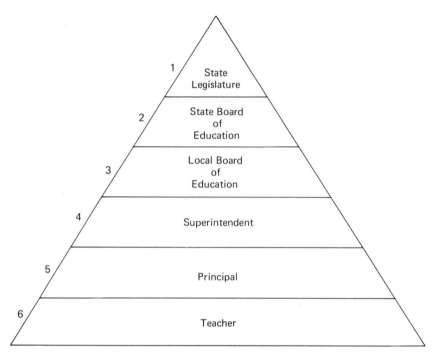

**Figure 1-1.** Power pyramid showing the formal hierarchical authority structure in education.

Some organizations can be classified as having a horizontal rather than hierarchical authority structure. In such organizations, no person possesses more authority than another. Persons do not tend to compete for positions whereby they can control others because no such positions exist. The medical profession offers a useful example of this concept.

The physician need not seek the approval of a superior before prescribing a drug or making an incision, although there is a formal hierarchical authority structure in hospitals that limits the authority of the independent physician. In the professional model, competition for power is lessened since all members have equal access to rewards and punishments. Neither can force the action of another. Since no one has more power than another, the feeling of superiority is lessened. Of course, an individual physician may gain power by virtue of his excellence in his specialty, but such power is not institutionalized.

In education, authority resides in various persons in the hierarchy, inevitably "above" the teacher. Thus, teachers have little autonomy, a major characteristic of professionals. "The formal and legal allocation of authority in school systems is monolithic, hierarchical, and centralized; official powers are focused at the apex of the structure."[3]

The risk involved in making a decision is another factor in reducing the authority of teachers. The amount of authority granted to someone or to a group of persons depends, in large part, upon the amount of gain or risk involved for the organization. In the case of an institution, there is an assessment of the anticipated gains weighed against the anticipated or possible loss. This assessment determines all aspects of authority, such as how much authority to grant, to whom to advance the authority, what are the returns for the investment, how long shall the authority be granted.

In education, the teacher gives a student more authority when the risk of a poor or potentially damaging decision by the student is reduced to what is considered a reasonable probability. In the process, the teacher assesses the possible disadvantages of not granting the authority, such as a student may not have the opportunity to practice decision making on his own, he may become belligerent, or he may make inappropriate decisions without consulting the teacher.

Anderson suggests several factors that mitigate or limit the investment of authority in teachers. Six factors seem especially critical.

1. Inability to measure performance and results.
2. Distrust of teacher motivation.
3. Lack of assurance by administrators that their interests will be preserved.
4. Imbalance between authority and expected returns. The teacher is responsible for the progress of his students, but he has little or no authority to control environmental factors.
5. The public's view of the critical nature of education.
6. Teacher authority is lessened because teachers' actions are subject to control by the board of education, state legislature, parents individually and through the PTA, plus many other groups in the community.[4]

Anderson concludes that "the result appears to be a withdrawal of authority invested in teachers due to the perceived risk involved."[5]

To gain a more relevant perspective of the limitations of teacher authority, one has merely to observe how teachers work with students. In the process of teaching, the teacher attempts to diagnose the student's learning difficulty and to identify a prescription from alternatives available. This process is repeated many times each day for each student. It is true that some teachers diagnose the class and not the individual student; however, the process is the same.

**Diagnosis.** It appears initially that few if any restraints exist in the teacher's role as diagnostician. Certainly, a teacher is free to diagnose any problem a student is having in school, within the limits of the teacher's diagnostic ability. In one sense, this is true, but in another sense, it is not because the teacher is unlikely to examine "every" facet of the student if he knows that his previous diagnoses have not resulted in prescriptions. Will a teacher continue to refine his diagnosis of a student's difficulty in mathematics, for example, when his last diagnosis required material such as Diene's multi-base arithmetic blocks or Cuisenaire Rods, but neither were available, nor was there any indication that they would be in the future? Substitutes can be found for Diene's blocks and Cuisenaire Rods. Indeed, a teacher can make his own, and some do. But when funds are not allocated for special equipment and materials, a teacher reverts normally to the ubiquitous graded textbook which makes diagnosis almost superfluous.

Management specialists find a similar situation in many organizations. A superior is criticized by subordinates because he never approves requests of subordinates. The superior often can show that he has approved a high percentage of requests over the last few months. Subordinates explain this seeming paradox with the simple explanation that they stopped making requests they knew in advance the superior would reject. Thus, the superior has a high percentage of acceptances. Similarly, the teacher stops making diagnoses that lead to prescriptions that are not available.

**Prescription.** Teachers have few prescriptions from which to choose once a diagnosis is made. The educational pharmacy in many schools consists of textbooks, workbooks, World Book encyclopedias, assorted globes and maps, and a bleak supply of instructional aids. Analogies to the medical profession are hazardous, but it is almost inconceivable for a physician to diagnose an illness and prescribe a drug and not have the drug available in a pharmacy, or available within a short time from a pharmaceutical house.

· The author recently visited a physician concerning a persistent sore throat. The physician prescribed declomycin. The sore throat went away the fifth day, but returned the seventh day. On a second visit, the physician prescribed pentids. Again, the sore throat went away after five days but returned after a week. On the third visit, the physician prescribed a chest x-ray, a throat culture, and a blood count. The throat culture "grew-out" a virus, and the physician prescribed ampicillin. The sore throat was cured within a few days.

In this relatively routine problem, the physician made five prescriptions and all were available (1) declomycin, (2) pentids, (3) chest x-ray, (4) blood count, (5) ampicillin. We both would have been astonished if the pharmacy had not filled the prescriptions, or if the laboratory had been unable to take the blood count and x-ray.

In education, the opposite is true. It is the rule rather than the exception. Not only are teachers unable to acquire routine instructional materials, but many have difficulty even getting pencils for all students. A student may want a book on ghosts, but the library does not have a book on ghosts, and there are no funds to order one. Indeed, in many elementary schools there are no libraries. Or, a teacher decides that a particular student in the fourth grade needs reading material on the second-grade level. In many schools, a second-grade reader would be difficult, although usually not impossible, to acquire. A teacher has a workshop in modern mathematics and wants to use some of the material from the University of Illinois Arithmetic Project or School Mathematics Project. This is not possible in states where the state adoption specifies one program and no other is supposed to be used;

the local board of education specifies one program; there are insufficient funds to buy these books; or there must be a uniform mathematics program throughout the school district.

The problem is not that adequate instructional materials do not exist, but that teachers are often unaware of them, and school districts do not have the funds to purchase them. Teachers know that funds for instructional materials are not available, so they make little effort to learn about them.

**Alternatives.** A further restraint on teacher authority exists in the alternative category. When a diagnosis has been made and prescriptions *are* available, it may be impossible to use the prescription. A teacher may wish to team teach with two other teachers, but this is not permitted because the superintendent or principal disapproves. A teacher may wish to transfer a student to another grade because he believes such a transfer is desirable for the student, but it may not be allowed. A teacher may wish for a student to engage in his individual project in social studies for a period of two hours each morning instead of formal reading, but this is not possible because he is scheduled into art on Tuesday and Thursday, and the state law requires 160 minutes of reading each week.

Table 1-2 shows a summary of the number of recommended percentages of time for courses in elementary and intermediate grades in the state of New York.

### Table 1-2. Percentage of Time Recommended for Primary and Intermediate Grades, State of New York, 1969

*Primary Grades*

| | |
|---|---|
| Language arts group—speech, conversation, discussion, reading writing, spelling, literature, language usage etc. | 30% |
| Social studies | 10% |
| Science, health teaching | 10% |
| Mathematics | 10% |
| Arts and crafts—music, drawing, painting, dramatization, building and constructing etc. | 20% |
| Physical activities—those not included in the above such as trips, games and others | 20% |

*Intermediate Grades*

| | |
|---|---|
| Language arts group | 30% |
| Social studies | 20% |
| Science, health teaching | 15% |
| Mathematics | 15% |
| Arts and crafts | 10% |
| Planned physical activities—trips, games etc. | 10% |

Source: "Letters to Supervisors," Series 3, No. 10, New York State Education Department, Division of Elementary Education, Bureau of Instructional Supervision, Albany, New York, reprinted 1969.

This document is atypical as it recommends rather than mandates. Often, however, these recommendations are viewed as certitudes by principals and teachers in local school districts. It is not uncommon to see these percentages translated into minutes and adhered to closely by teachers when visiting schools in the state of New York. Such specifications are common throughout the United States.

To mandate specific amounts of time for certain subjects from the state level, as is often the case, is a deterrent to the individualization of instruction. To require 10 percent of the time for mathematics for the primary grades is undesirable because some students need less time and others need more time. The same applies to all subjects. One can only pity teachers who work in schools where such anachronistic and inane recommendations are enforced to the letter of the law.

It is apparent that the teacher is handicapped severely in his attempt to engage in the normal teaching function. He is handicapped in his diagnosis; he has few prescriptions from which to choose; and even when available, he is often unable to use them. In effect, the restraints amount to an intellectual straight jacket for the creative and imaginative teacher, resulting in a structure that is conducive to mediocrity, boredom, and conformity for both teachers and students.

The fact that teachers' authority is limited in the classroom, does not mean that teachers do not make decisions important to students' education. Lindsey points out that "within the *narrow* (my emphasis) area of freedom for decision-making allowed the individual classroom teacher, decisions are made which have considerable influence on learning opportunities provided pupils in school."[6] She lists sixteen illustrative decision areas.

Shall I take time to discuss their questions, or shall I assume that if they don't get it as I demonstrated, they just won't get it?
Shall I listen to him or tell him to take his seat?
Shall I report this to his parents or try to discuss it with him?
Shall I look at these cumulative records, or will I be better off if I don't know their backgrounds?
Shall I try to help them understand why we are doing this or just tell them to do it?
Shall I have them go through the motions of this exercise even though I don't believe in it, or shall I skip it altogether?
Shall I have him work on that program alone or give him some help?
Shall I make the same assignment for all of them, or shall I try to make different ones for different pupils?
Shall I be severe with him and deny him opportunity to explain or try to understand why he did it?
Shall I use the televised lesson today, or shall I try to clear up some misunderstandings from yesterday's lesson?
Shall I take time to talk to each one about the composition I'm handing back or just hand them back?
Shall I give a test today or wait until next week?
How can I help these pupils to get hold of this idea?
What can I do to make this textbook explanation more meaningful to them?
Just how much should I expect from all these pupils?
Should I try to deal with this problem in the whole group or in subgroups?[7]

Moeller and Charters observe that teachers have considerable autonomy in their classrooms because of their physical insulation and strong professional norms.[8] Lortie makes essentially the same observation when he notes that the ecological patterning of students where students and staff are dispersed throughout separate buildings—in contrast to all employees being under one roof—reduces the possibility of close control by superintendents and thereby increases the amount of power held by individual schools.[9] He maintains further that the "relatively unrationalized nature of teaching techniques also restricts initiations by administrative superiors."[10] A principal who attempts to assist, reprimand, or discipline a teacher finds that he has few established principles of pedagogy to support his point.

The following comment by a teacher expresses this point of view quite well:

The teacher is a technician in all of the preliminary stages of his work. His course is outlined for him, his students selected for him, the length of time they will be with him is predetermined, what textbooks he will use, and often what tests to use. Routinization and standardization are true—to a point. And then individuality takes over. In the classroom, the teacher is the decision-maker, if for no other reason then that there is no one else available to make a decision.[11]

While teachers can make many decisions that are significant for the education of students, clearly they cannot make many decisions concerning their work. It is somewhat paradoxical, for example, that there is almost universal agreement that teachers should be permitted the "privilege" of deciding the students' letter grade for a lesson, a semester, or a year. However, they are usually permitted no more than an opinion (sometimes not even that and always with the understanding that the teacher has no authority) concerning many instructional decisions. As Johnson states,

it is a myth that the teacher is autonomous in his classroom. The bureaucratic requirements, the influence the national educational system has over instructional materials, the evaluation of performance by state and national examinations, all influence the teacher's behavior in his classroom. Perhaps the only two areas in which teachers can innovate are in presenting materials and in relating to pupils. Even in these areas, however, studies show that teachers are not innovators.[12]

The lack of teacher authority is a critical problem because it strikes at the heart of teacher professionalization. It is impossible for teachers to become further professionalized without an increase in their authority. The authority of the practitioner to follow his own dictates rather than being constrained by a superior, or even colleagues, is a basic characteristic of professionals. Virtually every sociologist of occupations places it high on the list of characteristics of a profession.

Professionals are relinquishing some of their authority to organizations—physicians to clinics and hospitals, lawyers to corporations, scientists to large research organizations—but they retain considerable authority. Teachers live in a different world than these occupational groups. Teachers live in a world where the organization has almost complete domination over their decisions.

In summary, the teacher is handicapped severely as he strives to make educational decisions in the classroom. The mammoth hierarchy of authority above the teacher—involving ten layers as a minimum and often more than twice that number—limits his decision making by preempting the teacher's decisions. Most significant, decisions are made for the teacher before he enters the classroom. In the classroom, he cannot engage in the normal teaching function because of restrictions on his diagnosis, a limited pharmacy of prescriptions, and restraints on alternatives available to him once a diagnosis and prescription have been made. The decisions left to the teacher in the classroom are limited and often dictated by rigid rules and procedures about which he has little knowledge and less commitment.

Teachers are part of a larger societal movement to decentralize authority in bureaucracies. The view that teachers should have more authority has received lip service from teacher associations for a long time. Teachers are in the process of making it an accomplished fact. Teacher authority will become a reality if teachers understand the characteristics of what constitutes a profession and work assiduously to move in that direction. The following chapter presents a description of the classic characteristics of professions, a model teachers need not follow explicitly, but one which serves as a useful guide.

# TWO
# PROFESSIONALIZATION

*"So much lip service is paid to the notion that the classroom teacher is the most important person in the educational process while in reality, the teacher is encouraged to leave the classroom by means of promotion, higher pay, and status. In fact, when a male teacher says he plans to stay in the class he is viewed with curiosity! But what happened to the concept that he was the most important person? If we really are that important, shouldn't we be encouraged and receive incentives to remain in the classroom? Shouldn't we have a real voice in school policy, the curriculum, and the running of the school? Shouldn't the present trend be reversed?"\**

*"Professionalism is a state of mind, not a reality. Neither statute nor regulation, neither code nor shibboleth will make a teacher a professional. If we are to pursue the cult of excellence, we will need a degree of dedication, an expenditure of money and energy and intellect, the like of which we have only the faintest notion at this time."\*\**

*"I take this opportunity to say that the educational conduct of the school, as well as its administration, the selection of subject-matter, and the working out of the course of study, as well as actual instruction of children, have been almost entirely in the hands of teachers of the school; and that there has been a gradual development of the educational principles and methods involved, not a fixed equipment. The teachers started with question marks, rather than fixed rules, and if any answers have been reached, it is the teachers in the school who have supplied them."\*\*\**

Profession, professional, professionalism, and professionalization are relatively new terms to many teachers, although Brubacher traces the word profession to the sixteenth century and the early development of professions to the Greco-Roman period.[1] Many of the articles that have appeared fairly regularly for the last fifty years about the professionalization of occupations have been concerned with defining these terms.[2]

Vollmer's and Mills' definitions are used in this book.

*Profession:* We avoid the use of the term 'profession', except as an 'ideal type' of occupational organization which does not exist in reality, but which provides the model of the form of occupational organization that would result if any occupational group became completely professionalized.

*Professionalization:* The dynamic *process* whereby many occupations can be observed to change certain crucial characteristics in the direction of a 'profession', even though some of these may not move very far in this direction. It follows that these crucial characteristics constitute specifiable criteria of professionalization.

*Professionalism:* An *ideology* and associated activities that can be found in many and diverse occupational groups where members aspire to professional status. Professionalism as an ideology may induce members of many occupational groups to strive to become professional, but at the same time we can see that many occupational groups that express the ideology of professionalism in reality may not be very advanced in regard to professionalization. Professionalism may be a necessary constituent of professionalization, but professionalism is not a sufficient cause for the entire professional process.

*Professional Group:* Associations of colleagues in an occupational context where we observe that a relatively high degree of professionalization has taken place.

*Professionals:* Those who are considered by their colleagues to be members of professional groups.[3]

Some important distinctions are made in these definitions. The most significant is that profession is a term applied to an *ideal* type of organization that does not exist in reality. Thus, *no* occupation is a profession. However, all occupations have some characteristics of a profession. As an occupation moves in the direction of meeting these characteristics, the process of professionalization takes place. Professionalism is an ideology that induces members of an occupation to strive to become professionals.

Much of the literature in education assumes that teachers are already professionals. In a survey released by the National Education Association in 1965, 80.4 percent of teachers indicated that teaching was a professional occupation; 3.2 percent indicated that it was a highly technical occupation; 13.7 percent indicated that it was a highly skilled occupation; and 2.1 percent indicated that it was just another occupation.[4] It is likely that the percentage of teachers who consider themselves professional has increased since 1965. Sociologists are far less unanimous, with several viewing teaching as a semi-profession (see Chapter Five). The belief that teachers are already professionals can be detrimental to teacher professionalization because persons seldom work very enthusiastically toward the attainment of something they consider an accomplished objective. It is wise to avoid a debate over whether teachers are professionals. It is more useful to concentrate on their degree of professionalization.

The word professional has been sorely abused in education. It has several connotations, often contradictory. Perhaps the most common description of a professional teacher is one who is dedicated to the field of teaching and who is kind to students. This description holds also that the professional teacher is competent and works earnestly toward becoming more competent. The professional teacher takes courses at universities, reads books and periodicals in his area of specialization, volunteers to work on committees, and does not gossip about fellow teachers and students.

There is also a fairly widespread definition of the nonprofessional teacher. Interestingly, it is not the opposite of the professional. The nonprofessional teacher is most often described as being concerned with teacher welfare "too much" of the time. The nonprofessional spends what is considered an inordinate amount of time questioning the decisions of the administrative staff, and the wisdom of district policies enacted by the board of education. Like the "professional," he may take courses, be helpful to students, volunteer for committees, refrain from gossiping about other teachers. He is labeled a nonprofessional because of his "negative attitude" and, interestingly, his constant concern for teacher welfare and the quality of the educational program.

The existence of two teacher associations has served to cloud the picture. The teacher who is a member of the American Federation of Teachers or is "union-oriented" is sometimes labeled nonprofessional because unions use strikes that are considered by some persons to be tactics of nonprofessional blue collar workers. The union-oriented teacher rejoins by rejecting the word professional as a tool of administrators to force teachers to comply with institutional policies rather than arguing that strikes are not nonprofessional. In the process, a clear definition of a professional, already vague to teachers, is muddled further.

Both the American Federation of Teachers and the National Education Association are interested in advancing teacher professionalization. Both favor coercive means for increasing teacher authority. The leadership and, in general, the membership of the AFT and the NEA want teachers to become more professionalized.

It is harmful for teachers to continue a dialogue that is divisive rather than conciliatory. The terms are so confusing that a teacher labeled a nonprofessional by other teachers might be viewed as highly professional by an outsider visiting the school. The seemingly nonprofessional teacher is often the one fighting for more autonomy, which is an essential principle of professionalization. Corwin's study revealed, for example, that the most professionally-oriented teachers are the most militant, and that professional movements require militant leaders.[5] Much of this confusion can be reduced by studying the research of sociologists of occupations, who have attempted over the past half century to identify the characteristics of a profession.

### Characteristics of a Profession

All occupations can be placed on a continuum from those that meet the fewest characteristics of a profession to those that meet the most. One would expect physicians and lawyers to be at one end of a continuum and unskilled laborers to be at the other.

Barber notes that "theoretical and methodological consensus is not yet so great among sociologists that there is an absolute agreement on the definition of 'the professions'."[6] Several reasons for disagreement are that some researchers have sought to identify ideal characteristics even though ideal models do not exist; others have sought to identify characteristics of what are thought to be professions; and still others have simply listed consequences of professionalization, such as professionals often occupy positions of power in the society. To add to the confusion, many authors have a mixture.

Flexner suggested characteristics more than a half century ago.

In his view, professional activity was basically *intellectual*, carrying with it great personal responsibility; it was *learned*, being based on great knowledge and not merely routine; it was *practical*, rather than academic or theoretical; its technique could be taught, this being the basis of professional education; it was strongly *organized* internally; it was motivated by *altruism*, the professionals viewing themselves as working for some aspect of the good society (italics in the original).[7]

While many authors have written on the subject since then, there is considerable similarity between Flexner's statement of characteristics and subsequent findings.

A detailed analysis of the conflicting views of leading sociologists would serve largely to confuse the reader. In truth, there is considerable agreement on the characteristics of a professional and, for the purpose of this book, it is not critical which list is used.

Thirteen characteristics of a profession are offered:

1. Knowledge based upon scientific theory.
2. Service orientation.
3. Function.
4. The profession determines its own standards of education and training.
5. The student professional goes through a more far-reaching adult socialization experience than the learner in other occupations.
6. Professional practice is often legally recognized by some form of licensure.
7. Licensing and admission boards are manned by members of the profession.
8. Most legislation concerned with the profession is shaped by that profession.
9. The occupation gains in income, power, and prestige ranking, and can demand higher caliber students.
10. The practitioner is relatively free of lay evaluation and control.
11. The norms of practice enforced by the profession are more stringent than legal controls.
12. Members are more strongly identified and affiliated with the profession than are members of other occupations with theirs.
13. The profession is more likely to be a terminal occupation. Members do not care to leave it, and a higher proportion assert that if they had it to do over again, they would again choose that type of work.[8]

Probably no sociologist of occupations would agree completely with this list of characteristics.[9] This list is used because it is advanced by an eminent sociologist and includes many characteristics or features rather than forcing several similar characteristics into a single category.

Some persons question the wisdom of determining the degree of professionalization of an occupation by comparing it to the characteristics of the established professions. They argue that the established professions do not meet all of the characteristics themselves; some of the characteristics are valid for only a few professions; or that professionalization is more attitudinal than structural.

Seymour has noted the emergence of technicians who have many of the characteristics of professionals, such as a specialized body of knowledge, control over standards and membership, control over setting fees or rates of service, a code of ethical relationships with customers, and some members who may be self-employed. He suggests that "attempts to define a profession in terms of characteristics can easily become an exercise in semantics."[10]

Despite the arguments of Seymour and others, it seems doubtful that teachers will become further professionalized if they do not acquire more of the characteristics of the established professions. The value of describing the characteristics of professions in this chapter, and assessing how teachers meet these characteristics in the following chapter, is that it brings a degree of order to the process of teacher professionalization. It provides some catch-hold points for teachers. As Greenwood notes:

In the construction of an ideal type some exaggeration of reality is unavoidable, since the intent is to achieve an internally coherent picture. One function of the ideal type is to structure reality in such manner that discrete, disparate, and dissimilar phenomena become organized, thereby bringing order out of apparent disorder. We now possess a model of a profession that is much sharper and clearer than the actuality that confronts us when we observe the occupational scene.[11]

## 1. Knowledge Based Upon Scientific Theory

Professionals have knowledge and skills that laymen do not possess, thus practice "rests upon some branch of knowledge to which the professionals are privy by virtue of long study and by initiation and apprenticeship under masters already members of the profession."[12] As a physician makes a diagnosis or performs an operation, he uses knowledge that is highly theoretical and that has been gained by several years of intensive training. The same is true of many occupations thought to be professional by a wide spectrum of the population.

Plumbers, carpenters, and bricklayers have skills that laymen do not possess, yet these occupations are not considered professional. Greenwood speaks to this point when he suggests that to focus upon skills per se in describing the profession is to miss the kernel of their uniqueness.

The crucial distinction is this: the skills that characterize a profession flow from and are supported by a fund of knowledge that has been organized into an internally consistent system, called a *body of theory*. A professional's underlying body of theory is a system of abstract propositions that describe in general terms the classes of phenomena comprising the profession's focus of interest. Theory serves as a base in terms of which the professional rationalizes his operations in concrete situations. Acquisition of the professional skill requires a prior or simultaneous mastery of the theory underlying that skill.[13]

Since it takes several years of study to learn a scientific body of knowledge, persons entering a given profession attend professional schools and often have a period of internship or apprenticeship at which time the student professional applies the knowledge gained in the professional schools. While there are professions that do not have formal professional schools, they are few and are generally in the arts: acting, painting, writing. These occupations are requiring increasingly formal education as the theoretical basis for their disciplines becomes more refined, and as practice in the art requires a better knowledge of theory. Some persons would question whether acting, painting, and writing are professional pursuits, but that is not the concern here. The point is that occupations that have gained acceptance as professions have a scientific body of knowledge, professional schools that require several years of attendance to learn this body of knowledge, and an internship or apprenticeship during which time this body of knowledge is applied.

## 2. Service Orientation

One of the most distinguishing characteristics of a profession is that it has a service orientation toward its clients. This means that professional decisions are not based primarily on the material interests or needs of the profession, but on the perceived needs of the client.

A professional's first allegiance is to his client. The service orientation of a profession is expressed in its code of ethics which, in part, identifies the relationship between the professional and his client and, in turn, society. It normally spells out the obligations of the professional to the public, to peers, and to clients.

The code embodies the terms of an implicit contract between the professional and the society, by which the professional agrees to prevent its members from exploiting a potentially helpless layman and in return receives many privileges.[14]

The code is a public record designed to ensure community confidence. It is true, of course, that many nonprofessional occupations have self-regulating codes. These codes, however, are less binding and have less altruistic references.

Greenwood notes that in a professional code, the professional must have an emotional neutrality toward the client. He must provide service to all who request it, regardless of race, religion, social status, sex, income, politics, or age. The professional must give maximum service to all clients. The professional must offer his service to all, even at his personal inconvenience.

A nonprofessional, by contrast, may or may not provide his services. He is interested primarily in his own self-interest. He can reduce the quality of his service to fit the client's fee.[15]

The service orientation of a profession does not mean that the practitioner is a selfless, humble servant of the people. Indeed, many professionals are inordinately interested in maximizing their personal income. It does mean, however, that the practitioner must, under some circumstances, sacrifice personal self-interest for the benefit of the client and must take steps to ensure that prospective members of the profession are capable.

## 3. Function

No occupation can become very professionalized unless it has a unique function to perform in society. Function concerns what the occupation seeks to accomplish for its clients and for society.

The professional and the layman must agree essentially on the function of an occupation. Thus, the layman understands that the function of physicians is to reduce illness and improve health. The function of lawyers is to uphold justice by offering clients protection under the constitution and the laws of the land. If the layman did not understand the function of physicians and lawyers, he might take his medical problems to lawyers and his legal problems to physicians. If this occurred, medical schools would need to include courses in contracts and torts, jurisprudence, trusts, and constitutional law; whereas, law schools would need to include courses in anatomy, physiology, and radiology. The point is, if the function of an occupation is not clear, professional schools would not know which courses to include in their curriculum, the type of student to accept for training, the length of training for students, or what to include in its code of ethics. "If there is disagreement and confusion and uncertainty about the functions of a profession, there is likely to be disagreement and confusion and uncertainty about every other aspect of the profession."[16]

### 4. Standards of Education and Training

Since professions have a monopoly on the knowledge associated with their field, only persons within the profession can determine the standards of education and training necessary to ensure that the knowledge of the field is attained. This includes determining standards for all specialties within a profession. No layman feels sufficiently well-informed in the field of law to suggest courses in which prospective lawyers need to be enrolled to learn the principles of law, or to suggest the number of years of training that should be required.

### 5. Long Adult Socialization Period

Since professions can be viewed as existing with a knowledge base composed of abstract principles, it follows that only more intelligent persons can learn this knowledge. This means that the selection of student professionals be controlled by the profession, and that the socialization be sufficiently long so that the knowledge can be gained. During this time, the student professional also learns the norms of the profession. In addition, this period offers senior professionals a long time to weed out prospective candidates who do not meet the established standards. This is in stark contrast with nonprofessional occupations, where many jobs can be learned in one day and almost all in a brief training program.

### 6. Licensure

The education and training of a professional lead to a license or certificate. A licensing agency issues a license in recognition of a person's competence to perform in the profession. This does not guarantee that the person is competent, but that is its intent.

The purpose of a license is to screen candidates for admission to a profession. In education, certification has been used in place of license. The two are similar, but not always identical. Anderson and Ertell indicate several differences.

1. Most teachers are public employees, whereas most other professional people are engaged in private practice.

2. The state's authority for teacher certification comes from the general authority for education; that for licensing from the police power.

3. Teacher-certification practices have usually originated at the local level and were subsequently extended to the state level, whereas licensing has typically begun at the state level.

4. The client (student) has no personal choice with respect to teachers; however, there is usually broad freedom to choose among physicians, lawyers, pharmacists, and dentists.

5. Licensure is usually carried out with the collaboration of the professions. On the other hand, teacher certification is usually administered by the state board of education or the chief state school officer.[17]

## 7. Licensing and Admission Boards

The terms license (licensure) and certificate (certification) are largely synonymous and interchangeable. The documents are issued by a legal agency, almost always the state. While the state retains legal control, it has become fairly standard practice for the agency responsible for licensing, admission, and expulsion of members of a specific profession, to be manned by practitioners of that profession.

Licensing and admission boards of professions are manned by members of the profession because non-members (laymen) are not prepared to determine the type of requirements necessary for licensing, admission, or expulsion of a professional. Since laymen are not prepared to determine the types of courses needed by a lawyer in a law school, or to determine those principles or theories that are essential for prospective lawyers, they are not qualified to be members of licensing and admission boards.

The situation is similar in education. Laymen do not know the types of courses needed for teachers. Indeed, some laymen would have teachers enroll in nothing but reading courses. Others would eliminate all methods courses. Some would eliminate all requirements for licensing. Laymen have little knowledge of the essential principles in learning theory, child development, child psychology, or the essential skills in teaching reading, writing, and mathematics. The rationale is simple. The professional's knowledge is esoteric and takes years to acquire. The layman has not spent years gaining the knowledge and, therefore, should not guide or govern the profession.

## 8. Legislation

A profession shapes legislation concerned with its profession. If a state legislature or any other legislative body composed of laymen, whether representative of the people or not, develops and proposes legislation for a particular profession, then the professional loses a degree of his autonomy and is subject to the control of laymen.

Not all laws passed by state legislatures governing occupations and professions are "good," either from the citizens' standpoint or from the occupation's standpoint. The quality of the law passed by a state legislature, however, is not the issue. The issue is the profession's right to govern its own affairs. Therefore, it is unwise for professionals to support the state legislature when it passes legislation they support, and then to criticize the state legislature when they propose legislation they do not support. All legislation concerned with a profession that is not shaped by the profession should be opposed vigorously as a matter of principle.

### 9. Income, Power, Prestige Ranking, and Students

As occupations become more professionalized, they gain in income, power, and prestige. In the process, they gain more control over licensing, training, legislation, and can demand higher caliber students. This results in part because the supply of prospective students exceeds greatly the demand.

Bennis notes that most organizations strive to gain employee incentive through economic rewards. Professionals, by contrast, seek the full utilization of their talent and training once economic rewards become equitable. In addition, they are often concerned with status outside the organization and with developing their learning.[18]

Income, power, and prestige are complementary. Income normally brings power, and power often increases income. Similarly, income and power normally result in a higher prestige ranking. Many would argue that income should not lead to power and that income and power should not lead to a higher prestige ranking, but it does in America and in almost every other nation of the world.

### 10. Lay Evaluation and Control

Professional occupations are autonomous. Autonomous is defined by Webster's as "(a) having the right or power of self-government (b) undertaken or carried on without outside control." Professionals command a wide range of decision making, often possessing literally hundreds of alternatives from which to choose in making a decision. The criminal lawyer, for example, must decide whether to enter a plea of guilty or innocent, of second degree murder or involuntary manslaughter, due to neglect or insanity, in said county, on said day, with said witnesses. The lawyer, like other professionals, resists strongly any supervision or review of his decisions.

This is in contrast with the nonprofessional worker who has little discretionary power because the job specifications have been designed deliberately so that errors can be detected, training provided, or replacements made. It is more accurate to speak of degrees of autonomy rather than as an all or nothing entity.[19]

Teachers have autonomy, as do students, superintendents, and custodians. Teachers are in the process of seeking more autonomy.

The professional gains autonomy largely because of his extensive knowledge in a specific area. The critical factor in this dimension may not be the amount of knowledge of the professional so much as the gap between the professional's knowledge and the layman's knowledge.

A nonprofessional occupation has customers; a professional occupation has clients. What is the difference? A customer determines what services and/or commodities he wants, and he shops around until he finds them. His freedom of decision rests upon the premise that he has the capacity to appraise his own needs and to judge the potential of the service or of the commodity to satisfy them. The infallibility of his decision is epitomized in the slogan: "The customer is always right!" In a professional relationship, however, the professional dictates what is good or evil for the client, who has no choice but to accede to professional judgment.[20]

A second feature is that every profession strives to persuade the community to sanction its authority within specified spheres by conferring upon the profession certain powers and privileges.[21] Chief among these are the profession's control over its training centers; the profession's control over admission into the profession; a licensing system established by the community but on behalf of the profession for screening those qualified to practice the professional skills; an examination, when required, before a board of inquiry whose personnel are members of the profession.

### 11. Norms

While legal controls exist for all professions, nonlegal norms enforced by the profession are far more stringent. The law is silent concerning norms such as professors accepting students regardless of sex, income, social status, or race; reacting objectively to all students' work; and sharing all research findings with colleagues. This characteristic includes a belief in self-regulation.[22] The person best qualified to judge a professional is a professional in the same specialty. Basically, it is a belief in collegial control.

### 12. Identification and Affiliation With the Profession

A common denominator of all professions is a professional association. From an attitudinal standpoint, this provides a sense of group identity.[23] The professional uses his profession and his colleagues as references in the conduct of his work and life. His colleagues provide the major source of ideas for the professional in his work.[24]

The professional culture is characterized as being all-embracing in the sense that professional pursuits often require sixty or more working hours a week and extend into social relationships as well. It is a total career commitment which sharply differentiates it from other occupational groups which are occupied by persons motivated largely by monetary compensations. The professional seeks wages or fees, but wages remain of secondary importance to him.

### 13. Lifelong Occupation

The professional views his work as lifelong or terminal. Rarely does a person leave his chosen field of practice. This is true because a professional has a long and often expensive training period, high status, power, and high income. He has a sense of calling to the field. This is reflected in the dedication of the professional to his work and the attitude that he would probably want to do the work even if fewer extrinsic rewards were available.

The idea of a sense of calling could be argued by many persons if this meant an inner drive to enter a field regardless of its income, status, and working conditions. In truth, the high income, status, and favorable working conditions serve to create a sense of calling to the field. In any event, professionals rarely leave their chosen profession.

This chapter has delineated the characteristics of a profession. The following chapter includes an analysis of the degree to which teachers meet these characteristics.

# THREE
# THE TEACHER AS A PROFESSIONAL

*"In the days of European yesteryear the supper table was divided according to where one sat relative to the salt. Those of low status sat below the salt and were forbidden its use. In terms of a place in the determination of their economic conditions, working conditions, and policy process, teachers have traditionally been seated below the salt. But this Middle Age symbol of servility, long since as dead as knighthood across the seas, is destined to be cast aside by the growth of militancy among teachers who now want to sit above the salt. And so they shall."\**

*"For decades teachers have subscribed to the idea that they have professional obligations (such as staying late to work with students); now they are demanding professional rights as well (such as the right to select their own teaching materials and methods)."\*\**

*"One thing has become crystal-clear. Public school teachers, once the docile handmaidens of public education, are no longer quiescent. Spearheaded by resolute state and local organizations and stimulated by the competition between the National Education Association (NEA) and the American Federation of Teachers (AFT), the 'teachers movement' is gaining strength nationwide. . . . Teachers, or at least their leaders, are beginning to envisage a full partnership in the educational enterprise. They are beginning to talk about rights, not privileges, and power, not consultation. Their actions indicate that they mean what they are saying, as they never meant it before."\*\*\**

Do teachers meet the characteristics of a profession as described in the previous chapter? Is education now a profession? Can it become a profession? If not, can it be further professionalized? Each of the thirteen characteristics of a profession will be examined to note the degree to which teachers meet each one.

### Knowledge Based Upon Scientific Theory

The teacher deals constantly with knowledge. Whether one views teaching as telling, coordinating, or synthesizing, all deal with knowledge. The teacher brings selected materials to the students, helps them search out material, arranges material so that it is more useful to students. He decides, within legal restrictions of the state and local school district, the topics that seem the most useful. He listens to students discuss the knowledge they have gained and evaluates the extent to which they have learned this knowledge.

Does this constant use of knowledge mean that teachers base their actions and behavior upon a scientific body of knowledge? The answer is no. While a teacher's actions in the classroom may sometimes be dictated by well-researched principles, more often than not they are based on what the teacher has found useful in his own experience with students. Indeed, it is often alleged by critics of schools of education and by teachers themselves that they are influenced more as a result of their own experiences in schools than from their training in colleges and universities. Speaking of elementary teachers, Lortie states:

That which is taught in elementary school is presumed to be known by almost all adults, and teachers have not been able to convince many critics—and more importantly, legislatures—that "methods courses" constitute a truly distinct and impressive body of knowledge.[1]

One is inclined to make a blanket assertion that there is no scientific body of knowledge in education. Even the professional schools with doctoral programs in educational administration, psychology, curriculum, and instruction admit to a lack of theory within their disciplines.

Etzioni [2] observes that one reason why schools are basically no different now than they were in the beginning of the nineteenth century is that administrators rely more on folk than on scientific knowledge. He notes that most decision making in meetings of boards and administrators does not compare favorably with the more rational decision making of industry, the military, or the space agency. Educators are not ignorant, but they draw on folk knowledge they acquired in their teaching, on discussions with teachers, and on personal observations. "These are relevant, but they are inferior ways of knowing as compared to scientific knowledge."[3]

Etzioni notes also that in education there is less scientific knowledge available to draw upon; investment in educational research is much smaller than in other areas; most of the educational research conducted is low in quality, in part, because the best minds have not been attracted to education.

If the field of education had knowledge that was based upon scientific theory, it would be taught in the professional courses in schools of education. Koerner comments that the professional courses required of public school teachers, "are not constructed around programs of proven worth. Rather, they represent a half century's haphazard accretions for which no very specific rationale, either theoretical or empirical exists."[4] In addition, "most education courses are vague, insipid, time-wasting adumbrations of the obvious and probably irrelevant to academic teaching."[5]

For those who consider Koerner biased, there is Conant's study that was published in the same year.

*Professors of education have not yet discovered or agreed upon a common body of knowledge that they all feel should be held by school teachers before the student takes his first full-time job.* (italics in the original) To put it another way, I find no reason to believe that students who have completed the sequence of courses in education in one college or university have considered the same, or even a similar, set of facts or principles as their contemporaries in another institution even in the same state.[6]

Teachers do not hold a monopoly on the knowledge and skills necessary for professional practice. Figure 3-1 is an announcement that appeared in a University of California Extension catalogue, Los Angeles. A workshop entitled "Understanding Poor Readers" would seem to require specialists in reading as instructors or resource persons. Among the fourteen instructors, there were no reading specialists in education. Nine were in some field of medicine.

Jackson studied a number of *outstanding* elementary school teachers and found that they lacked a technical vocabulary. They rarely used such terms as defense mechanism, group cohesiveness, reinforcement schedules, and role expectations. He also found that these teachers had conceptual simplicity; that is, an avoidance of complex ideas. They indicated an uncomplicated view of causality—one cause for a given behavior. Teachers' responses were intuitive rather than rational—basing responses on impulse rather than reflection and thought. Teachers were opinionated rather than open-minded. They had narrow working definitions of common terms—one term had one meaning.[7]

Haller sampled conversations from tape-recorded interviews with elementary teachers and compared them to the Thorndike-Lorge Word List, a listing of the frequency with which English words are used. He found that 89.6 percent of the words used in the interviews coincided with the 2,200 most commonly used words on the list. Such heavy use of common vocabulary in discussing their work does not support the belief that teachers possess and employ an extensive technical rhetoric.[8]

If a scientific body of knowledge is lacking, it is not surprising that teachers respond in different ways when faced with identical situations with students. What does the theory of instruction or child development direct the teacher to do, for example, when a student stands in the rear of the room and yells at the top of his voice? Some teachers would administer corporal punishment on the spot. Others would have the student wait until after school and then administer corporal punishment. Others would send the student to the office. Others would ignore it and talk quietly to the student later in the day. Others (not many) would smile in approval. In all probability, the responses would vary because research in education does not have a scientific body of knowledge to guide the teachers' actions.

If teaching had a scientific body of knowledge, teachers' responses to a given stimulus would be similar. If the teachers mentioned in the previous paragraph were asked why they responded as they did, would they support their actions on the basis of principles derived from a scientific body of knowledge? Teachers today are not able usually to cite principles of learning or pedagogy to support their actions.

Teachers do not possess a scientific body of knowledge in part because they are not theoretically-trained at colleges and universities. The task force of the NDEA National Institute for Advanced Study in Teaching Disadvantaged Youth notes the difference between teachers who are theoretically-trained and those who are not.

One of the chief differences between a teacher who is theoretically-trained and one who is not is that the theoretically-trained teacher will perform with a set of

Continuing Education in Medicine and Health Sciences
(Accredited by the American Medical Association) presents

## UNDERSTANDING POOR READERS**

Saturday, April 4, 8:30 a.m.-5:00 p.m.
Sunday, April 5, 9:00 a.m.-4:30 p.m.
Auditorium, Dickson Art Center, UCLA

Reading failures in children are a source of continuing concern to educators. The complexity of the problem and many possible contributing factors make analysis difficult.

This program considers some possible causes of reading problems in children and suggests methods of treatment.

COURSE CHAIRMEN
*Glenn O. Dayton, Jr., M.D.,* Associate Clinical Professor of Ophthalmology, School of Medicine, UCLA
*Margaret H. Jones, M.D.,* Professor of Pediatrics, School of Medicine, UCLA

PROGRAM
Saturday, April 4
Reading Problems as Seen by the Physician and the Nurse · Reading Problems as Seen by the Teacher · Etiological Factors in Learning Disorders · The Psychologist's Role in Evaluation of Learning Disorders · The Physician's Role in Reading Problems — The Pediatrician, The Neurologist, The Ophthalmologist, The Otologist · Congenital Dyslexia and Dominance · The Multiple Handicapped Child · Panel Discussion and Questions

Sunday, April 5
Problems of Attention · Auditory Factors in Early Reading Experiences · Use of Movement Games to Teach Better Concepts · The Psychology of Failure · Teaching Methods for Poor Readers · Comments, Panel Discussion, Questions · Examination for Credit Students

INSTRUCTIONAL STAFF
*Harold B. Alexander, M.D.,* Associate Clinical Professor of Ophthalmology, School of Medicine, UCLA
*Jean Ayers, Ph.D.,* Visiting Associate Professor of Education, University of Southern California, Los Angeles
*Richard T. Barton, M.D.,* Associate Consultant in Otolaryngology, UCLA Student Health Service; Consultant, Kennedy Child Center, Santa Monica
*Bryant J. Cratty, Ed.D.,* Associate Professor of Physical Education, UCLA
*Shelton P. Dawson, M.D.,* Assistant Clinical Professor of Pediatrics, School of Medicine, UCLA
*Glenn O. Dayton, Jr., M.D.*
*Richard M. Flower, Ph.D.,* Associate Professor of Speech and Audiology, Department of Otolaryngology, University of California, San Francisco Medical Center
*Helen Gofman, M.D.,* Associate Professor of Pediatrics and Director, Child Study Unit, University of California, San Francisco Medical Center
*Madeline C. Hunter, Ed.D.,* Principal, University Elementary School, UCLA
*Margaret H. Jones, M.D.*
*Barbara K. Keogh, Ph.D.,* Assistant Professor Education, UCLA
*Donald B. Lindsley, Ph.D.,* Professor of Physiology and Psychology, UCLA
*Richard J. Schain, M.D.,* Associate Professor of Pediatrics and Medicine (Neurology), School of Medicine, UCLA
*Henry H. Work, M.D.,* Professor of Psychiatry, School of Medicine, UCLA

FEE: $30.00          CREDIT: 1½ units (Med. X 403)
**If this course is to be taken for credit, see page 7
Visitors are not permitted — attendance is by enrollment only. No refunds are granted after the program begins.
NOTE: A list of restaurants near the Campus is available at the registration desk. You may bring your own lunch if you wish — coffee is served.
ENROLL BY MAIL: Use application on inside back cover.

**Figure 3–1.** Description of workshop, Understanding Poor Readers, University of California, Los Angeles, Extension Division.

sophisticated concepts taken from the underlying disciplines of pedagogy as well as from the pedagogical field itself. The teacher who is not theoretically-trained will interpret events and objects in terms of common sense concepts that have come from the experience of the race permeated with outmoded ideas about human behavior.[9]

While a scientific body of knowledge is lacking in education, advances have been made. Only one area (reading) will be considered as it is often accused of having no definitive principles. Jacobs describes some of the different types of reading methods in Figure 3-2. The list is not meant to be exhaustive. This brief summary is elementary, but it shows that reading is a complex process that requires a well-trained teacher. While many teachers "teach" reading without a thorough knowledge of reading, this does not mean that substantial knowledge does not exist.[10]

To be viewed as a profession, an occupation must not only have a scientific body of knowledge, but citizens need to acknowledge this fact. This is decidedly not the case in education. The prevailing belief is that teachers are not experts in their field. Parents are not unmindful of the low quality of training nor, as former students, do they believe teachers possess esoteric knowledge. This situation is changing, but the degree of change is not marked.[11]

An additional obstacle to advancing scientific research in the field of education is the negative attitude of teachers toward theory. Darland discusses this point:

. . . our colleges do such a poor job of assisting teachers and all of us in understanding the role and the importance of theory. I would argue that to denigrate importance of theory is an anti-intellectual pastime that the teaching profession cannot afford to engage. Yet most teachers do just that! Why?[12]

The lack of a scientific body of knowledge represents the principal obstacle to teacher professionalization. To help alleviate this situation, there needs to be additional funds allocated and more emphasis placed upon basic theoretical research; professional schools in graduate schools of education need to develop programs that are more, not less, theoretical; teacher training programs need to be improved; and inservice programs need to be expanded.

### Service Orientation

Teachers come closer to satisfying the characteristic of service orientation than any other. Teachers frequently give verbal testimony to the effect that their teaching is an important and necessary service to students and society. Hall conducted a study of eleven occupations, some established and others aspiring to become professions. From this study, he concludes that "on the belief in service to the public and sense of calling to the field attributes, both of which are related to a sense of dedication to the profession, the teachers, social workers, and nurses emerge as strongly professionalized."[13]

| | Method | Emphasis on | May Help With | Drawbacks |
|---|---|---|---|---|
| Decoding | ALPHABETIC | *Names* of letters<br>ar-ue-en = run<br>see-ae-tee = cat | Letter recognition, development of left to right sequence. Durrell has suggested all the consonants' letter names, except h, q, w, and y, contain their phoneme or sound plus an extraneous vowel: e.g., b-ee, s-ee for b, c, d, g, p, t, v, z; or eh-l, eh-m for f, l, m, n, s, x. | Alphabetic sequence (a, b, c, d) may be confusing: e.g., b and d near each other in order, sound and shape similar. Child may lose interest in material read if concentrating solely on letter recognition. Some children make idiosyncratic associations with letters which are no help with sound: e.g., *r* is like a hammer. |
| Decoding | PHONIC | *Sounds* of letters<br>ruh-uh-neh (r-u-n = run)<br>*or*<br>ruh-un (r-un = run)<br>*or*<br>ruh-neh (ru-n = run) | Useful for deciphering unfamiliar (from sight) word. Child can try out a word to see if it fits. Does not have to wait to be told. Phonics can be taught *systematically*: e.g., synthesis, word building, word families; *incidentally*: analytic, beginning sounds of familiar words. | Blending or synthesizing sounds can be difficult for some children. Need for fine auditory discrimination. Boys' auditory ability appears to develop later than girls'. "Irregularity" of English may lead to restriction of vocabulary in readers, artificial style. Child can pronounce unfamiliar word, may not be in oral vocabulary. |
| Reading for Meaning | WHOLE-WORD OR LOOK-AND-SAY | (illustration)<br>run<br>rabbit<br>rug (not mat!) | Use of meaningful words: e.g., ice cream. Often pictorial representation an additional clue. Word/picture association. Look-and-say used for non-pictorial words, also service words: e.g., *are, the, you* taught as sight words. | Individual letters may be ignored, particularly word endings, medial vowels. Leads to guessing. No means of deciphering unfamiliar words. Child waits to be "told." Dependency on teacher. Difficult to differentiate between words similar in length, configuration: e.g., *cat, cot* must keep meaning in the foreground. |
| Reading for Meaning | WHOLE-SENTENCE | The girls run round the tree.<br>(N.B. Not dance or skip) | Emphasis on whole sentence and phrases. Children's interests can be used. Meaningful. Fosters appreciation of importance of intonation, phrasing, and pitch when reading aloud. | Individual letters and words may be left out. Guessing. Written language structure may not be familiar, substitutions may be based on dialect differences: e.g., reads *we was* instead of *we were*; does not help build up letter/sound associations. |
| Multiple Clues | LINGUISTIC | The man will *run* in the race.<br>The man will r . . . (letter clue)<br>The man will *rabbit* (syntactically unacceptable)<br>The man will *reach* (semantically unacceptable)<br>The man will *roll* (not probable) | Language as communication. Oral language provides child with clues. Type of word which will make a good "fit." Word parts, endings, etc. Signal information, e.g., *ed* added to a word signals past tense. Written language presents letter strings which become familiar, build in sound expectations. | Reading materials sometimes based on word using common letter strings, can be artificial. Stressing letter patterns of similar form can be confusing: e.g., *name, same, bane*. Playing down the use of pictures (said to give extraneous cues) may make dull books. May underrate differences in speech patterns. |

**Figure 3–2.** Different Types of Reading Methods. Source: Leland B. Jacobs, "Humanism in Teaching Reading," *Phi Delta Kappan*, LII (April, 1971), 466.

While teachers have a high service orientation, they are lacking in one aspect of service—faculty selection and training. As Goode points out, professions make a considerable effort to seek superior candidates and to give them high quality training, even though this results in increased competition. If this is not done, the society will not grant the profession autonomy from their control.[14]

To date, teachers have not given sufficient attention to the education of prospective teachers although there has been substantial activity at the national level the past year. Teacher training institutions, certification, the training of prospective teachers, and inservice education are discussed in the final chapter.

## Function

One has only to read the current literature in education to discover that there is little agreement on the function of education. Neill maintains that education has no function beyond developing the individual child. Hutchins maintains that the function of education is to pass on to students the noblest ideas and ideals of man. Dewey maintains that the function of education is to create institutions that would set man free to develop his human capabilities in the light of his daily experiences. These traditional views all have modern-day spokesmen.

One might argue that these "competing" philosophies exist for all occupations and that teachers are no more influenced by their existence than any other. Unfortunately, this is not the case. The practice of scientists, physicians, and lawyers, for example, are not influenced directly by these philosophies. A scientist may have different views concerning the source of knowledge, the nature of man, and the future of man. These views may influence the church he attends or the friends he cultivates, but they have little to do with his work. A physician may be a naturalist, but this philosophy does not influence the type of drug he prescribes or the location of an incision for appendicitis. Exceptions in the field of medicine could be euthanasia, abortion, and birth control.

This is decidedly not the case in education. The philosophy that a teacher, a staff, or a community supports influences the goals for students, the method of instruction, and the type of punishment used.

Some may maintain that the function of education persons embrace, while obviously somewhat different, are substantially the same in many areas and do not represent a serious problem so far as agreeing upon an overall function of education. This is rather doubtful. There is a substantial difference in function between persons who argue for general education, and those who argue for vocational education. Similarly, there is often a sizable difference in function between those who believe that the early childhood phase of schooling should be skill development, and those who believe it should be socialization.

Disagreement over the function of education may be healthy in a democracy, but it is decidedly not healthy for the professionalization of teaching. There is a distinct conflict between vague and/or conflicting functions of an occupation and professionalization.

The most serious problem is not that educators disagree concerning the function of education, but that laymen do. Teachers presumably learn the principles and techniques of teaching in their professional schools. They assume a teaching position in a given community and expect to be able to use these principles and techniques in the classroom. The members of the community, however, often have a different view of the function of education than the teachers. These differences can lead to the elimination of sex education in the schools even though teachers believe a systematic program of sex education should be offered. It can lead to the elimination of new methods of school organization such as team teaching and modular scheduling. It can lead to the adoption or elimination of reading in the kindergarten. It can lead, as in the Los Angeles Unified School District, to phonics being instituted district wide for a period of time. It can lead to economics being required of all students in high school.

Lieberman notes that an occupation must have relatively specific functions if it is to be a profession.

Doctors do not have to wait until they are in a community to know what their functions will be. No matter in what medical school he received his training or where he practices medicine, the function of the doctor is relatively clear and definite. Medical schools can set up a program of medical education in the knowledge that it will for most practical purposes enable the person who takes it to practice medicine anywhere in the United States.[15]

### Standards of Education and Training

Teachers have little to say about their standards of education and training. Either the state board of education determines the standards for teachers, or it approves programs of colleges and universities preparing teachers. In either event, teachers do not have a vote and only rarely a voice in the determination of their standards of education. A conversation with most teachers reveals that they are dissatisfied with the teacher preparation program. Some maintain that all their courses in education were useless. At present, they are powerless to alter the courses or the requirements. The Teacher Standards and Licensure Commission is discussed and recommended in the final chapter. It would place the certification and pre-service education of teachers in the hands of teachers.

### Long Adult Socialization Period

While four years of college are required to receive a permanent teaching certificate in all but four states, and five years of college for beginning teachers in several states, this is not more training than is required for many occupations.

The Research Division, National Education Association, reports that 94.1 percent of elementary teachers and 98.8 percent of secondary teachers have a bachelor's degree or more. This has improved markedly in the past twelve years. As late as 1961, 20.3 percent of elementary teachers had no degree (see Appendix A).

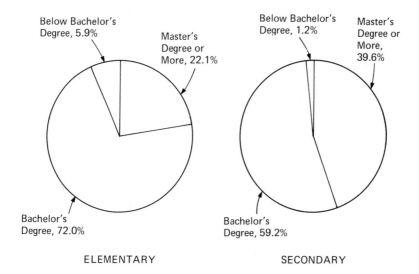

Below Bachelor's Degree, 5.9%

Master's Degree or More, 22.1%

Bachelor's Degree, 72.0%

ELEMENTARY

Below Bachelor's Degree, 1.2%

Master's Degree or More, 39.6%

Bachelor's Degree, 59.2%

SECONDARY

**Figure 3–3.** "Estimated National Distribution of Public-School Teachers by Their Highest Level of Academic Preparation, 1970," *NEA Research Bulletin*, XLIX (May, 1971), p. 56.

Figure 3–3 shows the national distribution of public school teachers by their highest level of academic preparation in 1970.

Teachers, then, go through a rather limited adult socialization period compared to many occupations thought of as professions. While four years of college education are required, only a part of the course work is associated directly with teaching, so it is inaccurate to view college as four years of socialization into teaching.

It should be pointed out, however, that all high school graduates have spent approximately 10,000 hours in close contact with teachers in the course of their schooling.[16] Thus, in that sense, teachers have the longest socialization period of any occupation.

### Licensure

Teachers, as a rule, give little thought to certification once they receive their own certificate.[17] This is not the case in other professions where certification is controlled by members of the profession, and where outstanding candidates are sought eagerly. Teachers, however, should be interested in certification because it offers both a means by which the competence of new teachers can be maximized, and a means of eliminating those who are incompetent and who might serve to undermine the profession.

Lieberman argues that teachers should be vitally concerned with maintaining a high level of competence for certification because teachers suffer more directly from the criticism of parents concerning incompetent teachers than the established professions where the client can simply select another professional. In education, parents cannot shop around for a competent teacher and, therefore, are much more·likely to become annoyed at having to send their children to a professional they believe incompetent.[18]

All of the fifty states require a teaching certificate, the equivalent of a license, to teach. The requirements for certification vary from state to state. "Indeed, among the 16 most populous states, no two states *have adopted exactly the same requirements for entry into the profession* on either the elementary or secondary level."[19] In 1970, four states (Nebraska, South Dakota, Vermont, Wisconsin) did not require a minimum of a bachelor's degree for beginning elementary school teachers for certification; while two states and the District of Columbia required five years of preparation for the certification of beginning secondary school teachers.[20] Appendix B shows the minimum requirements for lowest regular teaching certificates by states.

Anderson suggests that the requirements for certification are appallingly low, being less than a good baccalaureate program in the liberal arts, if the student majors in education at the undergraduate level. More significantly,

certification requirements are not rigidly enforced. On the pretense of filling shortages in instructional staffs, many local school districts easily circumvent state requirements by requesting "emergency" or "temporary" certificates.[21]

In education, certification is granted after completion of certain courses, not after passage of an examination at the end of a total program of study. It is a constraining instrument designed to keep out those persons who have not passed a prescribed number of courses or experiences. Certification is not a device that seeks to include and license all those who can achieve a stated level of performance. Certification today stands simply as a statement of input.[22]

At present, certification is determined by completion of state-specified course requirements. In approximately ten states, certification involves the person's completing specific courses required by the state. Approximately forty states have adopted the "approved-program" approach in which the state automatically issues a certificate to persons approved by colleges and universities that have met the standards established by the state. Conant discusses both approaches.

The policy of certification based on the completion of state-specified course requirements is bankrupt; of this I am convinced. Unfortunately, the newer approved-program approach, which is intended to afford increased flexibility and freedom, involves the State Department to such a degree that the dominant public school forces can use it to impose their own orthodoxy as easily as they used the older system. The specific course requirements and the approved-program approach as it is now developing have critical defects in common; they cannot be enforced in such a manner that the public can be assured of competent teachers . . .[23]

Regardless of whether certification is based on completion of state-specified requirements or the approved-program approach, the minimum qualifications for certification continue to increase. Stinnett found in his comprehensive analysis of teacher certification that twelve states required the completion of a fifth year of preparation, in most cases, for both elementary and secondary school teachers within a specified period of time.[24] Arizona, for example, requires the master's degree or equivalent in credits within a period of six years from the time of the enactment of the legislation for both elementary and secondary school teachers.

Teachers will not gain control over certification until a larger number of teachers evidence an interest in that area. Their lack of interest may be allied with their reluctance to gain control over the evaluation of fellow teachers. Teachers resist evaluating fellow teachers while agreeing that administrators do a poor job.

### Licensing and Admission Boards

On many occasions, teachers have asked me why teachers must control entry if teaching is to be regarded as a profession. The question is really like asking why a bridge player has to take thirteen tricks to make a grand slam. The fact that teachers think they are asking a question of fact instead of a question of meaning is in itself a reflection of their widespread naïveté concerning professionalism. By definition, an occupational group is a profession only when it controls entry to that occupation. To ask whether teachers should control entry to teaching is tantamount to asking whether teaching should be a profession at all; to oppose teacher control of entry while advocating that teaching be a profession is to be confused.[25]

Virtually all professional and several nonprofessional occupations that license practitioners have all or a majority of board members in that occupation. As early as 1952, nurses had a majority in forty-four states, barbers in forty-one, beauticians in thirty-eight, architects in thirty-four, while teachers had a majority of members in only five states.[26] Teachers not only do not have a majority of membership on state licensing boards, but they have little representation at all.

Teachers have little control over certification requirements. Professional accreditation agencies are largely composed of persons who are involved directly in establishing or administering teacher education programs. Teachers do not regulate the teacher education institutions upon which they rely for the professional training of practitioners. This process has resulted in the admission of teachers to the profession with questionable training and competence.[27]

Table 3-1 shows how licensure and accreditation are handled in several professions. All professions, except teaching, grant a license by boards composed of members of that occupation.

The argument advanced most frequently against teachers gaining control of entrance to the profession is that teachers are public employees. By gaining control of entry, they would be placing themselves (a private group) in a position

### Table 3-1. Licensure and Accreditation in Selected Professions

| Profession | Initial Legal Licensure | Accreditation of Preparation Institutions |
|---|---|---|
| Accountancy | By state boards of accountancy, all or majority of whom are practitioners nominated by profession; examination plus experience necessary for licensure in most jurisdictions. | Accreditation by American Association of Collegiate Schools of Business or Regional Accrediting Association or State Board Review. |
| Dentistry | By state boards of dental examiners, all or majority of whom are practitioners appointed by governors—in many states on recommendation of state dental societies. | National by Council on Dental Education, American Dental Association. States require graduation from accredited institutions for licensure. |
| Medicine | By state boards of medical examiners, all or majority of whom are practitioners nominated by profession. | National by Liaison Council on Medical Education, American Medical Association and Association of American Medical Colleges. Required. |
| Law | By state boards of bar examiners, all or majority of whom are practitioners appointed by state supreme court. | National by Council of the Section of Legal Education and Admissions to the Bar, American Bar Association. Required for licensure in most states. |
| Nursing | By state boards of nursing, all or majority of whom are practitioners nominated by profession. | State required by state board of nursing; national available on voluntary basis by National League for Nursing. |
| Osteopathic Medicine | By one of the following depending on the state: State board of osteopathic examiners State board of medical examiners Composite board of medical and osteopathic examiners. | National by American Osteopathic Association. Required. |
| Teaching | In most states, licensure and accreditation functions for elementary and secondary teachers are controlled by state boards of education whose members are laymen, not practitioners. (College teachers are not licensed.) National accreditation of preparation institutions by the National Council for Accreditation of Teacher Education is voluntary. Members of state boards of education are either appointed by the governor or elected by the general citizenry. | |
| Engineering | By state boards of engineering examiners, all or majority of whom are practitioners nominated by profession; license granted on demonstrated competence, including examination. | National by Engineers' Council for Professional Development. Voluntary. State also voluntary. |
| Architecture | By state boards of architectual examiners, all or majority of whom are practitioners nominated by profession; license granted on examination. | National by National Architectural Accrediting Board, Inc. Voluntary. |

Source: "Special Feature on Governance of the Profession," *Today's Education*, LX (December, 1971), 18–19.

to dictate to the public. Persons supporting such a position evidence little confidence in teachers. It may be that the public would be served best by having teachers control entry because they are best able to make decisions concerning other teachers. The fact that teachers are public employees is not relevant. Each year an increasing number of professions (notably physicians) become publicly employed. Does it follow then that entry into these professions be placed in the hands of laymen?

### Legislation

Educators have had success shaping legislation in several states. In general, however, legislators have not sought their advice on legislation concerning education. At the federal level, teacher associations were virtually ignored during the sixties. There are state laws in many states requiring specific subjects in schools. Not only are specific subjects required, but also the grades in which the subjects are to be taught. Indeed, some prescriptions exist in the state *constitution*, which means they cannot be modified by the legislative body. A state legislature should not prescribe legislation for a profession because it places the profession at the mercy of laymen; thus, the profession loses autonomy.

A state legislature can and should provide guidance to teachers by stating broad educational aims for the state, but it is hardly equipped to know what specific subjects would help attain these aims, and certainly not qualified to state at which grade level a specific course should be offered.

Prescribing specific courses is inadvisable also because knowledge is changing so rapidly that teachers need to make frequent changes in the curriculum and should not be required to wait until a bill reaches the state legislature to change a course of study.

### Income, Power, Prestige Ranking, and Students

The income of teachers has increased steadily during the twentieth century from an average of $1,420 in 1929, to $9,689 in 1970-71 [28] (see Appendix C). This increase corresponds to the increase in income of most occupations during the same time. While income increased, in dollars, 78 percent from the school year 1961-62 to 1971-72, it gained only 27.8 percent in actual purchasing power as measured by the Consumer Price Index.[29] Furthermore, as Lindman points out, most persons judge the adequacy of their income by comparing it to the earnings of their friends and neighbors. Have teachers' salaries improved in comparison to per capita income? From 1929 to the present, the ratio has been remarkably stable. Lindman concludes that the average annual salary paid to public school teachers has kept pace with other salaries since the 1930s, but that there has been no relative gain.[30] This corresponds with an AFT study in which Oliver concludes that teacher salaries have increased less than one percent per year in actual purchasing power since 1966.[31] Another study by Oliver in 1972, revealed that the nation's average classroom teacher faces an absolute decline in real spendable earnings for the first time in twenty or more years.[32]

How does the income of teachers compare to "nonprofessional" occupations? The Research Division, National Education Association reports that,

Average salaries of teachers in the public elementary and secondary school systems in 1969 were less than 7 percent above the average earnings of all wage and salary workers in all industries, including both professional and nonprofessional workers; and only 5.3 percent above earnings for employees in manufacturing.[33]

In 1969, public school teachers earned higher wages than only a few occupations—agriculture, forestry, and fisheries; printing and publishing; communication; finance, insurance, and real estate; banking; state and local government enterprises. They earned less than occupations such as mining, contract construction, machinery, and transportation equipment [34] (see Appendix D).

While the income of teachers has increased steadily and exceeds many nonprofessional occupations, Table 3-2 shows it does not compare favorably to those occupations thought of as professions and is less than many nonprofessional occupations in private industry. Elam notes the discrepancy and states:

Recently, we were intrigued to discover that the average net income of doctors of medicine in private practice rose by about $7,250 in the period from 1962 to 1967—from $25,000 to $32,000, that is. The *increase* happens to be almost exactly the *total* current average income for U.S. teachers. The standards of admission to the two professions are not *that* far apart, and shouldn't be. The economic gap represents a distortion of priorities which cannot long be tolerated in our society.[35]

Teachers do not fare too well in school districts with the *highest paid* salary schedules. The Research Division, NEA, reported recently on 174 school districts that responded to its request for information. The mean scheduled salary in 1970-71 for beginning teachers with a bachelor's degree was $7,961. The mean maximum scheduled salary for the master's degree was $15,180. The report points out that most of the districts are in suburban areas near or adjacent to large metropolitan areas. The New York City area accounted for 40.8 percent of the sample.[36]

Another indication of the low salary of teachers is the percentage of teachers who are moonlighting; that is, having two or more employers or being self-employed. A recent study by Michman reports that 39 percent of teachers were moonlighters.[37] Michman suggests that moonlighting may be on the increase as a comprehensive study by Guthrie, in 1965, found that 29 percent of teachers were moonlighting.[38]

Teacher power has increased through the use of strikes. From 1960 to 1970, there were more than 500 teacher strikes. Chapter Seven, on collective bargaining, treats this topic in detail. It is enough to say here that while teachers' power is increasing, it does not compare favorably to the power of many other occupations and professions.

Readings of occupational prestige have been taken over the past forty

## Table 3-2. Average Starting Salaries, School Year 1965-66—1972-73

Average starting salaries, school year,

| Group | 1965–66 | 1966–67 | 1967–68 | 1968–69 | 1969–70 | 1970–71 | 1971–72 | 1972–73* |
|---|---|---|---|---|---|---|---|---|
| | | | | *Men and Women Teachers with Bachelor's Degree* | | | | |
| Beginning teachers* | $4,928 | $5,144 | $5,523 | $5,941 | $6,383 | $ 6,850 | $ 7,061 | |
| | | | | *Men Graduates with Bachelor's Degree†* | | | | |
| Engineering | $7,548 | $8,112 | $8,772 | $9,312 | $9,960 | $10,476 | $10,500 | $10,608 |
| Accounting | 6,732 | 7,128 | 7,776 | 8,424 | 9,396 | 10,080 | 10,260 | 10,356 |
| Sales-Marketing | 6,276 | 6,774 | 7,044 | 7,620 | 8,088 | 8,580 | 8,736 | 8,904 |
| Business Administration | 6,240 | 6,576 | 7,140 | 7,560 | 8,100 | 8,124 | 8,424 | 8,568 |
| Liberal Arts | 6,216 | 6,432 | 6,780 | 7,368 | 7,980 | 8,184 | 8,292 | 8,328 |
| Production Management | 6,816 | 7,176 | 7,584 | 7,980 | 8,736 | 9,048 | 9,792 | 9,828 |
| Chemistry | 7,032 | 7,500 | 8,064 | 8,520 | 9,276 | 9,708 | 9,720 | 9,840 |
| Physics | 7,164 | 7,740 | 8,448 | 8,916 | 9,348 | 10,080 | 9,636 | 9,990 |
| Mathematics-Statistics | 6,672 | 7,260 | 7,944 | 8,412 | 8,952 | 9,468 | 9,192 | 9,276 |
| Economics-Finance | 6,600 | 6,732 | 7,416 | 7,800 | 8,304 | 8,880 | 9,216 | 9,240 |
| Other fields | 6,360 | 7,044 | 7,644 | 7,656 | 8,796 | 9,264 | 8,580 | 8,664 |
| Total, all fields (weighted average) | $6,792 | $7,248 | $7,836 | $8,391 | $8,985 | $ 9,361 | $ 9,534 | $ 9,682 |

*Women Graduates with Bachelor's Degree*

| | | $6,324 | $7,104 | $7,776 | $8,484 | $8,952 | $9,312 | $9,516 |
|---|---|---|---|---|---|---|---|---|
| Mathematics-Statistics | NA | | | | | | | |
| Economics— Finance | NA | 6,000 | 6,636 | 6,984 | 7,224 | 8,400 | 8,400 | ‡ |
| General Business | NA | 5,520 | 6,000 | 6,840 | 7,104 | 8,184 | 8,016 | 8,184 |
| Chemistry | NA | 7,056 | 7,452 | 8,280 | 8,532 | 9,180 | 9,744 | 9,816§ |
| Accounting | NA | 6,768 | 6,984 | 7,716 | 8,304 | 8,952 | 9,516 | 10,224 |
| Home Economics | NA | 5,664 | 6,276 | 6,660 | 7,056 | 7,380 | 7,932 | ‡ |
| Engineering— Technical Research | NA | 7,260 | 8,208 | 8,904 | 9,672 | 10,128 | 10,608 | 10,560 |

Source: Reported in *NEA Research Bulletin*, XLIX (October, 1971), Research Division, National Education Association, 75.

*In school systems enrolling 6,000 or more pupils.

†Average salaries shown for men for 1972-73 are based on hires made in November 1971 of men who will graduate in June 1972.

‡Not reported.

§For science graduates.

years in the United States. Teacher prestige has not increased significantly during this time. Teachers rank below most professional groups, but now rank above artistic and communication professions, i.e., artist, musician, author, journalist.[39] "Between 1947 and 1963, although not arriving in the league of the established professions, the prestige rating of teachers did improve (from a rank of 34 out of 90 to one of 27.5)."[40] Lortie notes that among women, teaching has high prestige; however, for men, teaching ranks significantly lower than top levels of work achievement.[41]

One factor that may negatively influence teacher prestige is the lack of maturity of the clients over whom they have control. There may be a scale of prestige based on the ages of the children being taught. Evidence of this feeling can be found in school systems where some high school teachers "look down upon" elementary teachers, and where some upper elementary teachers "look down upon" lower elementary teachers.

After reviewing the status of teachers, Gerstl felt obligated to state that if the status situation appears overly grim, it should be remembered that other more esteemed professions were the frame of reference and that teaching is more highly thought of than many types of work.[42]

Since teaching has comparatively low income, power, and prestige, it cannot demand high caliber students. Students planning graduate work in education represent lower socioeconomic backgrounds than students in other graduate fields. While it is not known what effect low socioeconomic origin has upon performance of teachers, Lieberman notes that,

If teachers are drawn largely from social classes which offer very limited opportunities for intellectual and cultural development, . . . it would be surprising for this to have no effect on the overall quality of educational services.[43]

Regardless of statements by educators that teachers compare favorably with members of other occupations in intellectual ability, there is much evidence that they do not. A smaller proportion of men and women in education are from the top fifth in academic performance, except for minor health fields, than in any other academic area. Men of higher intellectual ability are especially underrepresented.[44] "The low standing of education departments is reflective of the quality of their students. The inability to attract good students will, in turn, contribute to the vicious cycle of reinforced intellectual mediocrity."[45]

### Lay Evaluation and Control

The teacher is far from free of lay evaluation and control. Citizens, in part because they have spent twelve or more years in school, feel free to offer advice and criticism.

Many citizens can describe the characteristics of their best and worst teachers. They "know" how mathematics, social science, and art were taught to them, and most are able to offer criticism. They "know" the types of materials offered, as well as the rules and procedures employed to deal with recalcitrant and vociferous students. Parents can and do cite objections to some of these practices. Follow-up studies of high school graduates have revealed consistently that students have very definite views concerning teachers, the curriculum, co-curricular activities, and methods of instruction. The criticisms voiced by these students often parallel closely criticisms offered by educational reformers. Many parents feel especially free to offer suggestions and advice to teachers, since they consider themselves intellectually superior to teachers by virtue of more years of schooling. This situation is reinforced, interestingly, when teachers encourage parents to assist their child with his homework. If the parent can teach the child, then the parent is inclined to believe that he should be able to evaluate the teacher's and the school's performance.

The teacher is often something of a pawn of the patrons in the local school district. Gerstl observes that this is explained partly because the students belong to others, and there is the tendency to allow the layman to believe he knows what is best for his child.[46].

The parents and community are not the only influences that reduce the teacher's authority. The teacher does not have unlimited control over his clients, the students. The teacher must accept all students sent to him in all but a few school districts, even if he considers himself unable to teach them. One commonly hears teachers complain about having too many students with mental and/or emotional problems that require teachers with specialized training, or recalcitrant and belligerent students who render the teacher's instruction ineffective. Teachers are permitted to send such students to the office or "counselor," but they rarely do because they know the student will return the next day. Similarly, the teacher cannot expel a student from his class. In the intermediate and secondary schools, students may enroll in virtually any subject they wish regardless of the wishes of the teacher or counselor. Not uncommonly, intelligent students enroll in so-called easy courses or; conversely, less intelligent students enroll in courses too difficult for them.

The teacher's relationships to society reveals his lack of control. He teaches what he is told to teach. The prescription begins at the state legislature and extends all the way down to department chairmen. Textbooks, in many schools, are selected for the teacher or the teacher selects them from a list prepared by others. Supplementary materials used by teachers must often be approved before they are used. Material related even indirectly to communism, socialism, patriotism, sex, and evolution often arouses public concern and censorship. The teacher cannot simply turn to another client. He is reprimanded or dismissed. As Wittlin points out, lay boards have considerable authority over certification, salary, and the selection of instructional materials. Boards even reject recommendations to keep extremely deviant students out of regular classrooms. "No lay adviser would defy a hospital administrator or doctor with the immoral request of accommodating in a general ward patients suffering from an infectious or mental disease."[47]

The relation between public employees and governance needs to be examined. Some persons maintain that public employees receive their salary from the citizenry and thus should be beholden to them. The fact that teachers are paid public employees, however, does not mean that they should permit laymen to govern their profession. The public, through its board of education, can determine broad policy and the financial support it will provide a school district. But, it has no claim to make professional decisions in areas such as teacher training programs, certification, teacher selection and evaluation, specific courses of study, and the selection and use of instructional materials. The public can decide to build a bridge, but engineers decide how to build it; the public can establish a system of courts, but lawyers determine how they will try a case in court; the public can authorize the construction of a hospital, but physicians determine the equipment needed and the medical treatment to be used with patients. Similarly, the public can establish a public school system, but teachers should decide what students will study and which experiences are most useful.

The autonomy that is derived from expertise extends beyond professions. Most electricians would be startled if a layman tried to tell them how to wire a house. Many automobile mechanics become annoyed when customers tell them what needs to be repaired on their automobiles rather than describing the symptoms or dysfunctions. There is no reason why teachers as public employees should not seek to gain additional autonomy in the process of professionalization. Some citizens will undoubtedly object; but, in the long run, paradoxically, laymen will never view teachers with respect until teachers are liberated from lay interference in the governance of their profession.

### Norms

Teachers have norms, such as teachers should be kind to students, teachers should not criticize each other, teachers should not punish the class for an individual student's misbehavior, and teachers should continue their educational training.

The number of norms for teachers is no less than for established professions, but many are enforced by non-teachers. Some are enforced by law. The norms cited above, for example, are violated frequently and the violators are not subject to peer criticism. Also, teachers have few norms that are more stringent than legal controls, a condition that is reversed in the established professions.

### Identification and Affiliation With the Profession

It seems logical that an occupation with a high service orientation would tend to be identified strongly with the profession, but this does not explain why such a high percentage of teachers leave teaching. Some persons would maintain that any occupation with a high percentage of women will show a high number leaving that occupation. In truth, however, an extremely high percentage of men leave teaching as well. Hall contends that teaching is a secondary concern for many teachers. The first concern has to do with family and household responsibilities. It provides a paycheck to support these responsibilities. He maintains that teachers treat teaching as a job rather than as a career as evidenced by the large number of teachers who leave teaching.[48]

### Lifelong Occupation

"No occupational group can hope to attain recognition as a profession if a relatively large number of its practitioners are transients who do not look upon their work as a career."[49] The NEA reports that 78 percent of all teachers would choose teaching as a career if they had it to do over again.[50] A sizable number, however, leave teaching each year—women to be married, to have children, to become full-time housewives; and both men and women to become administrators, or to enter other occupations. Forty-five percent of married women leave the classroom for a year or more for maternity or child-rearing purposes. Fully 53.5 percent of married women have one or more absences. This compares to 46.1 percent for all women, and 19.4 percent for men.[51]

Unskilled workers shift from one job to another. Professionals, on the other hand, normally remain in one occupation. "So strong is this tendency that the ex-lawyer or ex-physician is likely to be regarded rather like an unfrocked priest, as a person who has proven unworthy of great responsibility."[52]

There is a tremendous attrition rate among teachers. At the end of five years, only about 20 percent of the incoming group are still in the classroom. Not only do teachers leave teaching at an alarming rate, but during the past ten years the percentage of certified teachers who actually entered teaching immediately following certification ranged from 74.1 to 83.2 percent for elementary, and 62.3 to 69.2 percent for high school teachers.[53]

An author with the AACTE maintains that the primary reason so many trained teachers never enter the classroom is a lack of commitment to teaching because of little investment in preparation for it. The amount of knowledge wasted is not considerable. Other professions have an extensive and strenuous training program. Teachers, by contrast, normally have a basic liberal arts program which includes a few courses in pedagogy. If a teacher decides to change his occupational goals after graduation he loses little, since his educational background is quite similar to that of a liberal arts major.[54]

A sizable number of teachers do not view teaching as a terminal occupation, but as Godine points out, "As conditions of employment improve and teachers acquire income commensurate with their professional status, more people will view teaching as an ultimate career rather than as a ladder to administrative advancement."[55] In addition, as teachers gain power and prestige, a higher percentage of men will tend to remain in teaching. As women become more liberated and seek to establish their identities outside of and independent of the home, they will be less inclined to relinquish a promising career to be housewives.

### Summary

Teachers do not meet many of the characteristics of a professional. They are in a particularly unenviable position regarding (1) function, (2) knowledge based upon scientific theory, (3) licensing and admission boards being manned by members of the profession, (4) income, power, prestige ranking, and demand for high caliber students, and (5) freedom from lay evaluation and control. Teachers rank high in perhaps only one characteristic, a service orientation. The remaining characteristics lie somewhere in between, although doubtless there would be considerable disagreement with any rank. Vander Werf, after noting five characteristics of a professional states, "Traditionally, teachers' organizations have paid little attention to any of these except perhaps in a small way to specialized knowledge and only recently to autonomy."[56]

Teachers need not necessarily satisfy all of the characteristics of a professional. To ape the established professional model is both unrealistic and unwise.

Our mistakes have been to equate the concept of professionalism with the particular way in which medicine and law are practiced. It would be more realistic to recognize that the teaching profession has characteristics of its own which dictate for teachers a different relationship to society. In other words, we have been using the wrong yardstick.[57]

While the preceding remarks have some validity, teachers should resist rejecting wholesale the idea that teaching is somehow peculiar from all other occupations. The traditional characteristics of professionals provide a useful framework against which all occupations can be analyzed and measured. Table 3-3 presents several contrasts between the education profession and other professions.

Becker has noted that authorities are unclear as to whether professions are to be defined by objective features of organizations and activity, or by the praiseworthy moral stance of their practitioners.[58] In the preceding two chapters, for example, thirteen characteristics of professions were analyzed to determine the degree to which teachers meet them. The assumption is that the closer an occupation gets to the attainment of these characteristics, the closer it will be to attaining professional status. Becker questions this assumption and suggests that professionalism is conferred by people on occupations that seem morally to deserve it. Medicine and law qualify. Teaching and plumbing do not. He tries to prove this in part by showing that physicians do not meet many of the characteristics of professions. He suggests that "educators might perform a great service by working out a symbol more closely related to the realities of work life practitioners confront, a symbol which could provide an intelligible and workable moral guide in problematic situations."[59]

Becker and Solomon do not confront the issue of why the public confers professional status on certain occupations and not on others. While they resist defining occupations by the degree to which they meet a set of characteristics, they offer no conceptualization or "symbol" to guide teachers in the years ahead. Without an alternative, teachers have little choice but to seek professional status by gaining in the characteristics discussed in the previous chapter.

Before teachers make too loud a claim to professional status, they need to

### Table 3-3. Table of Contrasts Between the Education Profession and other Professions

| *In the Education Profession:* | *In other Professions:* |
| --- | --- |
| The practitioner works with 30 or more clients simultaneously. | The practitioner deals with one client at a time. |
| The relationship is adult to child. | The relationships is adult to adult. |
| Treatment is conducted in a classroom with 29 or more other clients observing and hearing all that takes place. | Treatment is conducted in a private office. |
| Treatment continues six hours a day, 180 days a year. | Conference is held by appointment, and the period is normally brief. |
| A multitude of problems must be dealt with continuously and constantly. | The client consults the expert usually regarding one specific problem. |
| Results of treatment are long range and not immediately evident. | Expert's advice usually brings immediately identifiable results. |
| Results are intangible, concerning attitudes and behaviors. | Results are tangible, even immediately visible. |
| Compensation derives from public funds. | The client is expected to pay the expert directly. |
| The client is required to submit to treatment by law. | The client voluntarily seeks expert services. |
| Legal responsibility for the welfare of children is complex, i.e. involving parents. | Legal responsibility is direct and from adult to adult. |
| The client has little or no choice in the selection of the practitioner. | The client chooses his expert, changing his choice at will. |
| Communication to the adult world is through the minds of children, creating misunderstandings. | Communication is adult to adult, with no intermediary. |

Source: Eva Washington, "How Do We Compare?," *California Teachers Association Journal*, LXV (May, 1969), 18. Copyright 1969, by California Teachers Association.

become familiar with the arguments of those (often teachers) who view teachers as craftsmen, mired in a bureaucratic structure, unable to make critical decisions concerning their students and, in particular, their profession. The following chapter presents these points of view. Even if teachers reject the idea that they are functionaries, they need to realize the societal forces impinging upon the school and the teachers that serve to reinforce that image.

# FOUR
# THE TEACHER AS A FUNCTIONARY

*"I have been teaching eleven years and this—well—this is the first time my own views have been sought concerning any educational matter."\**

*"Mere educational anarchy would result if teachers were to construe . . . our consulting them in school matters as an invitation to take into their own hands and to act upon their individual initiative in such matters as are the proper duties of administrative officers. Reference is here made to such functions as the making and administering of courses of study, the choice of textbooks, the purchase of school aids and supplies, the selection and assignment of teachers."\*\**

*"Teachers who are poorly paid, treated as subordinates, and given little freedom and autonomy by the school administration cannot help but reflect their true position and reduce their influence in the pupil's eyes. A person must have a measure of self-respect and status before he can expect others to admire these traits in him."\*\*\**

*"We have to punch a time clock and abide by the Rules. We must make sure our students likewise abide, and that they sign the time sheet whenever they leave or reenter a room. We have keys but no locks (except in lavatories), blackboards but no chalk, students but no seats, teachers but no time to teach."\*\*\*\**

The thesis advanced in this chapter is not one that the author embraces, but it has the support of some scholars and a number of laymen. The thesis is that the teacher is a functionary or technician in a bureaucracy. This is not meant to suggest that teachers are intellectually incompetent or uncreative and lazy. Many competent persons are functionaries in bureaucracies; consider the millions of white collar workers in government and industry.

As a functionary, most significant decisions, even those related directly to his work, are made for him. Since they are made for him, they can be altered or abolished without his consent and even without consulting him for an opinion. A functionary is easily replaceable. While it is desirable that he be well trained, it is not imperative. The organization will continue, for example, even though the functionary does not know why he does what he does, which is often the case. He need not know how his particular job contributes to the welfare of the total organization.

The role of the teacher as a functionary is presented clearly by Wayland.

Essentially what I am saying is that the teacher is a subordinate member of an organization, a bureaucracy in the sociological sense, and that the basic definition of his role in that system is largely determined for him. Modifications in that role are made in the interest of the goals of the system, and the individual must either accept this role or seek a setting where the role is more to his liking.[1]

Similarly, Johnson notes that the record-keeping, the use of standardized instructional materials, the ritualized ways in which cognitive information is presented, the official timekeeping, and the control over supplies represent bureaucratic role expectations for teachers.[2] If a teacher is a functionary, it should be revealed by analyzing the daily activities of a typical classroom teacher, such as the schedule he follows, the decisions he makes, and the amount of control he has.

Many factors governing the behavior of teachers are outside their control. The teachers and students are required by law to be present, on time, and not leave early. The teacher must teach to the students assigned to him and at a prescribed time. The selection of subjects, the method of organizing teachers and students, and the establishment of rules and regulations are essentially outside the control of teachers. The remainder of this chapter presents a description and analysis of sixteen factors that limit the decision making of teachers.

### 1. The School as a Socializing Agent

Since the Industrial Revolution, schools have existed, in large part, to perpetuate the nation-state. The needs of society determine in large measure the philosophy of education, the kinds of educational opportunities available, the social groups to which they are available, and all elements of the educational system including methods of financing, administration, certification, curriculum, etc.

Citizens establish and finance the schools, and all children are obligated by law to attend. American courts have ruled consistently that children must attend school. At least part of the argument of the courts has been that an individual citizen has responsibilities toward the society (as opposed to self-development, per se), and that the child must attend school to learn these responsibilities. Some persons, such as Neill, Goodman, and Illich, maintain that schools should be concerned wholly with the development of the individual, but there is no likelihood that that point of view will be adopted widely in the United States.

Education exists, in large part, to perpetuate American values—a representative government, an informed electorate, a viable and expanding economic system. While education is legally the responsibility of the various states, these states and their local boards of education cannot or more often will not make a decision that is inconsistent with the goals of America. A teacher, for example, is not free to teach his students to overthrow the government, to disrespect the flag, or to support socialism. A board of education cannot abandon the teaching of reading, communication skills, or mathematics; nor is it free to provide education only for those intellectually capable.

In addition to the fact that schools exist in large measure to socialize young people into an adult society, the existing customs and mores of the people influence schools. A year-round school will become a reality only if parents are willing to give up summer vacations or take several vacations of shorter duration during the year. Similarly, a four-day school week will not likely become a reality until a large segment of the population is employed four days a week, or until the schools provide some system for taking care of children whose parents are at work.

## 2. Specific Function of the Schools

Schools are responsible for providing a "basic" program of studies in education. This restricts the decision making of all persons in education. A local board of education, for example, cannot decide that the students should work in the ghetto to decrease poverty, or work in the city parks to keep them clean. The teacher cannot decide that the students should work as nurses' aides all day instead of attending class. As Etzioni states: "Schools prosper only at the tolerance of the taxpayers, and hence must take into account community pressures to keep up the legitimation of their efforts."[3]

Some teachers believe that their lack of decision making is the result of principals or superintendents who consider themselves "Little Napoleons." Others blame board members or citizens who believe anyone can teach second-grade students. There is some truth to these allegations, but in general such blanket indictments represent a narrow and simplistic view of the dynamic role of the school in a social and cultural context. To cite persons such as principals, super-intendents, or board members as causal agents is to assume that they are free to redefine their roles. It is more accurate to view such persons as actors playing roles that have been assigned to them.

## 3. Goals of Local Community

The teacher's scope of decision making is limited by the desires of citizens in the community. The citizens of an upper-middle-class suburban community may reject courses in industrial arts or secretarial practices even though teachers believe many students could benefit by such courses. Conversely, citizens in lower socio-economic communities may place a disproportionate weight on the value of basic skills while teachers would prefer placing more emphasis on students developing a more wholesome concept of themselves and engaging in social interaction with peers.

In addition to the goals of the local community, individual parents exert influence on teachers. It is not uncommon for teachers and counselors at the intermediate and senior high schools to complain of parents who insist that their child enroll in courses for which he is not prepared, as well as the frequent complaint of parents regarding so-called controversial books assigned by teachers.

## 4. Teacher Competence

All teachers are not competent, just as all scientists and lawyers are not. Anyone who has been in an administrative or supervisory position or has had any contact with teachers (the typical adult has been a student of over forty teachers), knows that incompetent teachers exist. There are teachers who dislike students who are not intellectually capable, who have a limited knowledge of content and process, who are so bored and indifferent concerning their own lives that life in their classrooms are dull and unproductive. Because such teachers exist, all teachers are limited in their decision-making in order to protect students.

Leles conducted a study in Ohio that involved responses from 765 elementary and secondary school teachers. He found more than 200 pieces of data describing practices and situations in which educational purposes were perverted by the way teachers and other school personnel handled students.

Among these practices are prejudiced behavior toward children of lower social status or of less ability; extreme disciplinary measures; and negative self-images given to students, turning them away from school and learning.[4]

Some incompetent teachers will remain incompetent in spite of efforts to educate them. Tenure protects all teachers, even the extremely incompetent. The fact that there are incompetent teachers is not meant to be critical of all teachers or teacher preparation institutions. Nor is it seen as particularly atypical when compared to many other occupational groups. It is simply to acknowledge a fact. It is everyone's wish to reduce the number of sub-standard teachers, and everyone should feel a responsibility to assist. But it does no good to contend blindly that all teachers are competent. This being so, the argument follows that rules, policies, and procedures are needed to guide and occasionally control minimally competent teachers.

### 5. Teacher Turnover

When a functionary leaves an organization, the organization operates essentially without interruption. The AACTE reports that about 12 percent of all teachers leave schools at the end of each school year.[5] With the relatively high teacher turnover, the best prospect for stability and continuity is in an educational program that is independent of particular teachers. This stability and continuity can best be gained through fairly permanent rules and procedures that continue regardless of the staff. Thus a new teacher is likely to follow closely the state or local syllabus to be certain he does not interrupt or duplicate the sequence of experiences of the students. Without permanent rules and procedures, a school with a high teacher turnover would spend a disproportionately large amount of its time deciding routine problems and policies.

### 6. Time Limitation

Teachers have little time outside of their classrooms. This lack of time serves to limit the decision-making area for teachers. Bishop argues that teachers should spend no more than 50 percent of their time in front of children.[6] If the teacher had more time, he could enhance his competence. He might be able to review the latest research in areas such as mathematics, social science, language arts, science, learning, instructional materials. Time is simply not available. The teacher, therefore, welcomes the various curriculum guides prepared by others because he does not have the time to review and study all data and materials himself. The teacher, busy with students from 9:00 to 3:00 each day, has little enough time to plan exciting and useful learning opportunities for the students. If most of the decisions of teachers were not routinized, perhaps as high as 95 percent, teachers would be incapacitated by the sheer complexity of the operation.

### 7. Financial Limitations

Lack of financial support restricts the decision making of teachers. Every organization must operate within a budget. While teachers often seek additional funds, eventually a budget must be established which seldom provides all the materials, equipment, and supplies needed by teachers. While teachers might wish closed-circuit television, an enlarged library, and a computer program in mathematics, it is unlikely that they will get one, let alone all three.

A teacher working with inadequate facilities, a crowded room, one textbook per student, few instructional materials, no library, no audiovisual equipment, a broken-down tape recorder, inadequate supplies (even those who can teach under such conditions), has every excuse for playing the role of functionary.

### 8. Facilities Limitations

Facilities can limit the decision making of teachers. The teachers in an old comprehensive school, for example, may wish to adopt team teaching, but the facilities might be such that it is difficult to do so. Assuming that remodeling is not possible, the only remaining alternative is to construct a new facility. This is seldom possible. Similarly, many elementary schools do not have space for a library. One can always argue that space can be found somewhere, but this is not always true. This restraint is so obvious that it appears superfluous, yet it is a restraint and is cited frequently by teachers as a reason why an innovation cannot be adopted.

### 9. Complexity of Knowledge

It is impossible for an individual teacher or group of teachers to keep abreast of new programs and research findings. The elementary teacher cannot be knowledgeable in five or six disciplines of knowledge, in addition to knowing what is current in learning, psychology, human development, and pedagogy. The problem is as severe at the secondary level.

Teachers need assistance in determining fundamental and complex curriculum questions. What knowledge is of most worth for which individual?

Which of the traditional disciplines should be included in the curriculum? Which mode of inquiry will be applied once the disciplines are established? If the curriculum is not to be organized around the essential disciplines, how is it to be organized? What methods of learning are most effective in which discipline? These types of questions require the knowledge of many persons—university professors in disciplines such as pedagogy, psychology, and curriculum—as well as insightful practicing teachers. In the process of preparing and organizing the vast field of knowledge for teachers, many decisions must be made. This is inevitable and desirable. But, in the process of developing an institutional curriculum, teachers lose much of their freedom to make decisions regarding subject matter.

### 10. Need for Continuity and Sequence

The learning opportunities in which students engage should have continuity and sequence, that is, a student should be able to encounter a learning opportunity over and over for reinforcement, and it should become increasingly difficult.

If these principles are not taken into account, a teacher might repeat content already covered adequately by a previous teacher, or conversely, overlook significant content that needs to be covered. A fifth-grade teacher, for example, might decide not to offer numeration in mathematics to the students and thereby leave a twelve-month gap in continuity and sequence. The sequence of a subject should not be left to chance. Some type of central planning is necessary to guarantee that a regular sequence is being followed. But, once again, an institutionalized course of study that has continuity and sequence reduces the flexibility and freedom of the teacher.

### 11. The Assignment of Work in a Bureaucracy

Not only must the teacher fit his activities into a unified curriculum, but he must be willing to comply with the demands of the total organization, the complexity of which is somewhat startling to many persons. One can imagine, for example, a school system where no teacher wanted to teach kindergarten. Does that suggest kindergarten students be sent home? The solution is that some teacher who would prefer to teach upper elementary or second grade must teach kindergarten for a year until a teacher can be employed who wishes to work with younger children. Perhaps that is an unlikely example. It is certainly not uncommon for teachers to have assignments that are not of their choosing. There seems little chance that this situation will change. With the dynamic nature of our society, schools can change fairly drastically in a short period of time. An industry may move a plant into or out of a school district with a resulting change in the school's enrollment and financial resources. An unusually high number of resignations one year may require drastic shifts in personnel. The state or local school district may require a particular course for the first time. National curriculum studies such as SMSG, PSSC, BSCS, may reduce or increase the student-teacher ratio and require last minute changes. This suggests that centralized authority is necessary, and that the decision-making area of teachers must be restricted.

Persons in a bureaucracy are employed to accomplish the organization's goals. In times of crisis, individuals within the bureaucracy must be willing to relinquish some of their freedom of choice to comply with or to satisfy the needs of the organization.

## 12. Size of School Systems

Public school systems in operation have decreased from over 127,000 in 1931-32, to less than 18,000 today. Virtually every authority in education believes that the present number of school districts should be reduced even more, excepting large city school districts. Thus, school districts are decreasing in number and increasing in size. One can predict then that centralization will increase and with it, institutional procedures and rules. Once again, teachers will tend to lose authority.

## 13. Ripple Effect of Decisions

Once a decision is made it influences or forces other decisions. This ripple effect can limit severely the scope of decisions made by teachers. It is possible, for example, for a given faculty developing educational specifications for a new school, to design a structure with self-contained classrooms. In subsequent years, the teachers may decide they wish to engage in team teaching. This is possible, but only if funds are available to tear down some walls and purchase partitions or sight barriers. Thus, the initial decision to build a school with walls tends to limit the decisions of the faculty at a later date. The opposite can also be true—open space schools restrict those teachers who wish a self-contained classroom.

It is possible that the administration, working with a representative group of teachers, might decide to place increased emphasis on early childhood education—perhaps offering kindergarten. The funds allocated to this program indirectly and sometimes directly affect the educational program throughout the district. There is good reason to believe, for example, that kindergarten would affect the student-teacher ratio in most classrooms; it might reduce the amount of money allocated for supplies; and it might mean more crowded buildings. Thus, in a very real way, no one has complete control over all decisions. The vast hierarchy of authority seems to make this even more applicable to education.

## 14. Administrators

Administrators limit the decision making of teachers. It is the principal, quite often, who insists upon achievement groupings, an enlarged phonics program, the retention of the self-contained classroom or, conversely, adamantly decrees heterogeneous grouping, no phonics, and team teaching. Administrators in the central office often insist upon multi-itemed report cards four times a year in preference to parent-teacher conferences; suggest investing funds in bleachers for the football field rather than in libraries for the elementary school; adopt SMSG and impose it district wide rather than several programs, leaving the choice of programs to the discretion of individual faculties. An essential task, discussed more thoroughly in Chapter Eight, is to determine which decisions can be made most appropriately by administrators, and which decisions can be made most appropriately by teachers.

### 15. Tradition

Tradition dictates most of our actions. Most persons are incapable of considering objectively new solutions, approaches, and strategies for every problem they confront. Man falls back on tradition because of a lack of time and often energy. Many teachers teach like their former teachers because they lack the time to learn a variety of new approaches.

A person who wishes to change an educational practice must anticipate that persons will resist the innovation because it breaks with tradition. Thus, tradition limits the decision making of teachers.

The fifteen factors mentioned thus far serve to limit severely the decision making of teachers. An optimist might believe that the existing situation will improve, but the facts do not seem to warrant that belief. In addition to the factors just mentioned, the educational system is becoming national in character; thus, centralization of decision making is even more likely. The following section discusses the influence of the national educational system, which offers additional support for the role of the teacher as a functionary.

### 16. The Effect that the Emerging National Educational System Has on the Decision Making of Teachers

The emergence and persistence of a national educational system have relevance because centralization leads generally to the diminution of the authority of persons at the technical (lowest) level in an organization. One might argue that America does not have a national educational system but Campbell et al. argue:

So long as we persist in the folklore of localism we refuse to face up to the fact that we have always had some federal policy for education, that in recent decades this policy has grown appreciably, and that all evidence suggests that more national policy is inevitable. Somehow we must accept the fact that basic forces cannot be wished away, but that we have some alternatives in setting up arrangements for dealing with them.[7]

Wayland cites several factors that contribute to a national educational system.[8] The first three are developments in the general society which support the movement toward a national educational system. The remaining seven are factors outside the local school district, but within education, that support the movement toward a national educational system.

1. *Great mobility of the population.* The basically common character of our school systems makes possible movement without serious disturbance in the educational development of our youth.

2. *National character of labor market.* . . . the common educational program facilitates movement into the labor market wherever the jobs may be. . . .[9]

3. *Manpower shortage.* The acceleration in demand for highly competent and trained personnel is aggravating an already difficult problem of recruiting able people into the teaching field. . . .

4. *Our graduate and professional schools, and many of our colleges are national institutions.* . . . colleges have been moving toward a norm in their admission prerequisites and their curriculum which has its impact on the secondary school programs, and so on down the line.

5. *National testing programs.* Related to the foregoing development has been the increasingly widespread practice of national examinations for secondary students, e.g., the College Entrance Board and the National Merit Scholarship Corporation examinations. . . .[10]

6. *Federal actions.* The alacrity with which school systems set up language laboratories and science programs in keeping with the requirements of the federal government for assistance in money or in kind may be seen as an indicator of the willingness of schools to accept a new national norm.

7. *National textbook system.* The persistent and extensive reliance on the textbook as a central, if not the only instructional resource, has been noted by many. The national market of the textbook, therefore, serves as a major factor in providing a common educational experience across the country. . . .

8. *Television programming.* Although only regional at the moment, the assumption on which such programs operate is that a basically common program is being provided, and therefore common instructional assistance is appropriate.

9. *New programs developed by advanced specialists.* In a number of fields, such as physics, biology, mathematics, chemistry, and, more recently, economics, top authorities have been proceeding on the assumption that a common program ought to be, and could be, offered in schools throughout the country. They have therefore been supplying the curriculum to the teacher, rather than depending on the teacher to develop his own. For most of these programs, teachers are given short courses on how to use the new approaches. . . .

10. *Accrediting agencies and professional organizations.* Although the intent of the accrediting agencies is to establish a base, it seems likely that, in fact, the consequence has been to move schools in a common direction. In a similar way, professional organizations have not deliberately intended to establish a national system of education, but the effect of the communication and the leadership has led to the building of norms which influence the operation of school systems.[11]

Some persons will question the amount of control these groups or agencies have. Interestingly, Koerner lists many of the same conditions—testing agencies, accreditation associations, curriculum reform groups, foundations, citizens' advisory groups, other national groups and influences. Koerner believes, even after considering these influences, that professional educators have far too much control.[12]

It would seem that the picture could not be painted more bleak. The parameters for teacher decision making are drawn so tightly that no further restrictions are possible. These factors are cited not as conditions that *should* exist, but that do exist.

Before teachers gain increased authority in the classroom, they will need to deal with these factors. The task seems overwhelming. Several of these factors taken alone would pose a serious obstacle to teachers gaining increased authority. The chief value of listing the various limiting factors is that it brings them to a conscious level where they can be analyzed and confronted. *They will not be overcome by imagining they do not exist.*

# FIVE
# THE TEACHER AS A SEMI-PROFESSIONAL [1]

*"The policy recommendation which obviously emerges is for these middle-status [occupations] to acknowledge their position, to seek to improve their status rather than to try to pass for another. They are semi-professionals. . . . The main point is that the membership must realize that there is a distinct middle ground from which these groupings neither can nor need to break out."\**

*"The administration may face conflict whenever it attempts to provide extensive supervision of the activities of professionals. Teachers in many public schools are not treated as professionals in this respect, for they are extensively supervised and given directives on the carrying out of their tasks. In addition, they are expected to perform many tasks, such as collecting milk funds, taking up tickets, etc., that are not related to teaching."\*\**

*"It is truly depressing to hear people discuss what the schools or teachers 'should be doing' in abysmal ignorance of the [working] conditions which prevail in education. One might as well discuss what a farmer should produce in complete ignorance of the soil and moisture conditions which prevail on his farm, or criticize him for not cultivating something which these conditions have ruled out as impossible. Absurd as this might be, people continually criticize teachers for not accomplishing educational objectives which simply cannot be achieved under the prevailing [working] conditions in education."\*\*\**

*"A single teacher deals with at least fifteen hundred children during his career. . . . Under stress and fatigue they turn into husks in human shape and react no longer to all signals of inquiry or of distress which come from their pupils."\*\*\*\**

*"The right to exercise professional judgment, the right to a voice in selecting teaching materials and planning the curriculum, the right to some say on class size and non-teaching assignments, the right to a major voice in setting salaries and related welfare benefits—all are being claimed by leaders of the two national organizations. This boils down to an increasing demand by teachers for a larger share of authority and a greater role in educational decision-making."\*\*\*\*\**

Carr-Saunders was the first person to use the term semi-profession to describe an occupational group. He differentiated four major types of professions.

1. *The established professions*—law, medicine, and the church share two basic attributes; their practice is based upon the theoretical study of a department of learning; and the members of these professions feel bound to follow a certain mode of behavior.

2. *The new professions*—those which are based on their own fundamental studies such as engineering, chemistry, accounting, and the natural and social sciences.

3. *The semi-professions*—those which replace theoretical study by the acquisition of technical skill. Technical practice and knowledge is the basis of semi-professions such as nursing, pharmacy, optometry, and social work.

4. *The would-be professions*—those which require neither theoretical study nor the acquisition of exact techniques, but rather a familiarity with modern practices in business, administrative practices, and current conventions. Examples of these are hospital, sales, and work managers.

The major difference between the established professions and the remaining categories is knowledge—professional practice is based upon theoretical principles, while semi-professions use technical skills. Carr-Saunders considers teachers semi-professionals.[2]

Sussmann and O'Brien use the term quasi-professional when referring to teachers. They note that schools of education socialize students for the behavior appropriate to a bureaucratic rather than professional organization.[3]

Etzioni and several other scholars maintain that teachers, nurses, and social workers are semi-professionals.[4] They view this categorization as the permanent or ultimate position for these occupations, not a transitional stage leading to full professionalization. These occupations will become more professionalized in the future. They will gain increased scientific knowledge, increase their autonomy, and extend their training period; however, these changes will not be so significant as to classify them as professions.

### Differences Between Professionals and Semi-Professionals

Etzioni and his colleagues do not offer a precise list of differences between professionals and semi-professionals, although many differences are discussed. Eight categories emerge from their analysis: (1) knowledge, (2) privileged communication, (3) concern with life or death, (4) autonomy, (5) control by whom, (6) organization in which practitioner works, (7) sex, (8) years of training.[5]

The categories identified are not definitive, of equal weight, or always mutually exclusive. Their identification is intended to place the model of a semi-professional into sharper focus. Table 5-1 shows how professionals and semi-professionals compare in these categories. Each category will be discussed briefly.

### 1. Knowledge

As noted in Chapters Two and Three, autonomy depends in large measure on the amount of scientific knowledge that an occupation possesses. Educational practice is not based upon a body of scientific principles. More important, teachers do not create knowledge, they communicate it. Indeed, many teachers are critical of the "theoretical" knowledge they receive at colleges and universities.

**Table 5-1. Differences Between Professionals and Semi-Professionals in Eight Categories**

| Category | Professional | Semi-Professional |
|---|---|---|
| 1. Knowledge | Creation & Application | Communication |
| 2. Privileged Communication | Protected | Less Likely to be Protected |
| 3. Concern with Life and Death | Often | Seldom |
| 4. Autonomy | Considerable | Lacking |
| 5. Control by Whom | Internal (Himself) | External (Administrators, Lay Boards) |
| 6. Organization in Which Practitioner Works | Independent or less Bureaucratized | Bureaucratic |
| 7. Sex | Predominately Male | Predominately Female |
| 8. Years of Training | Five Years or More | Five Years or Less |

Source: Derived from the analysis of semi-professionals by Amitai Etzioni (ed.), *The Semi-Professions and Their Organization: Teachers, Nurses, Social Workers* (New York: The Free Press, 1969).

Etzioni differentiates between those occupations that create and apply knowledge and those that simply communicate it. He notes that "pure" professions do the former; semi-professions the latter.[6]

### 2. Privileged Communication

The established professions are protected generally in their practice by the guarantee of privileged communication. This is part and parcel of autonomy. Semi-professions do not place as much emphasis on privileged communication. Teachers often discuss openly students by name with colleagues, and problem students are often sent to non-teachers (administrators) for discipline and sometimes academic purposes.

### 3. Concern with Life and Death

Etzioni believes that the society is more likely to confer professional status on occupations concerned with life and death. He notes that semi-professions are rarely associated with these. As Lortie points out, "No one ever died of a split infinitive."[7]

Etzioni does not explain the existence of several professions (such as certified public accountants, nuclear physicists) which are not concerned with life or death, yet are professionals. Neither does he explain the existence of several occupations such as firemen, forestry men, and policemen which are concerned with life and death, but are not accorded professional status.

### 4. Autonomy

Teachers' lack of autonomy was discussed thoroughly in the last three chapters. A great deal more need not be said. Compared to professional employees, semi-professionals lack autonomy and are told what to do and how to do it. They have considerably more autonomy than blue collar workers and many white collar workers, but far less than professionals.

### 5. Control by Whom

Not only do teachers lack autonomy, but their control is external and hierarchical; that is, control is often enforced outside the profession by lay boards or superiors. In professions, control, to the degree it exists, is within the profession and is collegial rather than hierarchical.

In education, the control by superiors includes course requirements set down by departments of education; certification by boards of laymen; and hiring by personnel officers, principals and superintendents of schools, and lay boards.

There are some exceptions to these practices, but in general the working life of teachers is externally controlled.

### 6. Organization in Which Practitioner Works

As noted in Chapter Two, the teacher is at the bottom of a hierarchy of offices with the governor and state legislature at the top. Each layer slices off a portion of power, so relatively few decisions are left to the teacher. A principal exists in large part to ensure that rules, procedures, and policies developed by the state department of education are enforced. The education code often serves to restrict needed changes in educational programs.

Another difference between professional and semi-professional organizations is the behavior of administrators—in professional organizations they continue their practice, but in semi-professional organizations they "leave" their practice to become administrators.

In education, administrators who do no teaching enjoy greater status than teachers. Such a reward system encourages the stress on rules and hierarchical accountability and reduces dispositions toward employee autonomy.

### 7. Sex

It is not known whether women have caused certain occupations to take on the characteristics of semi-professions, or whether certain occupations attract women because of certain characteristics in the occupation. It is true, however, that women predominate in the three occupations Etzioni and associates identify as semi-professions—elementary teaching, nursing, and social work.

Data for 1970–71 show that 84.4 percent of elementary teachers and 46.3 percent of secondary teachers are women.[8] Women constitute 67.2 percent of all teachers.[9] Since so many teachers are women, a specific section concerning women in semi-professions follows this section.

### 8. Years of Training

All of the established professions require more than five years of training. Often there is an internship where practice is observed closely by existing practitioners. Even with this lengthy training, specialization requires one to three years of additional training. The general practitioner is only minimally trained after his regular medical training.

The semi-professional, by contrast, normally requires four years of college education, although a fifth year is now required in a few states, and will be required in twelve states within a few years. Most teachers have what amounts to a two-year training program somewhat evenly divided between education and "academic" courses.

Many factors that limit the professionalization of teachers are woven into the history if not mores of the occupational group. Stinchcombe maintains that the conditions concerning an organizations founding have a lasting effect on its future development.[10] Teachers were poorly trained in Colonial America. They had little status. They were viewed as low salaried, marginally intelligent, passive, female, and under the control of administrators. Not only were teachers socialized to this role, but also citizens.

One additional "peculiarity" of semi-professions should be noted. There may be a conflict between the values of professionals and of semi-professionals. Hall's study indicates that teachers have a high service orientation as do nurses and social workers.[11] Many professionals are motivated by applying knowledge, often dispassionately, and by maximizing salaries. One would expect, therefore, that teachers might resist professionalization if they thought it might lead to the lessening of their service orientation toward students. It will be interesting to see if this indeed is the case.

### Women and Semi-Professionals

Not all the differences between professional and semi-professional organizations can be traced to the differences in the nature of the professional authority. Part of the difference is due to the fact that the typical professional is a male whereas the typical semi-professional is a female.[12]

Etzioni also notes that:

Despite the effects of emancipation, women on the average are more amenable to administrative control than men. It seems that on the average, women are also less conscious of organizational status and more submissive in this context than men. They also, on the average, have fewer years of higher education than men, and their acceptance into the medical profession or university teaching is sharply limited. [13]

Simpson and Simpson discuss more than ten factors or forces affecting women in occupations.[14] Most of the studies they cite are concerned with a cross-section of women and are obviously not applicable to all women. Four causal factors have been derived from their analysis. These factors are: (1) a woman's primary attachment to the family role; (2) cultural norm that women should defer to men and that men are superior; (3) desire for sociability; (4) holistic rather than particularistic orientation.

*A Woman's Primary Attachment to the Family Role*

The view that women's primary attachment is to their family role has far-reaching ramifications so far as their career development is concerned. Seventy-seven percent of women teachers are married.[15] This often establishes a conflict between the home and job.

When home and work obligations conflict, the home has to take precedence. Women's self-images are built chiefly around their family roles, whereas men's are conditioned more by occupational roles.[16]

*Cultural Norm that Women Should Defer to Men and that Men are Superior*

The cultural norm that women should defer to men is changing, fortunately, but the degree of change is not yet known. In past years, many females considered males superior. Many men state they would not work for a woman, and, paradoxically, many women make the same statement. As a result of this norm, the public is less willing to grant autonomy to an occupation that is composed largely of women. Though there is little current valid data available, it is possible that this attitude has changed significantly in the past few years.

In the past, and too often today, administrators and boards of education have had a paternal attitude toward teachers. This type of relationship is antithetical to a professional occupation where teachers strive to gain autonomy to enable them, rather than laymen and administrators, to make decisions governing their work.

*Desire for Sociability*

The desire for pleasant relationships with colleagues at work seems to be more important to females than to males. It would seem to follow that women desire sociability more than men because many women are less intrinsically motivated in their work. Caring less about what happens in certain types of work, they seek to avoid conflicts on the job. This may indicate why teachers have resisted assiduously evaluating each other's performance.

Professionals often have a particularistic orientation. A scientist can study the four-leaf clover or the topography of the ocean floor for years on end with little, if any, visible concern for how his research affects man. Anyone who has been in a court of law senses this very quickly. The client often becomes a minor irritant as lawyers and judges adjudicate a case.

Semi-professionals, by contrast, tend to have a holistic orientation. They have a deep desire to help individual clients and to give service. They more often feel a personal interest in their clients. It is often emotional and all-embracing. Established professionals have a service orientation, but they seek to avoid personalizing their relationships with clients.

The following comment by Lortie gives a good summary of the preceding four points:

As far as elementary teaching is concerned, it is clearly congruent with feminine socialization, work styles, and familial roles. Compared to other realistic alternatives for women, teaching offers attractive prestige and money. The decentralized nature of school organization means local hiring in almost every community; teaching is thus accessible to women who are relatively immobile members of the work force. The absence of interpersonal rivalry for monetary rewards fits the socialization experiences Caplow attributed to American women. The work schedule of teachers facilitates the participation of women with school-age children—their work hours coincide with those during which their children are outside the home. The slow-changing technology of teaching permits teachers to be away for protracted periods (as during the early years of child rearing) and to return without excessive loss of skill. An obvious but important correlative fact should also be mentioned; in our society, as in most, the care of small children is culturally defined as women's work.[17]

Thus, there may be a circuitous, cumulative effect. Women have gone into teaching because it is conducive to their socialization, work style, and familial roles. This reinforces and solidifies the perception of the laymen concerning elementary teachers. Men are discouraged from entering a field that remains feminine.

It needs to be emphasized that the sociologists whose views are reported, do not suggest that this is the way women *should* be, only that, for a majority, this is the way they are. In addition, they are referring to the average woman, not those who are extremely conventional or those who are extremely liberated. If women are as reported, it is because of the culture in which they are raised.

## Factors that Cause Teachers to Be Semi-Professionals

Simpson and Simpson suggest three factors that tend to maintain an occupation as semi-professional: (1) lack of mandate; (2) necessity for bureaucratic control; (3) weak orientation toward autonomy.[18]

The public accords an occupation professional status because of the superior knowledge of its practitioners. Since the public does not believe semi-professionals base their practice upon a scientific body of knowledge, they do not accord them professional status. Because semi-professionals lack a scientific body of knowledge, the public believes they must be controlled by lay boards. The administrators in semi-professional occupations have considerable control because they, like the public, do not have confidence in the decisions made by semi-professionals, and because they are more accountable to the public.

Bureaucratic control over semi-professionals is necessary because many semi-professionals lack intrinsic motivation. They have few group norms to govern their work and no colleague reference groups to set standards.

Semi-professionals do not demand autonomy or resist strongly control by superiors. This may be because they have less intrinsic commitment to their work; they lack a strong feeling of identity with colleagues; and they realize they are not sufficiently competent to be granted autonomy. While many teachers may feel deserving of autonomy, they are not so certain about all teachers, and many will admit that unless some controls are built into the existing structure, additional autonomy may not be advantageous for the profession generally.

### Secondary Teachers as Semi-Professionals

In considering the teacher as a semi-professional, Etzioni and his associates confine their analysis to elementary school teachers. This raises the question of whether teachers in the secondary schools are more professionalized than their colleagues in the elementary schools. If secondary teachers are more professionalized, it should be apparent by noting the degree to which they meet the factors of semi-professionals discussed previously.

Of the eight categories, there seems to be little, if any, difference in privileged communication, concern with life and death, or autonomy. There does appear to be a difference in five of the categories.

The level of complexity of knowledge is more advanced in the secondary school. This is not necessarily because physics and calculus are inherently more complex than, for example, a knowledge of how to teach reading. It is true, however, that physics and calculus are based upon a firmer foundation of scientific knowledge than the expanded neighborhood concept in the early elementary phase of schooling. Also, secondary teachers' knowledge of their subjects is, on the average, more fully developed than the teachers' knowledge at the elementary school level because they have a longer training period. The use of knowledge at the elementary and secondary level is virtually identical; that is, communication rather than creation.

Secondary school teachers appear to have less external control than elementary school teachers because, on the average, the subjects taught are based more upon a scientific body of knowledge, teachers have a longer training period, the physical plant is larger, and there is a higher percentage of men.

While both the elementary and secondary schools are bureaucratized, the secondary school by virtue of its size, specialization, and large number of precise rules and procedures is more bureaucratic than the elementary school.

As noted earlier, 15.6 percent of elementary teachers are male, and 53.7 percent of secondary teachers are male. If the view of women expressed previously is valid, it has implications for teacher professionalization. Many male teachers are more aggressive than female teachers; they are more motivated to changing a system that compensates them poorly in wages; they can devote more time to their profession because of the lack of household and child-rearing responsibilities; they do not need to interrupt their professional career more than a couple of days when children arrive; they are more likely to make their occupation life-long; and they have a longer training period.

Elementary teachers have fewer years of training than secondary teachers. For elementary teachers, 72 percent have a bachelor's degree and 22.1 percent have a bachelor's degree plus thirty hours. For secondary teachers, 59.2 percent have a bachelor's degree and 39.6 percent have a master's degree.[19]

Thus, secondary teachers appear to be somewhat more professionalized than elementary teachers. The one category where secondary school teachers appear to have less claim to professional status than elementary teachers is bureaucratization.

### Summary

Etzioni suggests that semi-professionals aspire to full-fledged professional status despite the fact that they know they do not deserve such a status, and despite the fact that they do not qualify.[20] He suggests that this may be because the only alternative is nonprofessional status which they resist because they feel that they are "more" than salesclerks and office clerks. Thus, they persist in maintaining they are professionals.

Does it make any difference whether teachers think of themselves or are thought of as professionals or semi-professionals? Is any harm done by letting teachers continue to think of themselves as professionals? Etzioni maintains that unrealistic aspirations are not without costs. "The costs are those typically associated with persons seeking to pass for what they are not: a guilty feeling for floating a status claim without sufficient base and a rejection by those who hold the status legitimately."[21] He argues for semi-professionals to acknowledge their middle-status group rather than trying to pass for professionals.

A strong case can be made for viewing the teacher as a semi-professional. It is clearly impossible to argue that the teacher meets the characteristics of the established professions or the opposite extreme, a craft or trade. Yet the term semi-profession has a negative connotation that Etzioni acknowledges and one he would like semi-professionals to overlook. But they are not likely to do so. It is difficult to inspire teachers by challenging them with the status of semi-professionals.

More important, teachers are not interested in aping either the established professions or the semi-professions. Perhaps teachers do not want the public distrust that often comes from being a lawyer; the widespread disgust that comes from being a rich physician; the shallowness of bargaining solely for improved welfare benefits from being a craft. Rather, they need to be alerted to the characteristics of a profession, seeking to advance in those areas that lead toward improved working conditions and an improved educational program.

# SIX
# THE SCHOOL AS A BUREAUCRACY

*"A third of a century of centralized power and responsibility in Washington has produced a bureaucratic monstrosity, cumbersome, unresponsive, and inefficient."\**

*"Teachers come into the field with high hopes, but the system kills them. The process of psychic self-protection sets in, creating internal defenses necessary to survive in the face of continued failure."\*\**

*"There is a need for change in a system which, to a marked degree, measures teacher performance in terms of obedience, respect for authority, and adherence to bureaucratic rules and regulations as much or more than in terms of intellectual achievement and a desire to experiment."\*\*\**

*"The overwhelming danger is that many teachers whose professional expectations are frustrated abandon them, accepting instead a more rewarding bureaucratic orientation characterized by apathy, a rigid legalistic adherence to rules and regulations, an impersonal attitude toward students, and an 'upward-looking posture' that looks to school administrators for cues before decisions are made. These unprofessional attitudes, although decried by school administrators, school boards, and the public, are unanticipated results of bureaucratically structured school systems that inadvertently foster and reward such behavior."\*\*\*\**

*"If an association is established for the purpose of deciding upon common goals and courses of action to implement them, which is the function of democratic government, . . . the free expression of opinion must be safeguarded against other considerations, including those of efficiency. Since bureaucratization prevents the attainment of this objective, it must be avoided at all cost."\*\*\*\*\**

Teachers work in a formal organization in which students report to teachers, teachers report to principals, principals report to superintendents, superintendents report to boards of education, boards of education report to state departments of education, state departments report to the state legislature. This bureaucratic structure hinders the teachers' path to professional status because the decisions made at each level in the hierarchy reduce the decision making of teachers. If teachers are to increase their scope of decision making, it is necessary to understand the school as an organization, the place of the school in the total educational hierarchy, the decision-making power of persons occupying positions at the various levels, and the effect of bureaucratic organizations on the professionalization of teachers.

## The Existing Structure

The organization of schools in the early history of America consisted mainly of one teacher in a one-room school. The teacher's word was virtually sacrosanct in the classroom from the Colonial Period to mid-nineteenth century. The organization of students, the time schedule followed by students, and to a large extent, the curriculum, were determined by the teacher. Teachers were given this authority because educational practices were fairly uniform and established, and citizens felt assured that the teacher would convey them.

During the latter part of the nineteenth century, cities and school systems began to grow in size and enrollment. Gradually, a graded school emerged and with it, the need for centralized control of the curriculum and instructional practices. Teachers, along with principals, superintendents, and even boards of education, lost much of their authority to the state.[1]

As schools grew in enrollment, administrators were required to direct, coordinate, and control the schools. Teachers saw their decision-making authority diminish. First, the curriculum was taken over by the principal and later by the district office and board of education. The method of school organization became the province of the principal because it was thought that teachers did not possess as global a perspective of the educational program. With the advent of textbooks, workbooks, filmstrips and films, and later with programed instruction, the curricular responsibilities of the teacher diminished even more.

A complex hierarchy of authority has developed in education during the twentieth century. At the top is the state legislature and the state department of education; at the bottom, teachers and students. An army of bureaucrats has crept in between ostensibly to assist the teacher; but, too often it has simply enforced rules and procedures and resisted change.

The responsibilities of the state department of education, the county board of education, and the local board of education are not understood by all persons, not even by those who occupy positions in these agencies. Superintendents from one school district have different responsibilities than superintendents from an adjacent school district. Principals have different views of their responsibilities depending upon the superintendent to whom they report or the district in which they are employed. Teachers are given considerable authority in their classrooms in some schools and very little in others.

Aside from the vast differences that exist when comparing legislatures or school districts, there are also differences within the same legislature or school district from year to year. A state legislature may repeal legislation that enjoyed widespread support in the former legislative session. A superintendent of schools may abandon educational programs instituted by his predecessor. The situation is similar throughout the entire educational hierarchy with the result that persons at the bottom of the hierarchy—the teachers and the students—are at the mercy of a host of persons and agencies above them who can and often do alter policies and practices without consulting them.

It is surprising how little the typical teacher knows about the educational structure of which he is a member. Admittedly, this situation is changing. Many teachers do not know, for example, that the state ultimately has absolute control over education; that the local board of education has jurisdiction only within its district and exists at the pleasure of the state; that education must compete with dozens of other services for tax dollars; and that the superintendent of schools is the chief administrative officer of the board, not of the teachers. In addition, many teachers have a limited understanding of the nature of bureaucracies and the conflict between the professional and the organization.

Figure 6-1 shows the existing hierarchy in education. This is a skeletal outline and does not include all the offices that actually exist. Between the teacher and the principal, for example, is often a vice-principal. Between the principal and the assistant superintendent for curriculum and instruction is often the director of elementary education. Between the assistant superintendent for curriculum and instruction and the superintendent is often an administrative assistant or an area superintendent. In a large school district such as New York City or Los Angeles, the organization chart is similar to that of a large corporation. The following section explains briefly the function of each level in the hierarchy.

*Citizenry*

It is sometimes forgotten, but never for long, that schools exist at the pleasure of society. The fact that citizens view education as instrumental, i.e., as a means for preparing students to be responsible and productive adult members of society, serves to restrict the decision making of all persons associated with schools. To prepare students to be responsible and productive citizens tends to make citizens demand a balanced educational program. The students and teachers cannot ignore English, physical education, or mathematics in favor of music or art. Neither can they ignore American history, driver education, or drug education.[2] Citizens have a significant voice in the operation of the schools. Their demands often reduce the autonomy of teachers and thus impede their professionalization.

*State Legislature*

There is no mention of education in the United States Constitution. Education is the responsibility of each of the fifty states. While there have been some inroads into state control of education through the National Defense Education Act of 1958, and the Elementary and Secondary Education Act of 1965, these inroads have not been substantial when compared to the total expenditures for education.

The responsibilities of state legislatures differ from state to state, but they are more alike than different. Campbell et al., divide the decisions of the state legislature into five areas: the program, certification of personnel, building

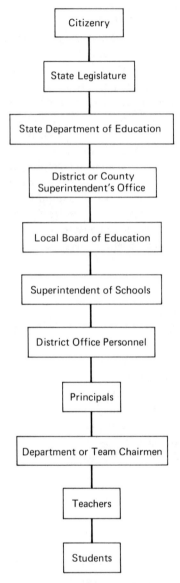

Citizenry

State Legislature

State Department of Education

District or County
Superintendent's Office

Local Board of Education

Superintendent of Schools

District Office Personnel

Principals

Department or Team Chairmen

Teachers

Students

**Figure 6–1.** The formal structure of education for states.

standards, financial support, and nonpublic schools. Programs, to examine just one decision area, include items such as (1) the scope or extent of the program, (2) standards for the program, (3) education for exceptional students, (4) textbook selection policies, and (5) instructional programs.[3]

The state legislature has almost unlimited power to control not only the schools but also the curriculum. Forty-three of the states require some type of state authority for approval to establish required courses in local schools; thirty-four states require approval for nonrequired courses.[4] There is an increase in the number of statutory enactments for public school curriculum and the subject requirements for high school graduation.

The authority of the state legislature is enormous. A memorandum, putting into effect a California state legislature's ten-minute extension of the school day, had such power that its influence was felt immediately in all elementary schools in that state. This type of memorandum is so routine that it is accepted without hesitation.

## State Department of Education

Every state has the equivalent of a department of education, a state board of education, and a chief state school officer. The functions of state boards vary greatly; however, the trend is toward designating the state board as the legislative component of the central education agency, with full responsibility for the legislative policy-making functions.[5] The board has control over certification, the authority to fix requirements, and to issue, reissue, and revoke certificates. It also formulates educational policies, recommends legislation, submits a budget to the governor, and appoints the state department of education staff.[6]

State regulations can be viewed broadly or strictly. Personnel within the state department exert authority, sometimes going beyond the regulations imposed by requiring compliance to the "letter of the law." Many forward-looking educational programs have been abandoned because a state official ruled them violations of the education code. Even when a progressive, chief state school officer assumes leadership, it is difficult for him to influence state officials with tenure who follow the education code as if it were a bible.

## Intermediate Unit

Twenty-seven states provide intermediate units between themselves and local districts to assist in the administration of schools.[7] These are normally organized along county lines; thus, some districts from sparsely populated counties in northwest Nebraska have a part-time county superintendent of schools, while densely populated counties in southern California have staffs totaling hundreds of persons with doctoral degrees in specialized areas.

County boards of education prepare information and make reports to the state department of education, sometimes reorganize school districts, register teachers' certificates, supervise rural schools, provide some in-service education of teachers, and give special services to weak districts.[8] Generally speaking, however, intermediate units of government in education do not provide significant leadership or assistance to teachers. The trend over the last fifty years has been in the direction of reducing the power of intermediate units.

## Local Boards of Education

The local board of education, while having to operate within the restraints of the state legislature and the state department of education, has considerable power. In a very real sense, assuming the support of the local patrons, it can develop a fairly unique program for the students in its immediate jurisdiction.

It is an indictment of boards of education and the educational community as well, that the educational offerings are so similar from district to district. An examination of the educational programs reveals that although authority is decentralized to 17,218 school districts in 1971-72, [9] a national curriculum has evolved just as surely as if it had been dictated from Washington, D.C.

Local boards' decision making is not restricted to educational programs or the purchasing of supplies and equipment. In fact, one is hardly able to suggest an educational decision that some local board of education has not made, including use or rejection of new mathematics and science programs, or the type of school organization.[10] All of these decisions serve to undermine the authority of administrators and teachers.

## Superintendent of Schools

Almost every operating school district of any size has a superintendent of schools. The superintendent occupies a position of considerable power. He recommends administrators and teachers for appointment and dismissal; he approves all supplies and equipment for purchase; he approves all courses of study; and, until recently, he alone recommended formal policies for consideration and adoption by the board of education.

The superintendent's influence can be pervasive. He can impair seriously the adoption of any new program by simply voicing his resistance to it, or institute programs he considers desirable by making his wishes known. Although his power is not absolute, his influence is substantial.

## District Office Personnel

Most superintendents, even in smaller districts, have an administrative staff. Campbell suggests these total nearly 60,000 persons including 13,500 superintendents.[11] The district office staff most often includes assistant superintendent for finance, assistant superintendent for curriculum and instruction; but it can also include dozens of other persons. Generally, those persons serve in a staff rather than a line capacity; i.e., they provide the superintendent and others with information rather than direct the work of others. Nevertheless, they represent a level between the building administrator and the superintendent of schools and can sometimes influence decisions.

## Principal

Almost every school has a principal to whom teachers are responsible. It is considered inappropriate for teachers to report directly to persons above the principal without the principal's consent. This policy has been circumvented during the last decade with the advent of more active teacher associations which usually make recommendations directly to the superintendent or board of education. Principals normally report directly to the superintendent in smaller school districts, and to assistant or area supervisors in larger districts.

The superintendent has more power than a building principal. To the teacher, however, the power of some principals can be awesome indeed. While principals do not often have the opportunity to make decisions that should be made at a higher level, they often do not hesitate to make decisions that should be made at a lower level. Also, the close proximity of the principal to teachers tends to increase his control over them.

## Department or Team Chairmen

While teachers generally report directly to a principal, department chairmen or team chairmen sometimes come between the teacher and the principal. These persons normally have some authority in the hierarchical ladder. Depending upon the school, they decide the classes that a teacher shall teach, the textbooks and instructional materials to be used, and sometimes the assignment of students to classes. The relationship between a teacher and chairman can be highly collegial but not always so.

## Teachers

The last person on the hierarchical ladder is the teacher, excepting teacher aides and students. It is not surprising, therefore, that teachers are rebelling as they lack power, status, and money. While the teacher has some autonomy in the classroom, it is apparent that the authority possessed by persons operating at higher levels restricts severely the authority of teachers.

This condition does not exist by design. No board of education has adopted an explicit policy that teachers should be powerless. What has occurred in education has occurred in many other organizations. It involves a variety of factors related to specialization, efficiency, and division of labor brought about by the demands of a growing technological society. Historically, power has been centralized at the top of the hierarchy. Only occasionally has power trickled down through the various layers to reach teachers. Thus, teachers work in a vast bureaucracy. The following section discusses the characteristics of a bureaucracy. The subsequent section considers to what degree education meets these characteristics.

### The Nature of a Bureaucracy

Bureaucracies are as inevitable as big business and big government, but there is no universal agreement on the definition or characteristics of bureaucracies.[12] Most authorities would agree, however, that a bureaucracy is a form of administrative organization that seeks to achieve efficiency of operaion through the rationalization of organizational behavior. The primary objective of a bureaucracy is to eliminate irrationality. It puts a high premium on continuity, control by experts, and discretion. It also claims to provide optimal returns on inputs. Bureaucratic organizations are considered more likely than other organizations to maximize efficiency and to attain the goals of the organization with the least cost. Blau and Scott [13] discuss Weber's initial characteristics of bureaucracies: (a) specialization of work, (b) hierarchical authority structure, (c) rules and regulations, (d) emphasis on personal detachment, and (e) employment based on technical qualifications.

a. Specialization of work is concerned with the manner in which tasks in an organization are distributed to the various positions as duties. This means that there is a clear-cut division of labor.

b. Hierarchical authority structure is concerned with the formal arrangement of superiors and subordinates in an organization.

c. Rules and regulations govern all official decisions and actions within the organization. These rules are often precise and ensure a high degree of rationality for the decisions made. In addition, they maximize control through an impersonal and rational means.

d. Personal detachment on the part of officials within a bureaucracy is expected toward both clients and other officials within the organization. This requirement makes it easier for an official to make decisions beneficial to the organization, without having concern for friends, colleagues, and other personnel unduly influence his decisions.

e. The assignment of persons within the bureaucracy is based on technical qualifications which are ascertained through highly formalized and impersonal procedures. The benefits of this are (i) elimination of nepotism and favoritism, (ii) elimination of class privilege, (iii) members have lifelong tenure, maximizing vocational security that tends to ensure their service without regard to extraneous pressure.

It is clear, then, that bureaucracies can be viewed as an organizational structure that leads to precision, reliability, and efficiency. Any organizational structure with such grandiose characteristics should have the everlasting respect of persons who work in them. This is decidedly not the case. Indeed, it is difficult to find anyone willing to extol the virtues of bureaucracies. Why have bureaucracies not lived up to Weber's expectations?

Three dysfunctions of bureaucracies have been considered in detail by sociologists and economists. These dysfunctions are trained incapacity, displacement of goals, and conformity. Within these three categories reside numerous lesser ills that have been identified by scholars or by persons who find themselves at odds with a bureaucracy.

**Trained Incapacity.** Trained incapacity comes into play when one's ability functions as an inadequacy. The worker's obligation to observe rules becomes transformed into a personal *devotion* to the rigid enforcement of regulations under any condition. When a new condition arises which is not recognized as substantially different, previous training may lead to the use of the wrong procedures.[14]

Instances of trained incapacity abound in education. Most principals and teachers, for example, are trained to work in a graded school system. If nongrading becomes a goal, they often continue to assign only graded materials for students; they require the same objectives for all students; they retain the A to F grading; and they persist thinking in terms of questions such as, Whom shall we retain this year? Their training, then, becomes an incapacity because it is directed to practices that no longer exist.

In the years ahead, principals and other administrators will have many instances of trained incapacity when confronted with increased teacher demand for decision making. Principals' training programs, both in professional schools and on the job, have assumed generally that teachers were semi-professionals or functionaries. As principals use this type of training in schools, it will lead increasingly to their incapacity because these activities are appropriate for an administrator of semi-professionals or craft workers.

**Displacement of Goals.** A second disadvantage of bureaucracies is displacement of goals. For the bureaucracy to operate effectively, it must have reliability of behavior and conformity with prescribed patterns of action. Displacement occurs when means to attain goals become goals themselves.

Persons in a bureaucracy, often low in the hierarchy, glorify routine procedures. What results from this is only too familiar. The person's extreme conformity to the rules interferes with the attainment of the goals of the organization. Red tape abounds with persons who never forget a rule or a procedure but, paradoxically, are unable to be of use to the organization.

This process is painfully apparent in education. Administrators in some school districts continue to require weekly, if not daily, lesson plans from teachers. Principals who obey such policies and require these lesson plans overlook the fact that, by and large, they serve no goal of the organization. The lesson plans, almost never used by teachers or read by anyone, become ends in themselves.

**Conformity.** Another dysfunction of bureaucracies is that they encourage conformity upon the office holder.

In education, teachers learn to follow institutional procedures and rules that encourage conformity. All students must see the nurse before re-entering school after an illness; spelling is from 9:00 to 9:15 each day; students who forget their gym shoes cannot participate.

The following section considers to what degree the characteristics of bureaucracies exist in education.

### Education and Bureaucracy

Education has many of the characteristics of bureaucracies. School systems have numerous policies, rules, and procedures to ensure similar or identical responses to problems. There is a clear-cut division of labor. There is a minimum of personal contact. Assignments are based on technical qualifications and are highly formalized. Teachers have tenure. Promotion is based upon seniority or achievement. Each office has a specified sphere of authority.

Bidwell states that school systems display, at least in rudimentary form, the following characteristics: (1) a functional division of labor, (2) the differentiation of staff roles as offices, (3) the hierarchical ordering of offices, (4) operation according to rules of procedure.[15] School systems do not possess two characteristics of bureaucracies: teachers have few specialized offices, and there is no bureaucratic career possible; and school systems have a structural looseness by virtue of decentralized schools existing throughout a school district.

Solomon (as well as Gerstl, Moeller, and Corwin) sees the schools as bureaucratized and operating within a framework of laws, codes, rules, and regulations produced by the legislature, the board of education, the superintendent, and intermediate and lower-level officials. This makes school systems as subject to bureaucratic malaise as organizations in any other field.[16]

While Bidwell acknowledges that schools are somewhat bureaucratized, he takes care to point out that teachers have considerable autonomy in the classroom. He believes that teachers gain this autonomy by working alone within the classroom relatively hidden from colleagues and superiors. Similarly, the school is relatively hidden from superiors. This "hiddenness" expands the autonomy of teachers and principals and allows them substantial control over curricula and teaching methods.[17]

In summary, schools have many of the characteristics of bureaucracies. The degree of teacher autonomy in the classroom is an area for further research, but there is no disagreement that until quite recently teachers have had little authority outside of the classroom to govern their affairs as professionals.

### Professionalization and Bureaucratization

Some persons maintain that teachers cannot become professionals because the requirements for professionalization are irreconcilable with the demands of bureaucracies. Many sociologists do not support the position that the two are irreconcilable, [18] but many do see a conflict or strain between these two "institutions."

If the demands of the school as a bureaucracy are in conflict with the requirements for the professionalization of teachers, then the bureaucracy must be altered, circumvented, or teachers must remain a semi-professional or craft occupation. While teachers are not "pure" professionals and schools are not "pure" bureaucracies, it should be useful to examine the strain that exists between teachers and the organization in which they work.

Corwin believes that in education and in many organizations the essential conflict is not between the demands of the organization and the needs of the individual or between labor and management, but rather between two entirely different bases of authority—professional versus bureaucratic.[19] Similarly, Anderson [20] and Thompson [21] both maintain that the critical problem for organizations involves reconciling the growing professionalism of individuals who seek individual autonomy and the central control demands of bureaucratic hierarchies which demand conformity and uniformity. The professional and bureaucratic models provide alternative approaches to the organization of complex tasks.[22] In fact, two institutions may be involved.[23]

In Table 6-1 Corwin suggests contrasting characteristics of professional and employee modes of organization: routine of work, continuity of procedure, specificity of rules, specialization on the basis of function, monopoly of knowledge, responsibility for decision-making, centralization of authority, basis of authority. Which of the two modes most closely fits teachers?

*Routine of Work*

Many teachers attempt to individualize instruction, stressing the uniqueness of each student's problems. Much more stress is placed on individualizing the rate of learning than on individualizing the ends; that is, teachers often work individually with students at their level of ability, but the student has little to say about the desirability of having reading or the age of exploration as areas of study. Teachers generally individualize means, not ends.

Many institutional restraints hamper the teachers who wish to individualize. Textbooks are often selected uniformly, often on a state or county level. National curriculum projects serve to standardize the course of study. The use of national tests, such as the Scholastic Aptitude Test, standardize the program as do state examinations, such as the New York State Regents'. Local school districts procedures and rules are often applied arbitrarily to all.

The individualization of instruction is also made difficult by the number of clients a teacher serves. There are approximately thirty students in elementary school classrooms, but secondary teachers often have as many as 150 students a day. While notable exceptions exist, in general, there is little individualization. Students are on the same page of the same textbook and are being evaluated by the norm of the class.

## Table 6-1. Contrasting Characteristics of Professional and Employee Modes of Organization

| Continuum[a] | Bureaucratic-Employee Expectations | | Professional Expectations | |
|---|---|---|---|---|
| | High | Low | High | Low |
| | Stress on uniformity of client's problems. | | Stress on uniqueness of client's problems. | |
| | *Routine of Work* | | | |
| Standardization | Stress on records and files. | | Stress on research and change. | |
| | *Continuity of Procedure* | | | |
| | Rules stated as univerals or rules specific. | | Rules stated as alternatives or rule diffuse. | |
| | *Specificity of Rules* | | | |
| | Stress on efficiency of technique. Task orientation. | | Stress on achievement of goals. Client orientation. | |
| | *Specialization on the Basis of Function* | | | |
| Specialization | Skill based primarily on practice. | | Skill based primarily on knowledge. | |
| | *Monopoly of Knowledge* | | | |
| | Decisions concerning application of rules to routine problems. | | Decisions concerning professional policy and unique problems. | |
| | *Responsibility for Decision-Making* | | | |
| | Punishment centered administration. | | Representative administration. | |
| | *Centralization of Authority* | | | |
| Authority | Rules sanctioned by the public. | | Rules sanctioned by powerful and legally sanctioned professions. | |
| | Loyalty to the organization and to superiors. Authority from office. | | Loyalty to professional associations and clients. Authority from personal competence. | |
| | *Basis of Authority* | | | |

Source: Ronald G. Corwin, *A Sociology of Education: Emerging Patterns of Class, Status, and Power in the Public Schools* (New York: Appleton-Century-Crofts, 1965), p. 232. By permission of Appleton-Century-Crofts, Educational Division, Meredith Corporation.

[a]Read each of the *variables* listed opposite the major continua as follows:
1. On the left hand side of the dotted line, employee expectations are on a scale from "high" (on the left) to "low" (on the right).
2. On the right hand side of the dotted line, professional expectations are measured as a scale from "high" (on the left) to "low" (on the right).
3. Note that the professional and the employee variables are treated as separate variables, each ranging from high to low.

## Continuity of Procedure

Permanent change and innovation are not characteristic of teaching in American schools. Teachers, on the average, are using substantially the same methods of instruction in their classroom that prevailed twenty years ago. Research, which should result in change in any organization, is sadly lacking in education. The small amount of money spent annually for educational research compared to that which is spent by industry takes its toll. Schoolmen wishing to change the educational program find that there is often a lack of research and, more often, no intermediate agency whose job it is to translate the theoretical research from universities into a form that is usable in the classroom.

## Specificity of Rules

Many teachers know what is required to provide useful experiences for students, but bureaucratic rules limit the teachers' opportunity to provide those experiences. Teachers question seriously not only the subjects required for students, but also their sequence during the day. Bureaucratic rules do not permit them to make changes in subject or sequence. A growing number of teachers prefer hetero-geneous rather than homogeneous ability grouping, multi-age grouping to single-grade grouping. Bureaucratic rules often do not permit such changes.

Teachers are so "hemmed in" by rules and regulations that most have stopped questioning them and comply obediently because it seems nothing can be done about them. Increasingly, however, teachers are beginning to feel the strain that comes from complying with organizational rules that are dysfunctional to the education of students and to the development of a profession.

## Specialization on the Basis of Function

Employees in bureaucracies place stress on the efficiency of their technique and on the completion of specific tasks rather than the achievement of a goal. Thus, the bureaucrat is task-oriented while the professional is client-oriented.

Teachers are not client-oriented because few teachers are wholly respon-sible for the entire educational program of a student. The teacher in a self-contained classroom is responsible for thirty students for a year, but the total number of self-contained classrooms is decreasing in the elementary schools as departmentali-zation is more widely applied; as various types of team teaching come into wide-spread use; and as specialization becomes more prevalent. Increasingly, teachers are responsible for a part but not all of the students' schooling.

## Monopoly of Knowledge

A fairly thorough discussion of the lack of scientific knowledge was presented in Chapter Three. It is generally agreed that education courses in colleges and universities are not based upon a scientific body of knowledge; that students enrolled in schools of education are scholastically below students from other professional groups; that professors of education have nearly the lowest academic standing of all professors. This suggests that the actions of teachers in the classroom are not based upon an esoteric body of knowledge gained from university courses or inservice workshops. Instead, teachers' actions represent some promising, logical, and sometimes valid principles that are proposed by persons who have had experience working with students.

## Responsibility for Decision Making

As noted in Chapters One and Four, teachers have limited responsibility for decision making either in or out of their classrooms. It is sometimes difficult for many teachers to believe this because they make decisions in the classroom every day. These decisions, however, are made within fairly narrow limits and are concerned largely with life in the classroom. They have virtually no control concerning certification, the programs offered at teacher training institutions, the selection and evaluation of fellow teachers, their inservice education, the deployment of teachers, the grouping of students, and often, even the selection of textbooks and instructional supplies.

## Centralization of Authority

Bureaucracies place problems or issues into discrete categories where they can be handled with established procedures and rules. Since all issues falling within one category are dealt with identically, authority can remain centralized. Professionals, by contrast, encounter more unique problems and must, therefore, have the authority to apply a variety of actions. Teachers deal with students who are unique; but, interestingly, they are usually grouped by age and use a graded textbook. This virtually forces all but the most dedicated and creative teacher to deal with them as a group.

## Basis of Authority

The professional is controlled by his colleagues according to norms developed by the professionals. Thus, the professional has self-control. The bureaucrat, by contrast, is governed by a hierarchy of authority.

As noted before, the bureaucrat gains his authority by virtue of his office while the professional gains his authority through his knowledge. The bureaucrat may be competent, but the amount of deference due him increases directly with his rank rather than his personal or technical competence.[24] Scott suggests that the professional has conditional loyalty to the bureaucracy. He is concerned largely with his reputation among peers rather than with pleasing his organizational superiors.[25]

In the past, teachers have been willing to comply with the supervision of the building principal and superintendent. Increasingly, this has not been the case. Almost twenty years ago, Becker found that conflict arose when the principal ignored the needs of teachers for professional independence.[26] This conflict is on the rise and will increase significantly in the 1970s.

## Summary

It appears that teachers come closer to fitting the bureaucratic-employee expectations than the professional expectations. The fact that there is a strain between the bureaucracy and the professional does not mean that the two institutions should be separated. Indeed, they will not be. Increasingly, professionals are being employed in bureaucracies. These professionals earn salaries and are often responsible to nonprofessional supervisors who evaluate the professional's contribution. In addition, the supervisor often controls the professional by regulating which project is to be advanced, and which area is to be researched. These practices are in conflict with the professionals' traditional autonomy to govern themselves rather than be governed by others.[27]

Blau and Scott, in fact, point out six characteristics of professionals and bureaucrats and found five of them to be similar. For example, both the professional and bureaucrat (1) are governed by universalistic standards, that is, they are based on certain objective criteria which are independent of the particular case under consideration; (2) both are experts in their area of specialization; (3) both encourage affective neutrality with clients, that is, no personal involvement with clients; (4) both gain authority by means of their technical qualifications; (5) neither base their actions on their own self-interest. The only characteristic they found dissimilar was that the source of discipline within a bureaucracy is not the colleague group but the hierarchy of authority.[28]

While there may not be agreement on the exact nature of the strain between professionals and bureaucracies, it is apparent that two modes or institutions exist. Efforts in the future will not be directed toward reducing the number of professionals in bureaucracies but toward minimizing the conflicts that inevitably exist with the development of dual lines of authority. The bureaucratic and collegial authority systems must somehow coexist in the school organizations of the future.[29]

Teachers will not be able to choose between these two extremes. Instead, they can be expected to experiment with a variety of new structures to accommodate differences. Considerable imagination and hard work will be required by teachers to create an organization that will be responsible to the society's legitimate desire for quality education for its children but, at the same time, conducive to the growth and development of teachers as professionals.

# SEVEN
# COLLECTIVE BARGAINING

*"Professional negotiation must mean something more than the right to be heard. Most teachers associations have had this right for years. The right only to be heard might be simply an annual supplicatory pilgrimage to the board of education, resulting only in warm expressions of gratitude and goodwill by both parties. This routine could consist of a polite presentation by the teachers, blank stares from the board, a polite 'thank you.' Then follows an interminable wait by the teachers; and finally reading of the board's action in the local newspaper or via the superintendent's bulletin with any connection between teachers' requests and board action strictly coincidental. This, of course, is not professional negotiation."\**

*"We went through a miserable time period of so-called 'co-operative determination' which smacked in every sense the characteristics of paternalism. The one major difference between the two was that the school board and superintendent under cooperative determination would let us come in, sit down at the table, listen to our comments, then proceed to tell us what we would be getting. Under paternalism they just told us what we were getting."\*\**

*"The fact is, professional negotiations probably hold a greater potential for the improvement of education than any series of events or activities which have occurred in the last fifty years."\*\*\**

*"In its role as employer, government should accept the principle of union organization among its employees. Like any other employer it should bargain in good faith with the duly certified representatives of its workers. In cases where the public health, safety, and security are not at stake, such collective bargaining process may legitimately include the right to strike."\*\*\*\**

The Taft-Hartley Act provides the standard definition of collective bargaining. It is

the performance of the mutual obligation of the employer and the representatives of the employees to meet at reasonable times and confer in good faith with respect to wages, hours, and other terms and conditions of employment, or the negotiation of any agreement, or any question arising thereunder, and the execution of a written contract incorporating any agreement reached, if requested by either party, but such obligation does not compel either party to agree to a proposal or require the making of a concession.[1, 2]

Collective bargaining is concerned with mediating differences between employers and employees. It is more than a procedure for giving teachers a chance to be consulted on school affairs. Collective bargaining reduces and, in some areas, eliminates the decision-making power normally assigned to administrators and boards of education. This is the principal reason why collective bargaining is so often resisted by boards of education and administrators.

The difference between the traditional approach to school personnel administration and collective bargaining is marked. Nolte reports that with the traditional approach, the board could act unilaterally without consultation with its employees, allow only one-way communication, always have the last word, lack good faith, ignore divergencies between policy and practice, and retain a power relationship that is unilateral, paternalistic, and authoritarian. Using collective bargaining, however, the board is required to consult with employees, communication is two-way, impasse procedures are provided, good faith bargaining is mandated, constant dialogue requires the board to discuss divergencies between policy and practice, and the power relationship is bilateral, cooperative, and democratic.[3] Appendix E shows Nolte's complete analysis comparing the traditional approach to school personnel administration with the collective bargaining approach.

Collective bargaining increases the power of teachers.

*Power is the ability, either real or imputed, which when possessed by one entity enables that entity to cause another entity to behave in a manner in which it would not have behaved if the threat or actual application of action of the first entity were not possible.* Stated simply, entity #1 has power over entity #2 if it can somehow cause entity #2 to behave in a manner in which it would not otherwise have behaved.[4]

Teacher power, then, is the ability of teachers to cause others (against their will) to behave in a manner teachers desire. The relationship between collective bargaining and teacher power is that through collective bargaining, teachers seek to increase their power.

### Need for Collective Bargaining

There are literally hundreds of issues that are of concern to teachers and that can be negotiated. They are divided into three broad categories—teacher welfare (often termed trade union) objectives, service objectives, and professional objectives.

### Teacher Welfare Objectives

Teacher welfare objectives assist teachers personally. These include issues such as salary, sick leave, duties, benefits (insurance, health plans, retirement plans), released time, and such miscellaneous items as working conditions, use of teacher aides, tuition reimbursement for advanced credits, provision of preparation time, etc.

### Service Objectives

Service objectives are those which assist students. They include matters relating to number of school districts, obtaining additional funds, free textbooks and supplies, quality of textbooks, courses of study and sequence of courses, libraries and library hours, remedial programs, guidance and counseling, etc.

### Professional Objectives

Professional objectives are those which further professionalize teachers as an occupational group. These include some of the following:

a. Passage of a federal statute requiring school boards to negotiate with teachers' bargaining agents; recognize the rights of teachers to take collective action if talks fail; and establish a Professional Employees Relations Commission to mediate disputes between school boards and teacher organizations.

b. Professional negotiations agreements at the local level.

c. Teacher control over recruitment, selection, evaluation, and tenure, of fellow teachers, including substitute teachers.

d. Teacher control over selection of department chairmen and supervisors.

e. School time and resources for development of in-service education programs to be conducted on school time during the regular school year.

f. Legislation to give school teaching legal status as a recognized profession under a professional board of preparation and licensing representatives of the teaching profession and having responsibility to define and maintain standards of admission to and licensing of the teaching profession.

There is often an overlap within these three objectives, and some clauses advance all three areas. All of these issues have been subject to collective bargaining in some school district. Some are applicable to local school districts and some to states.

Some teachers and citizens believe teacher welfare or trade union objectives are antithetical to service objectives. In point of fact, however, trade union objectives often enhance service objectives. Class size can be viewed as a trade union objective, but it can also be viewed as a service objective. There is contradictory evidence concerning class size and learning, but the point is that teachers propose smaller classes principally because they believe such classes will permit them to do a more effective job, not because smaller classes will make their work easier.

Trade union objectives can also enhance professional objectives. Free health and accident insurance protection, increased salaries, and an hour for lunch advance teacher professionalization because they serve to make the occupation more attractive to persons who contemplate entering the field; they encourage teachers to remain in the field; and they remind citizens that the occupation is important enough to merit such benefits.

Teachers should avoid advancing *only* trade union objectives because the realization of these objectives will not by themselves advance the professionalization of teachers.

### Extent of Teacher Power

Over ten years ago, Lieberman stated that because teacher associations are weak, "teachers are without power; because they are without power, power is exercised upon them to weaken and to corrupt public education."[5] This situation has changed during the last decade. Teacher associations are no longer weak, but it is not known exactly how much power they have gained. Gittell reported, in 1968, that her own studies of six *large city systems* suggested that teacher associations play a relatively limited role in the broader area of school policy-making.[6]

If teachers do not have the power, who does? Rosenthal undertook a study of five large school systems where he analyzed the distribution of power. The five cities were New York, Boston, Chicago, San Francisco, and Atlanta. He sought to determine which participants had the greatest influence in determining school policy.

Through a leadership survey, the leaders of nine teacher organizations were asked to assess whether several listed individuals and groups had "much," "some," or "little" power in deciding various kinds of educational policy. To standardize power attributes and facilitate comparisons, he constructed an index of relative power.[7] To facilitate comparisons, the data have been placed on a chart (see Figure 7-1), showing the *mean* index of relative power score for all persons and groups. The data revealed that *teacher leaders* thought teachers had less influence in all areas except salary. Their power slightly outranked principals. The superintendent and the board of education shared most of the power, whereas the principal and teacher had far less. Indeed, the teachers were near the bottom while the superintendent was near the top.

These results take on added significance when one recalls that the respondents were leaders of teacher organizations who would be inclined to exaggerate rather than underestimate their power. In addition, these data were from five large cities where teacher militancy had been pronounced. If this is the extent of teacher power in New York and San Francisco, what must it be in Sacramento, Waco, Dayton, or in the thousands of very small school districts throughout America? Rosenthal concludes:

. . . in contrast to the established governors of public education, teacher groups have little to say about educational policies, with the possible exception of salaries and related matters. They are still far short of achieving a commanding position, controlling educational policy, or exercising major influence in the area of school decision-making. The old regimes may be shaken, but they have not been toppled.[8]

Some teachers and parents believe teachers are not yet deserving or ready for increased power. When they are, the public and its local boards of education will permit teachers to govern themselves. Lieberman notes, however, that no one thought the Negroes ready to integrate schools and sit in the front of buses in 1954; no one thought Kennedy ready for the Presidency; no one thought labor unions ready to assume power.[9]

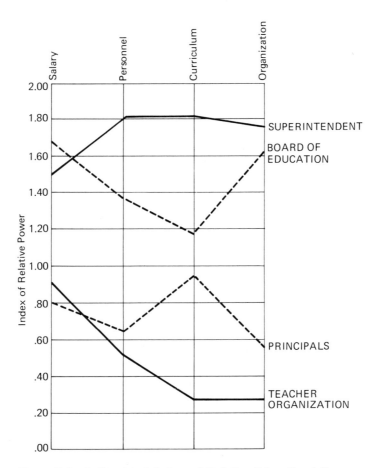

**Figure 7–1.** A Graphical Index of Relative Educational Power. Data derived from Table 26, "An Index of Relative Educational Power," in Alan Rosenthal, *Pedagogues and Power: Teacher Groups in School Politics* (Syracuse, New York: Syracuse University Press, 1969), p. 131.

### Extent of Strikes and Collective Bargaining

While little evidence is available, it would probably be safe to say that teacher strikes were considered unethical, if not repugnant, by a majority of teachers before 1960. That attitude has changed markedly during the last ten years.

The number of strikes, work stoppages, and interruptions of service has increased each year from 1962–63 (when there were two strikes), to 1969–70 (when there were 181). In 1970–71 there was a decline to 130 strikes.[10] Appendix F shows a summary of teacher strikes, work stoppages, and interruptions of service by type of organization involved, January 1940 through June 1971. Appendix G shows similar data but provides detailed information since 1960–61.

A second indication of the extent of strikes and collective bargaining is the increase in the number of state legislatures enacting laws granting collective bargaining rights to public employees. The first act was enacted by Wisconsin in 1959. By July, 1972, twenty-six states had collective bargaining legislation for teachers. Four states (Florida, Nebraska, New Hampshire, and Texas) have permissive legislation. The type of legislation varies considerably in scope but, in general, is as broad as that granted the private sector.

It is now apparent, however, that the lack of enabling legislation does not prevent collective bargaining. Arizona, for example, has no legislation concerning collective bargaining rights for teachers, but 68.9 percent of the instructional personnel were engaged in bargaining. Similarly, Colorado had 82.4 percent; Illinois, 65.5 percent; Kansas, 62.5 percent; and Ohio, 69.1 percent of their instructional personnel engaged in bargaining. None of these states has collective bargaining rights for teachers.[11]

A third indication of the extent of collective bargaining is the number of classroom teacher negotiation agreements and the number of school systems having comprehensive classroom teacher agreements. A classroom teacher agreement is "one to which a classroom teacher bargaining unit is party, whether this unit consists exclusively of classroom teachers or includes classroom teachers and other school-board employees, such as central-office administrators or principals."[12]

A comprehensive classroom agreement is

one which contains some of the provisions found in procedural agreements (recognition of an employee organization, negotiation procedures, and procedures for the resolution of impasse), as well as specific items related to personnel and conditions of employment which are negotiated and agreed upon by the parties involved.[13]

The number of teacher agreements has increased from a total of 1,531 in 1967, to 3,045 in 1969. The number of comprehensive classroom teacher agreements has increased from 389 in 1966–67, to 1,040 in 1968–69.[14]

In the 1970–71 school year, an estimated 3,522 public school systems with an enrollment of 1,000 or more, were operating under a written negotiation agreement. This is a 130 percent increase over 1966–67, and comprises 57.3 percent responding systems employing 63.6 percent of all instructional personnel employed in responding systems.[15]

Finally, there is a fourth sign of the extent of strikes and collective bargaining. It is the appearance of professional negotiation specialists used by school districts. The Educational Research Services sent questionnaires to 122 school systems with pupil enrollment in excess of 50,000. Of this number, 21 reported having full-time professional negotiation specialists; 32 reported having an employee with professional negotiation responsibilities in addition to other duties; 21 reported using a part-time outside specialist; and 5 reported co-chairmen, a part-time outsider working with a member of the central administrative staff. In all, 79 of 122 districts reported having a full-time or part-time professional negotiation specialist.[16]

Collective action has taken the form of strikes and state sanctions. Other means of pressure have been used as well. Moskow notes several: slowdowns, investigations, professional holidays, work stoppages, mass resignations, recommendations that no new teachers accept assignments in a state or local school system, the withholding of salary agreements, campaigns in school board or municipal elections, criticisms of school authorities, packing public meetings of the board of education, picketing, refusal to participate in extracurricular activities.[17]

There is no doubt that teachers will continue to use collective bargaining and strikes in attempting to gain their demands. Having emerged from a world of benevolent dictatorship, they are not likely to relinquish their new-found power and sense of freedom.

It is important to know why teachers have suddenly begun to use collective bargaining and strikes. If the factors are not fundamental, that is, rooted in fairly widespread societal movements, they are likely to be short-lived. The following section deals with this topic.

## Conditions Affecting Teacher Militancy [18]

Many citizens, board members, and administrators have wondered why teachers have become more militant. A superficial analysis of the causes would prompt one to consider the rising power of the American Federation of Teachers or the inadequate salaries of teachers. While these are probably sufficiently adequate explanations for the layman, they represent a naive view of the conditions that have tended to support this rather widespread effort.

As many as twenty-four authors have sought to identify the factors that have effected teacher militancy. After reviewing many of these, Williams identified three internal and three external causes. I have condensed his analysis.

1. *Civil Disobedience.* The successes of those using civil disobedience have not been ignored by teachers.
2. *The American Labor Movement.* Teachers are not unmindful of the labor movement's success in improving the wages and working conditions of its members.
3. *Dissatisfaction with Schools.* Many educators believe that the schools are not making the appropriate contribution to society. This creates a climate of dissatisfaction for change and tends to legitimize teacher militancy.
4. *Changing Character of the Teaching Profession.* There has been a change from a female- to a male-dominated profession. The impact of this was discussed in Chapter Five.

5. *Inadequate Teacher Compensation.*

6. *Professionals in the Organization.* As teachers gain in power and ability, they will increasingly view themselves as professionals. Consequently, they will put pressure on administrators and increase the tension between management and labor.[19]

Four additional external factors are worthy of mention.

7. *Larger and More Bureaucratic Systems.* The steady decline in the number of school districts has resulted in an increase in the size of school districts. Many advantages accrue to larger school districts, but one disadvantage may be that they tend to reduce the decision-making authority of teachers. As school districts have become larger, there has been a resultant loss of identity by teachers. In a sense, one can view the rising power of teachers as a direct response to the rising size of the bureaucracy.

8. *Societal Demands Toward More Democratic Institutions.* The societal thrust toward more democratic institutions is evidenced by factors such as the reduced number of autocratic heads of nations, the lessening number of colonial possessions throughout the world, and the ecumenical movement.

In October, 1969, *Time* magazine reported that an assemblage of 144 prelates resulted in a groping first step toward something resembling parliamentary government in the Roman Catholic Church.[20] It would be unwise to take sides on this issue, but its development in such a well-established institution, if only by a minority, affects all institutions. Teachers are swept up in this movement. "Seeing and experiencing the benefits of some democracy, teachers do not rest content. They aspire to and work toward greater democracy in the public schools."[21]

9. *Struggle Between the AFT and the NEA.* The emergence of the AFT, and its resultant conflict with the NEA, have greatly stimulated teacher militancy. Indeed, it is apparent that the two groups are striving for the support of teachers, often by being more militant. This rivalry will not likely be a factor in the future since the two organizations appear on the verge of merger.

10. *Countervailing Power.* Galbraith notes that countervailing power occurs when one section of the economy gains a disproportionate amount of control or power over a second section. In time, this second section tries to equalize that power. As one segment assumes a disproportionate amount of power over a second segment, the latter develops various mechanisms to equalize the power.[22] Teachers have gained a position of countervailing power in education. It is a direct response to the power of monopoly held by boards of education.[23] Thus, one can expect conflict to continue until a "balance" or accommodation has been reached. In many states, it is not even in sight.

*Civil Disobedience and Teachers*

It appears that the collective bargaining of teachers is grounded on some fundamental societal movements. It has not happened by chance or because of the efforts of a few dynamic leaders, not that capable leadership has not had positive results. But, will collective bargaining continue to be a useful device for teachers? Smythe posits five conditions that relate to a group's potential for forcing employers' concessions to employment demands.

1. Employees must be irreplaceable—either their skill must be so specialized that they cannot be replaced or their employers do not dare replace them.
2. Employees must be essential to the operation of the organization, i.e., the organization must be unable to function in the absence of the employees.
3. The cost of continued disagreement must exceed the cost of agreement —dissension must be too damaging to management for it to allow the impasse to continue.
4. Employees must be aware that they possess the first three strengths above.
5. Employees must be sufficiently militant and cohesive to bring effective pressure on the employer. The employer must realize that the employees will "hit the bricks," if necessary, to force their demands.[24]

If teachers satisfy these conditions, they will be in a strong position to gain their goals through the use of strikes. In general, teachers fit the criteria. Teachers are essentially irreplaceable. In large city school systems, qualified replacement would be difficult to find. In suburban school districts with fewer teachers, a board of education could conceivably find replacements for striking teachers, but it is very doubtful that it would want to do so in view of the educational problems created for students and the predictable sanctions by teacher associations.

Teachers are essential to the operation of the organization. Most teaching takes place in a single room with thirty students and one teacher. Teachers rarely leave the students alone for fear of administrative reprimand and the possibility of liability action as a result of a student's injury. In addition, to date, there are few automated devices whereby students can learn on their own.

In industry, management is forced to agree with union demands in large part because a continued strike will generally reduce profit. This does not apply to education. Members of the board of education do not lose profit as a result of strikes. Indeed, the only loss, if any, is political. Political loss can be sizable for persons with political ambitions but not for those without such ambitions. The fact that politics plays a role in the actions of some board members does not ensure that they will favor ending a strike when teachers are concerned with issues that will increase the school budget and taxes. A board member's constituency may wish for him to hold out. It is not certain, then, whether the cost of continued disagreement exceeds the cost of agreement.

Teachers in increasing numbers favor collective bargaining. An NEA report shows that 74.1 percent of teachers thought they should strike after all other means failed.[25] The successes of strikes in several large urban areas serve to reinforce this view.

The trend is toward increased militancy. The strikes in Florida in 1968, and Los Angeles in 1970 reveal, however, that many teachers will not "hit the bricks." In Los Angeles, for example, many elementary schools carried on business as usual.

It would appear, then, that teachers possess the conditions necessary to improve significantly their benefits and to alter the operation of the school. There is enough of a doubt, however, to cause teachers to take each strike one at a time and for them to question the strike as the sole means of gaining their objectives. It is worth noting that the number of strikes, which had been increasing over the past ten years, decreased for the first time in 1971.

While the number of teachers who have engaged in collective action and strikes continues to rise, this does not necessarily mean that all teachers support collective bargaining; nor does it mean that those who join strikes embrace whole-heartedly all aspects of the union model.

### Attitudes of Teachers Toward Collective Bargaining

The attitudes of teachers influence the degree to which they enter into collective bargaining and strikes. Teachers' attitudes toward collective bargaining have changed substantially the last few years. Teachers who are members of the AFT have embraced the use of collective bargaining and strikes for many years, but union-affiliated teachers were a comparatively unheard of minority until the United Federation of Teachers' strike in New York City in 1961.

Almost all teachers in 1961 were members of the NEA, whose leadership and membership were unalterably opposed to collective bargaining and strikes. While 1962 is seen as the year the NEA Representative Assembly approved of collective bargaining, the wording of the resolution (eliminated two years later) was reflective of their attitude toward labor.

Under no circumstances should the resolution of differences between professional associations and boards of education be sought through channels set up for handling industrial disputes. The teacher's situation is completely unlike that of an industrial employee. A board of education is completely unlike that of an industrial employer. A board of education is not a private employer, and a teacher is not a private employee. Both are public servants. Both are committed to serve the common indivisible interest of all persons and groups in the community in the best possible education for their children. Teachers and boards of education can perform their indispensable functions only if they act in terms of identity of purpose in carrying out this commitment. Industrial-disputes conciliation machinery, which assumes a conflict of interest and a diversity of purpose between persons and groups, is not appropriate to professional negotiations in public education.[26]

Since 1962, support for collective action and strikes has increased sub-stantially. As noted before, 74.1 percent of teachers thought they should strike after all other means failed. This corresponds to 53.3 percent in 1965.[27] Teachers now support collective bargaining and some form of force like strikes and sanctions. They have learned to wield the power they have.

#### Negative Attitudes Toward Collective Bargaining

Historically, teachers have viewed both collective bargaining and strikes as undesirable, considering them as motivated by self-interest, nonprofessional, and inappropriate for public employees.

**Motivated by Self-interest.** Collective bargaining is often used for personal gains. No one will deny that collective bargaining, strikes, and sanctions have been used to gain higher salaries and improved working conditions. Self-interest is not reprehensible, but the public often reacts negatively to teachers' desire for more pay and better working conditions, even though these same goals on the part of any other group of workers do not surprise them.

The argument that strikes serve only to assist teachers is spurious; however, it has some credibility as a majority of the issues bargained for to date have been concerned with teacher welfare. Collective bargaining for self-interest is not nonprofessional. Competent and dedicated teachers may be more likely to engage in collective bargaining and strikes. Cass observed that,

of the teachers who walked out of their classrooms, a substantial proportion (though by no means all) were among the better teachers in the schools—the ones who felt most keenly the inadequacies of time and facilities for teaching. (The deadwood and marginal performers are less likely to be moved by professional frustrations to risk their careers in seeking reform.)[28]

Considering teachers' high service orientation, it seems unlikely that they will be content to concentrate on self-interest for very long in deference to educational improvement and their professionalization.

**Nonprofessional.** The argument that collective bargaining is nonprofessional originates from the belief that historically blue collar workers engaged in collective bargaining and used strikes as a means of gaining many of their demands. Many persons view strikes as a tactic of nonprofessional workers.

It is often thought that unions, per se, are nonprofessional. But what is a union? Is the National Education Association any less a union because it says it is not? There are more similarities than differences between the American Medical Association and most unions. Furthermore, most large occupational groups have professional associations or unions. Literally dozens of organizations of engineers and scientists are certified as collective bargaining representatives by the National Labor Relations Board.

Undoubtedly there will always be persons who view collective bargaining and strikes as nonprofessional. It seems safe to predict that the number supporting this view will diminish considerably in the next few years because "some form of sanction, economic, political, or otherwise, must be available to the teaching staff if negotiations are to be successful, since the process assumes relative power equivalence on the parts of the protagonists."[29]

**Inappropriate for Public Employees.** Almost every state has enacted statutes permitting collective bargaining by public employees. Former Secretary of Labor Wirtz asserts that, *"It should be accepted generally, and removed from controversy, that some effective form of bi-lateral and representation labor relations is inevitable, proper, and desirable in public employment in this country."*[30]

The Citizens Committee for Equal Justice for Public Employees maintains that collective bargaining is not a perfect instrument for resolving conflict between employers and employees, but it is the best instrument yet devised.[31] The alternative places all power in management that is concerned primarily with maximizing profit and only secondarily interested in providing adequate wages and working conditions for employees. Too often the public supports no collective bargaining for public employees because it serves to keep budgets and tax rates low.

There is far less unanimity concerning the right of public employees to strike. This resistance revolves around one central theme—that public employees have more ability to paralyze a society, i.e., in many instances, alternative services are not available.

The strike, however, is the only genuine base of power for teachers. Without strikes, management can refuse to listen seriously to teachers' demands. Teachers have been through a long period of powerlessness. Having once gained some power, they are not likely to relinquish it without a struggle, especially since it has proven useful in gaining their goals.

It is noteworthy that courts have been reluctant to force public employees back to work. Former precedence is apparently giving way, forcing judges to hesitate to employ the full power of the courts on public employees. There have been notable exceptions to this with teacher leaders spending several weeks in jail.

### Alternative Models for Teacher Participation

There is no doubt that teachers are increasing their participation in school affairs. The question is, Which model of teacher participation will emerge? Williams describes four models that have been used to resolve the problem of professional decision making: the self-employed professional, the modified hierarchical, the academic, and the union models.[32]

#### Self-Employed Professional Model

The established professions, such as law and medicine, fit the self-employed professional model. Its adoption in education is extremely doubtful. It is difficult, for example, to reconcile the fact that schools exist as a public monopoly with the self-employed professional model. Students within a particular community need teachers living within a reasonable distance. They cannot depend upon the independent, fee-charging teacher to offer services at his convenience. The self-employed professional model in medicine, for example, has resulted in many rural communities being deprived of a physician. This situation could not be allowed to exist in education or, for that matter, should it be allowed in medicine.

In addition, the model is in sharp contrast with the prevailing notion that schooling must be substantially standardized. It in no way recognizes the existing level of competence of teachers. It makes the assumption that all teachers either are or can soon become competent.

It is apparent that the independent, fee-charging, self-employed professional model is not applicable to education although some characteristics of this model, such as increased autonomy and control over certification, are necessary ingredients.

### Modified Hierarchical Model

Since the modified hierarchical model exists today, it is not surprising to find that it accommodates itself quite well to the existing constraints. Indeed, it is an outgrowth of these constraints. The model functions with the recognition that the schools are public monopolies; that the parents, in large part, are the clients; that the educational program is similar, if not identical, in many districts; that teachers vary in competence and thus need supervision by administrators who vary in their competence.

Williams suggests that the model is reasonably efficient, that it presupposes a cooperative relationship between labor and management and thus minimizes internal conflict.

The principal weakness of the modified hierarchical model is that it has not shown itself to be responsive sufficiently to change. The fact that teachers are better trained now than they were ten or twenty years ago has not resulted in enlarging substantially the decision-making authority of teachers. The fact that a larger percentage of men have entered the field has not altered significantly the salaries of teachers. The fact that the technical theoretical knowledge in education has enlarged has not been accompanied by a rapid change in the curriculum. The fact that workers in all occupations have gained a variety of employee benefits has not resulted in similar benefits being offered to teachers. In all, while institutions throughout the world (churches, government, corporations) are beginning to re-examine the traditional authority structure, the modified hierarchical model in education persists.

Teachers are demanding substantial changes in this model, however, and it is unlikely that they will be willing to operate within this model in the future. Teachers are demanding more autonomy than this model provides.

### The Academic Model

The academic model differs from the professional model in many ways. Most significantly, it recognizes the existence of the formal bureaucracy and assumes the need for some management control. It differs from the modified hierarchical model in that it specifies functions and relates these to specific persons in groups rather than assuming that management has wide decision-making authority in all areas. Specifically, it grants teachers increased authority in academic areas. This results in a diminution of authority for administrators in this area. Administrators, however, maintain authority in management.

*The Union Model*

The union model exists normally within the modified hierarchical model in that it recognizes the existence and need for a hierarchy in education. Thus, the union model has many of the advantages of the modified hierarchical model. In this regard, it is much less of a dramatic departure from what exists today than the professional or academic model. The major change, therefore, is that teachers bargain collectively with boards of education or even higher offices. But, they accept the hierarchy. After all, they have to negotiate with someone and that someone is management.

When the union attempts to gain more authority in academic areas and negotiates for them, it is recognizing a major part of the academic model which sharply divides functions and puts academic authority in the hands of teachers.

*Academic Union Model*

Corwin was correct when he asserted that the teacher's professional authority will be in jeopardy until it is supported by the structure of the organization itself.[33] Which structure will provide teachers with this authority? Some conclusions seem inevitable. The self-employed professional model is not possible for reasons which have been discussed already. The existing modified hierarchical model is not possible because teachers will not accept it. The use of the union model will increase because it has proven successful. Whether the academic model will provide a useful alternative for teachers is not known. It may be more useful if incorporated with the union model. Thus, an academic union model emerges.

The academic union model encompasses the characteristics of the academic model but uses collective bargaining as a coercive means of gaining and maintaining teacher authority. In this model, teachers would have the responsibility through collective bargaining for making academic decisions (such as staff selection, promotion, and evaluation; curriculum; selection of materials and supplies; instructional decisions; school organization) and would negotiate with management concerning salary and working conditions. These decisions must be agreed upon by administrators and teachers.

Williams suggests that supervisory and administrative authority may be clearly differentiated in the future. Supervisory authority is defined as "responsibility for the governance of professional activities of teachers, including teaching competence, curriculum determination, and staff selection."[34] Administrative authority "refers to responsibility for such matters as plant maintenance, schedules, budget, administration, and supervision of nonprofessional employees."[35] Administrators carry out administrative functions; teachers carry out supervisory functions.

This is a broad classification and will doubtless need to be further refined. Some terms will need to be operationally defined; e.g., administration and curriculum determination. But the idea of separating administrative authority from supervisory authority is a promising alternative because it allows teachers to make educational or supervisory decisions, yet acknowledges the fact that some decisions are beyond the scope of individual teachers.

The model would be pyramidal, as schools and teachers exist in a hierarchical structure that cannot be willed away anymore than can the hierarchical structure that exists in teacher associations. The difference is that dual lines of authority would be determined. Thus, the model would look like Figure 7-2.

The academic union model resembles the model of authority structure that exists in most hospitals and large universities in which separate spheres of authority (dual lines of authority) have been identified. In these organizations, professionals are under no obligation to take the advice of administrators concerning client care. This arrangement does not preclude persons *offering* advice in any area. In Figure 7-2 the solid arrows represent official authority; the jagged arrows represent an advisory relationship.

Collective bargaining is essential for the academic union model to function effectively for teachers because it offers a form of sanction that elevates teachers to a power plane equivalent to management. Management has been reluctant historically to share its power. Thus, collective bargaining is forced upon workers.

The academic union model can evolve in many ways. It need not be an uncontrollable movement. It is not too late to influence teachers and their associations. Indeed, one purpose of this book is to provide information that might serve to influence teachers and leaders of teacher associations to consider the implications of their actions for the ultimate benefit of teachers and students.

Initial steps call for teacher associations to begin determining those academic areas over which the teacher would have control and those that are administrative (budget, maintenance, coordination, community agent, overall scheduling, supervision of nonprofessional personnel, etc.), over which the principal would have control. This has already begun, but it is not sufficiently systematic.

The academic union model does not permit the practitioner the same freedom as the self-employed professional model. The self-employed professional has almost complete freedom. The academic model places authority not so much in the hands of the individual practitioner as it does in the hands of fellow practitioners. Thus, the teacher might be required to use a specific science program, but that decision would have been made by groups of teachers rather than the state board of education, local board of education, or administrative staff. The academic union model, of course, increases the decision making of the individual practitioner, but the professional "hierarchy" retains some authority. This is extremely important because no model of decision making for teachers can ignore the fact that some teachers are unwilling or, in some cases, unable to make intelligent decisions regarding the education of students. If management loses authority in the existing modified hierarchical model, teacher associations must assume this authority.

It is difficult to assess which model is most beneficial for teachers. Advantages and disadvantages of each depend upon a variety of factors, such as one's perception of the competence of teachers and one's view of the role of the citizen in public education. What is apparent, however, is that the rigid adherence

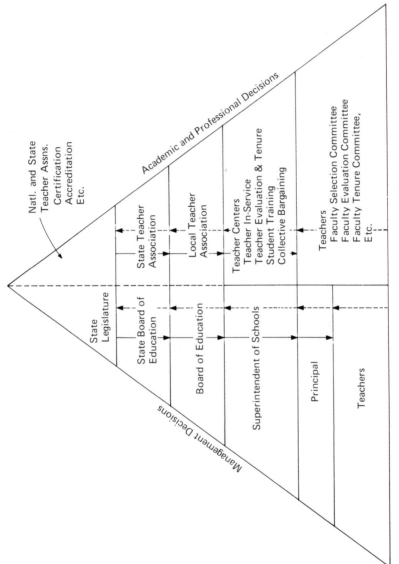

**Figure 7-2.** Academic Union Model.

Natl. and State Teacher Assns. Certification Accreditation Etc.

Academic and Professional Decisions

State Teacher Association

Local Teacher Association

Teacher Centers
Teacher In-Service
Teacher Evaluation & Tenure
Student Training
Collective Bargaining

Teachers
Faculty Selection Committee
Faculty Evaluation Committee
Faculty Tenure Committee,
Etc.

State Legislature

State Board of Education

Board of Education

Superintendent of Schools

Principal

Teachers

Management Decisions

to any one model will reduce the alternatives available to teachers. This is the time to posit promising alternatives, not stubbornly embrace one. This means, for example, that those who prefer the existing structure or the modified hierarchical structure will need to realize the economic plight of teachers as well as their lack of authority. It means that union advocates not be blind to the negative consequences of the model. In reality, it means that teachers must not ape the traditional and established professions such as medicine and law, but develop a powerful and effective collectivity.

### Stages of Collective Bargaining

It is difficult to predict which model will evolve in the years ahead. It is apparent, however, that teachers will use collective bargaining. Teachers and administrators will initially become adversaries, at least during negotiations. If this adversary stance continues after a contract has been developed, it will be harmful to the educational program. More than likely, the adversary stage will be followed by a more constructive understanding of the process of collective bargaining.

Carlton suggests a sequence of stages through which collective bargaining may pass: stage one—nativity, stage two—adolescence, stage three—productive and cooperative.[36] He points out that in stage one, teachers feel guilty about the need for using militant tactics to achieve trade union or self-interest goals. Stage two has much adversity and hostility as teachers feel their "backs are to the wall." This stage is much in evidence now in education. Stage three assumes a model of operation maximizing mutual benefits. Carlton suggests that many teachers believe that adolescence is the final stage, but unless teachers progress to the third stage, they can expect considerable hostility from a public that will hold teachers responsible for causing the deterioration of the public schools.[37]

Teachers negotiate with management—the board of education and their chief administrative officer, the superintendent of schools. But teachers work daily with building principals. Normally only teacher association leaders have contact with the central administration. An understanding of teacher professionalization and collective bargaining would be incomplete without an analysis of the situation in which principals exist. The following chapter is designed to give teachers and principals an understanding of the complex world facing principals and other administrators today.

# EIGHT
# IMPLICATIONS FOR ADMINISTRATORS

*"Teachers are beginning to question in what respects the principal, who may have been a very good football coach, qualifies to observe a French lesson and then to evaluate the teachers' performance. Teachers are evidencing a growing concern about areas of competence. For example, they ask why—if they are supposed to be competent within their area—they must draw lines in a plan book, three inches by two inches for each hour of the school day, for the approval of the principal."\**

*"Regardless of how suspicious we are of analogies which link the problems of the school with the experience of private industry, there is a parallel too close to be ignored between the first and second line supervisors of industry and the principals and department chairmen in our schools. For years, industrial supervisors, who are crucial in maintaining an efficient and productive operation, have stood by helplessly as new relationships between labor and management were carved out at the bargaining table without them. Without exaggerating the analogy, we have seen a similar exclusion take place in education. About all that can be said definitively, for the present at least, is that if the principal is to be heard, he must be heard as a member of the administrative team rather than as a spokesman for the teachers."\*\**

*"Hey, you administrators out there—listen to what Dylan's telling you. 'The times they are a'changing.' All over this society, power is shifting from the establishment to the people. The reason for this is that you have failed—you told us we were going to utopia and we wound up living on the city dump. You just can't share responsibility for such a colossal failure and expect to survive with all of your establishment power intact. Also, you must admit that the teachers can hardly do worse than you have done. It might even be the case that they can salvage the system and save your jobs."\*\*\**

*"In considering potential reorganization of large scale systems, administrators will have to take into account one of the most powerful phenomena of our times—the professional organization of employees."\*\*\*\**

Administrators have been shunted aside as adversaries in the process of collective bargaining. Most do not feel like adversaries, having entered administration, in part, because they enjoyed working with teachers and desired to have a more widespread influence. Many principals are becoming concerned, however, that their power is decreasing so rapidly that genuine leadership may become impossible.

Unless the self-employed, fee-charging professional model is used in education, with its one-to-one client relationship, teachers will continue to teach in schools with principals, and in school districts with superintendents of schools. The nature of the administrator's work may change, but some administrative authority is required to at least coordinate diverse activities, handle routine matters, and provide for the maintenance of the facility.

### The Principal's Power

The principal's power is dependent largely upon the degree of centralization that exists. If rules and policies are centralized, the principal loses authority; if decentralized, he gains. For example, if district policy requires twenty minutes of physical education per day, the principal and his staff lose their authority to have fifty minutes of physical education on Tuesdays and Thursdays. If district policy requires SMSG mathematics, the principal and his staff lose their authority to experiment with other programs.

The principal's power is dependent largely upon the degree of authority gained by teachers. If teachers gain authority, the principal normally loses it; if teachers lose authority, he normally gains authority. Sometimes, of course, teachers gain power from the board of education and superintendent without the principal losing power.

During the last ten years, both the central administration and teachers have gained power at the expense of the principal. Lutz, Kleinman, and Evans note that the principal operates from a powerless base. The central administration has stripped him of most of his power. He is neither a part of the administrative team nor the teacher association.[1] They go on to say,

Many teachers realize that although their building principal functions in the formal organization as the communication link in the line between themselves and the central administration, they can more readily achieve their goals via the informal communication channels maintained among teacher organization leaders, chief administrators, and board members. . . .[2]

Traditionally, if the individual teacher or group of teachers had a grievance, it would be discussed with their school principal. He would either resolve the problem or make a request to his immediate superior—the superintendent of schools in a small district, an assistant superintendent or area supervisor in a large district. With collective bargaining, this is no longer the case. Increasingly, teachers who have grievances communicate directly with the grievance committee which then communicates with the board of education or superintendent. The principal, who formerly had control over some areas, now finds teachers negotiating directly with higher officials. There is a power realignment taking place in the governing of schools. Teachers now negotiate issues such as class size, length of school day, transfer, grouping policies, and similar issues.

Beck speaks of the use of rewards and punishment, noting that the principal has no rewards for his staff because he is not in a position to hire them, set their salaries, establish fringe benefits, provide them bonuses, or lessen their work load. He cannot punish them because he cannot fire them, reduce their salaries, increase their work load appreciably, require them to work overtime, or discriminate in pupil load. He is powerless to reward or punish.[3]

In education, administrators lose considerable control because of the principle of equality or sameness; the manner in which teachers are paid, promoted, dismissed, and granted tenure; and the rhythm of allocative decisions in schools. Lortie notes that the allocations of teachers and resources to individual schools are determined by objective formulas such as the number of students enrolled. Additional resources to one school may lead to favoritism. Thus, experimentation is reduced. He notes also that equality is evident in the way teachers are paid—by a salary schedule that pays everyone the same regardless of competence, subject area, or grade level.[4] Most significantly, perhaps, "the rhythm of allocative decisions in schools is intermittent and infrequent in comparison with many other types of organization."[5] Allocations occur annually, and once school begins only minor changes are possible.

Not only is the principal powerless, but he is placed in a dilemma. He is a member of the administration, yet he must deal effectively with teachers. If he sides with management during a strike, he jeopardizes his relations with teachers. If he sides with teachers, he runs the risk of "betraying the confidence" of the man who hired and can fire him. If he works well with teachers, he is effective during the day. If he "plays ball" with the superintendent, he may receive a raise in salary and a promotion.

The principal's waning power over students has reduced his power as well. The courts have limited the alternatives available to principals by defending the constitutional rights of students. The day has passed when a principal could send a boy home to get his hair cut, or examine the personal belongings of students.[6]

While principals are losing formal power, they still have power irrespective of their offices. Guba developed the model shown in Figure 8-1. In this model, power is two-dimensional. It resides in the role of the person; i.e., in the principal's official capacity as a line officer in a bureaucracy *and* in the person of the principal irrespective of the office. Another way of viewing this model is that the *role* dimension is "given" the principal; the *person* dimension must be earned. Administrators will continue to have power in their official role, but power will decrease as teachers gain power. This does not mean that the principal will lose power in his personal dimension. The principal who wishes to influence the conduct of education in a school will want to concentrate on developing this personal dimension. While all principals have the potential for gaining power by virtue of their person, many teachers are unwilling to grant such power because they do not have confidence in the principal's ability.

As late as 1970, however, 42.8 percent of a nationwide sample of public school teachers thought their central office conferred considerable autonomy and initiative to principals; 45.7 percent thought their central office conferred some autonomy and initiative to principals; and 11.2 percent thought their central office conferred little autonomy and initiative to principals. Thus, about one teacher in ten perceived the principal as having little official autonomy and initiative.[7]

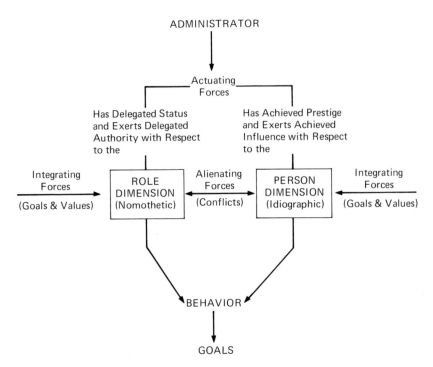

**Figure 8-1.** Model of Internal Administrative Relationships. Source: Egon G. Guba, "Research in Internal Administration— What Do We Know?," *Administrative Theory as a Guide to Action*, ed. Roald F. Campbell and James M. Lipham (Chicago: Midwest Administration Center, The University of Chicago, 1960), p. 124.

This does not mean that the 42.8 percent of the principals *have* considerable autonomy and initiative. It reveals teachers' perceptions of the views of their central office. Teachers have much to say about principal autonomy and, increasingly, their efforts lessen the authority of principals regardless of the wishes of the central office.

Thus far the data suggest that principals are losing power, but that does not mean they are powerless. Bidwell suggests that since the principal has a strong voice in the assignment of teachers to his school, he gains a measure of control over them.[8] In addition, he can make frequent and sensitive adjustments of teaching procedures. This is possible because most schools, especially elementary schools, are relatively small organizations in which close surveillance is possible.

The analysis thus far rests upon the assumption that a system has a fixed amount of power and exists as a finite sum in a closed system. But the school is extremely open. The rapid response of Congress to Sputnik and the increase of citizen involvement in the schools are evidence of its openness.

Smith and Tannenbaum believe that an increase in the control by one group does not imply decrease in control by others.[9] Erickson states this clearly, "When teachers, parents and student groups began wresting power for themselves, it has generally been discovered that there is more than enough to go around."[10] His empirical observations working with local teacher associations are supported in the theoretical work of Walton and McKersie who differentiate distribute bargaining, integrative bargaining, attitudinal structuring, and intraorganizational bargaining. In the latter, the resolution of issues may benefit both sides. In effect, it suggests that everyone may get a larger piece of the pie.[11] This suggests that an increase in power by teachers does not necessarily mean a decrease in the power of administrators.

The careful research of these investigators cannot be passed off lightly, yet the evidence to date, so far as schools are concerned, seems to indicate that principals have lost much of their power. Hopefully, additional research will help clarify this area.

Principals are losing power, but they still have some control over teachers. The critical issue for principals and teachers alike is to determine the type of control maximally useful in an organization that includes teachers who are diverse in their interest and competence.

### Control

The shift in authority requires the principal to use different methods of control. Etzioni has classified control into three analytical categories: physical, material, and symbolic.[12] Control based on the use of physical means is described as coercive power. Control based upon the use of material means is utilitarian power. Control based on charisma or collegial means constitutes normative power.

The principal does not have the opportunity to use utilitarian power since he has little control over "goods" and "services." Instructional materials are usually distributed uniformly from the district office, advances on the salary schedule are largely beyond the control of the principal, and the budget over which the principal has actual control is very limited.

Principals, then, have access to coercive and normative control. Obviously no principal uses either method of control under all circumstances. It seems useful, then, to establish two middle categories: normative-coercive and coercive-normative. Thus, the continuum from coercive to normative would be as follows:

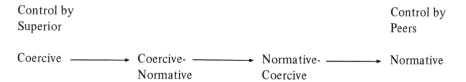

Control by
Superior

Control by
Peers

Coercive ⟶ Coercive-Normative ⟶ Normative-Coercive ⟶ Normative

The issue is not to determine the type of control a principal should use but rather the effect of various means of control on teachers who have varying competencies. No one mode of control is applicable to all teachers since teachers differ enormously in intelligence, enthusiasm, dedication, ability, personality, age, to name only a few characteristics.

Since there is a wide range of teacher ability and dedication in most schools, a type of control is needed that will serve to assist all of them. Many well-intending principals, trained in a graduate school to avoid coercive control, adopt normative control and treat teachers as professionals. They are surprised and often annoyed to find that some teachers do not desire it. In addition, they find that it does not necessarily result in achieving more efficiently the goals of the school. Principals have the same problem with their staff that teachers have with students; namely, neither teachers nor students are homogeneous. Thus, the type of control for one teacher may be dysfunctional for another.

How can the principal work most effectively with teachers who range from professional, to semi-professional, to functionary? To adopt the same leadership style with all teachers will almost certainly cause disorganization.

The *professional* teacher demands more authority to make most of the decisions affecting his work with students. He will not usually seek the principal's advice or tolerate the principal making decisions for him. He insists upon considerable freedom in his classroom and demands a voice in all affairs of the schools that immediately affect his work. For example, he wants to be consulted on all matters concerning school organization, budget, salaries, the community, and curriculum development.

The *functionary* teacher needs to be controlled to some degree by the principal because the functionary can make decisions that could be detrimental to students. The amount of control of the principal will depend upon the competence of the functionary. The fact that the principal needs to gain a measure of control does not mean that he interferes consistently with the decisions of teachers. Instead, he establishes policies or procedures that limit teachers' breadth of decision making.

The *semi-professional* teacher presents a vexing problem for principals. The semi-professional wants and often even demands extensive authority in the classroom. Yet, lacking certain skills of the professional, he needs some supervision. The principal is in the unenviable position of having to relate to some persons as professionals and to others as functionaries.

What is the most useful method of control? Coercive control is seldom useful because, among other things, teachers will not accept it. Aspects of coercive control, however, must be retained because there are societal expectations in a public bureaucracy, not the least of which is that teachers will be at work, on time, the 180-odd days prescribed by law. Normative control is not always useful because it often allows too much freedom for persons who are not yet prepared to assume full responsibility for their actions. Aspects of normative control must be used, however, because some teachers are already "professional," and almost all teachers are demanding increasingly more of a role in decision making.

## The Principal's Role

It is apparent that the principal's role is being altered dramatically in many schools. The principalship is being challenged by "superiors" and "subordinates." A new type of model needs to be developed. Klein, [13] and probably most authorities in educational administration, predicts that collegially-inclined leaders will have the best chance to succeed and survive in the coming decade.

Godine notes that two behaviors have dominated official conduct in the past—benevolent paternalism and authoritarianism. He notes, however, that teaching is attracting an increasing number of persons who will not be patronized or intimidated by "authoritarian" domination. [14]

The change from administrative and supervisory control to administrative control will not be easy for all principals, especially those who have been principals for many years. A recent study by Bridges suggests that the elementary principal's behavior is affected, perhaps molded, by the length of time he spends in a bureaucracy. The longer he spends in the bureaucracy, the less likely he is to satisfy the role of the office.

Initially, the individual may stamp his particular role with the unique style of his own characteristic pattern of expressive behavior. However, with increased exposure to the expectations associated with the bureaucratic role, the personality of the principal becomes submerged. [15]

The finding is predictable. A bureaucracy demands office holders to be methodical and disciplined. It demands that problems be handled in a uniform manner. It demands office holders to depersonalize their relations with clients. In addition, seniority, pensions, tenure, and incremental salaries within a bureaucracy encourage conformity.

## Transitional Steps

Principals can be expected to use methods of control that fit into the normative-coercive or coercive-normative range. Also, widespread adoption of participatory decision making can be expected. Participatory decision making is based on the assumption that a group can make a wiser decision than a single executive. Management retains control, but in certain circumstances, the control is more illusory than real. In this same vein, the principal should be a procedural administrator enforcing rational procedures of decision making but allowing teachers to make the actual decisions. [16]

It can be argued that procedural administration places too much control in the hands of the principal. The amount of control, however, depends in large part on who develops the procedures. If the procedures are developed by teachers, as they often will be, the principal does not have control because teachers are free to change the procedures. The principals who retain tight control over decisions are those who assiduously require every procedure to be followed literally. Once again, however, this type of behavior would prompt teachers to abolish the procedures or make them less rigid.

The role of the principal as a monitor of decisions and group processes corresponds to the role of the principal as convener of organizational problem solving. This new role

involves *convening others for problem solving and group decision making.* It functions within a team of staff members to broaden the locus of decision making to make use of the strengths and resources of the faculty. The principal as a single role taker makes fewer decisions on his own compared with a traditional role-model. Mostly, he guides groups through problem solving and stimulates all members to participate actively.[17]

Rich envisions a "substantive" as well as process role for the principal. He suggests that principals should control through prescriptions based on evaluation, which result in a prescriptive statement. "A prescriptive statement is a value judgment that contextually implies that one has engaged in a reasoning process before making the recommendation."[18] Prescriptive recommendations need not be complied with by teachers. They are recommendations only. The principal, however, does not have a sufficiently thorough knowledge in areas such as spelling, reading, and mathematics to make a recommendation. He will be forced to seek advice from teachers. If he has to solicit advice from teachers, why not let them make their own decisions rather than recommendations?

An initial structure for moving from coercive to normative control is through a representative educational council of teachers vested with broad decision-making authority. The use of educational councils will increase significantly in the years ahead. Educational councils are different than teacher advisory committees in that the former is a policy-making council. This does not mean that the educational council has unlimited power. It cannot, for example, vote to dismiss all students, have teachers report to work at noon, violate state laws governing education, or violate local board policies and procedures governing the operation of the school district.

The principal who wishes to move in the direction of increased teacher participation in decision making may wish to form an advisory group first and then an educational council. Indeed, most alert principals already have an advisory committee of teachers.

Almost all models of participatory decision making assume that the problem is one of improving administration. However, teachers seem increasingly to reject both "good" and "bad" administration. This is not simply a problem of creating good administrators. The problem is that professional status is designed to eliminate benevolent authoritarian administration because it is dependent upon the discretion of administrators.[19] Teachers today, however, are seeking a restructuring of the organization's authority system.

*Administrative Training Programs*

What is apparent is that administrative training programs at universities need to be changed dramatically. Goldhammer and Becker's study confirmed what many practicing administrators and professors in educational administration have suspected for many years, that "Principals who were effective could not be distinguished from those who were not on the basis of their formal preparation."[20]

First, administrators need to learn a great deal more than they know at present about teacher professionalization. Few departments of educational administration, as a result of increased teacher militancy, have changed their programs to provide studies in professionalization and collective bargaining. A course on "how to" engage in collective bargaining is not suggested. Collective bargaining, at least at this stage of development, is a skill that administrators understand, but bureaucratization and professionalization are the substantive areas of study.

Second, there needs to be more concentration on the concept of control. It is easy to suggest that administrators need to use some model of participatory decision making (sneaky telling to some critics). Indeed, that has been evident for over three decades. But which model? Does management need to retain control?

What disadvantages accrue to placing authority in the hands of teachers? How can principals encourage rather than resist efforts of teachers to gain control over hiring, dismissal, evaluation, promotion, while maintaining an educational program of top quality?

Also, if educational programs are decentralized, the principal could become a peer to teachers. He would gain power if he were one of them or elected by them.

Third, there is a need for more emphasis on an understanding of the concept of conflict. It is evident that disequilibrium as a result of conflict is necessary and desirable but, in general, administrators have sought to "keep a lid" on conflict especially between the teachers and the hierarchy, or between teachers and teachers. It is perhaps inevitable that practicing administrators, faced with many problems, will tend to discourage conflict. One hopes that graduate schools of educational administration will not. Corwin speaks to this point:

If conflict is a routine and normal occurrence within the administrative process, then administrative training programs should address themselves systematically to the proper role of conflict—its positive as well as its negative functions.[21]

Allied with conflict is the area of control. Does the administrator have control now? Perhaps he has nothing to lose. Bridges re-examines Simon's and Bernard's classic analysis concerning the source of authority.[22] He suggests that administrators are guided, shaped, and controlled by certain external agents; namely, subordinates. Thus, the administrator is a pawn as well as an originator of activities and programs.

Azzarelli offers perhaps the most coherent framework to those involved in preparing administrators and supervisors. He suggests the following:

1. Social and philosophical foundations of education including the sociology of the educational profession, the politics of power, etc.;

2. Behavioral sciences foundations including the psychology of group relations, sensitivity training and conflict analysis, human relations, power system analysis, etc.; and

3.   Technological foundations in the methods of resolving personnel problems including economics of public education, personnel relations, labor legislation, methods of contract negotiations.[23]

Some departments of educational administration have gone far beyond the issues raised in this chapter. It is safe to say, however, that the only evidence of change in most departments has been the addition of a course in collective bargaining. Departments need considerable reorganization if they are to adequately prepare administrators and supervisors. As a bare minimum, they need to include substantial work in superior-subordinate relationships in complex social organizations.[24] Departments of educational administration are not alone in this regard. Departments concerned with curriculum development have severely slighted the school as a formal bureaucratic institution and the decision-making responsibilities of curriculum supervisors. Seemingly, these are things one picks-up on the job.

### Superintendent of Schools [25]

Much of what has been said concerning principals can be applied to superintendents. They are losing power and are often bewildered by the new roles required of them. Many are fearful for the educational program, and some for their jobs. Perhaps most telling of all, they do not command the respect from teachers they once enjoyed. Rather than being bitter, many are simply regretful.

The transition from patriarch to negotiator will not be easy for superintendents.

Most superintendents have developed a system of values that includes the concept that they should serve as the leader of the professional staff. When a superintendent has worked diligently, perhaps for many years, to establish himself as patriarch to the teachers, it is easy to imagine the trauma he experiences when he is confronted with the insistence by the teachers that a formal negotiation situation be established. To him it seems like treason and implies that teachers don't trust his leadership— and they don't.[26]

Bernard E. Donovan, former superintendent of schools in New York City, has many battle scars. He suggests that training programs for superintendents be changed to include negotiation skills, employee-employer relationships, and the ability to analyze financial demands.[27]

### Boards of Education

The concern thus far has been primarily with the roles of teachers and administrators in collective bargaining. Some mention needs to be made about the roles of boards of education, inasmuch as the behavior of boards influences the conduct of other persons in the organization.

Board members can be excused for being confused. Before the 1960s, board members could rightly consider administrators and teachers as their employees for they hired them, conferred tenure, set salaries, approved the curriculum, selected instructional materials, passed judgment on the administrative staff, and, when necessary, fired persons. While they exercised these responsibilities, they more often than not simply rubber-stamped the recommendations of the superintendent. Indeed, many of the more competent superintendents of schools made it apparent that if their recommendations were overridden by the board, the board should hire another superintendent. Thus, boards "melted into the woodwork" in some school districts even though they continued to enjoy outward status in the eyes of the community and, indeed, in the eyes of the uninformed teacher.

Now boards are being thrust into the center of education, driven from their secure and paternalistic, legalistic, peripheral position of the past several decades. They are being asked to make judgments on a variety of topics because teacher associations will not negotiate with persons who do not have the power to make a decision. Increasingly, it is becoming evident that only the board has this necessary power.

This situation places boards in a difficult position. They are being pressured by external forces (chamber of commerce, parent taxpayers' groups, citizens generally) to maintain but not increase expenditures for schools. They are being pressured by internal forces (administrators, teacher associations, superintendents) to increase expenditures for schools.

In the process, board members are becoming frustrated and angry. Persons cannot retain an optimistic and constructive stance toward the educational problems at hand with two forces bombarding them with contradictory demands and often contradictory facts. It is likely that sides will be taken and objectivity reduced.

Citizen organizations and teacher associations are becoming quite aggressive. Teachers no longer come forward with hat in hand, a catch in their voice, and knees trembling. Often they march in as one of a bargaining team that is well-trained, efficient, and downright pushy. If any knees are trembling, they belong to the superintendent and members of the board.

The truth of the matter is that most board members do not have the time to gain command of the area of collective bargaining. Boards desiring to minimize conflicts and to take advantage of the knowledge of the professional staff should recognize the increased ability of the professional staff to govern themselves.

It is going to be extremely difficult for boards of education to bargain with teacher associations in the future. The percentage of boards, as sole negotiators, has decreased from 33.2 percent in 1966–67, to 13.2 percent in 1970–71.[28] Boards will be forced to use full-time negotiators who will be given wide discretionary power. The negotiator will work with the board of education and superintendent. One negotiator will grow into a team of negotiators which will work from January through December each year in preparation for the next contract.

Board members have adjusted to the reality of collective bargaining. There is every reason to believe, however, that the situation is changing again. It appears that in the future teacher associations will ignore local boards of education and bargain with the state legislature. This leads Iannacone to suggest that local school boards will become mere ceremonial bodies by 1980, roughly comparable to the existing responsibilities of county superintendents' offices in some states.[29]

In summary, collective bargaining is changing the authority structure in schools. Administrators are losing power. To retain authority, they will be required to concentrate on models of participatory decision making with teachers, strengthen their personal authority, learn a great deal more about the control over fairly diverse "employees," and understand more thoroughly the conflicts that exist when professionals work in a bureaucracy.

# NINE
# PROBLEMS AND ISSUES

*"Will the [union] model result in a narrow self-interest by teachers that will freeze the schools in a myriad of rules, regulations, and procedures resulting in continually deteriorating schools? Or will it result in teachers continuing to grow in responsibility and stature, making demands not only upon the public and on school management, but on themselves as well to insure that the public schools are responsive, creative, and relevant?"* *

*"In my book, when a teacher commits himself to break the law, this is probably the greatest sacrifice that that teacher is asked to make for that child. . . . In one particular instance we went through a period of time in which science books printed in 1942 were being used in 1961. We went through a period of time in which every April teachers ran out of paper, in which they did not get chalk, in which windows were broken and not repaired— right down the line. We went through a period of time that was, as far as the teachers were concerned, insurmountable. They exhausted the remedies provided for them under the law. . . . They were committed to a point where they had to admit that in order to improve the quality of education in that city they had to break the law."* **

*"Our theory suggests that public schools must either rapidly and broadly increase their legitimation, relying on old and new consensus-building mechanisms, or else financial shortage, riots, and alienation of citizens, parents, and students will severely constrict their very ability to function."* ***

It is hazardous to identify problems and issues concerned with teacher professionalization and collective bargaining because of the great diversity in the ability and attitude of teachers. Some teachers do not seek higher salaries, improved working conditions, or increased autonomy. Some are satisfied with the existing system. Those who are dissatisfied vary from being mildly discontent with the progress being made, to militants who fight vigorously for reform. In addition to the diversity of teachers, states vary in terms of wealth, population, citizen interest in education, and legislators' receptiveness to teacher collective bargaining. Similarly, school districts vary.

This diversity encourages teacher associations to concentrate their attention and energy on pressing local problems. This is understandable and defensible; however, local problems should not command the complete attention of teachers because teachers can gain autonomy only through a united profession.

This chapter discusses thirteen problems and issues that confront the entire profession and should command the attention of all teachers.

### Right of Collective Bargaining

The need for collective bargaining is an established fact, and it is time to consider issues upon which there is disagreement. Unfortunately, all state legislatures have not passed legislation to legalize collective bargaining for teachers. This is and should continue to be a priority for teacher associations at the state and national level.

States that have adopted legislation such as California's Winton Act (which assumes a cooperative position on the part of management and labor and retains management authority), will gradually be forced to adopt the private sector conflict-of-interest model.[1]

Teachers will continue to use strikes as coercive means for gaining their demands. The strike is an enormously powerful weapon for occupations engaged in services of which disruption will lead to great inconvenience for consumers or great loss of profit to investors or management. While education is essential for the well-being of the society, strikes do not inconvenience a great many persons (none for those adults without children, and little to the more affluent parents who often send their children to private schools), and they do not result in a loss of profit for management. Indeed, management often gains funds from a strike through a savings in salaries.

Looking back over the past several years, it is apparent that some strikes have been successful while others have not. In the future, increased attention needs to be given to whether a strike is likely to succeed and under which circumstances.

In speaking about the disadvantages of the Florida strike, Cass notes that the employment of untrained laymen to man the classrooms essentially tells the public that anyone can teach. He suggests that the long-term effect on the public attitude cannot yet be assessed, but it is not likely to be positive.[2]

Strikes always have some negative consequences. The essential question is whether the advantages outweigh the disadvantages. Statewide strikes are enormously expensive in terms of the loss of teachers' salaries. A better tactic may be to concentrate strikes in the major cities where the public is more sympathetic to striking workers, where control can be maintained more effectively, and where organized labor is often available for support when needed.

Teachers should demand unashamedly increased salaries and improved employee benefits regardless of the cost and possible negative effects on the education of students.[3] Salaries need to be increased, and teachers need to receive benefits similar to those enjoyed by millions of other persons.

Teachers need offer no justification for demanding increased salaries and improved working conditions. The appalling conditions under which teachers work presently is reason enough. There are, however, other defensible reasons for increased salaries and improved working conditions if teachers aspire to professional status. High salaries and good working conditions tend to attract more competent persons, male and female, into a field. In addition, higher salaries reduce the need for teachers to seek part-time work which drains energy from teaching and reduces the time that might be spent reading, assisting students, engaging in in-service activities, talking with colleagues, attending a course or lecture at a university, seeking a higher degree, or attending enriching cultural activities.

Teachers will want to increase the use of the various coercive means at their command. The time may come when teacher associations will want to ask whether their demands are in the public interest. To date, few instances of abused power are evident. There are, however, thousands of instances when teachers have lacked the courage to use the power at their command. This timidity has resulted in a weakened profession and a weakened educational program for students.

Critics will maintain that such a welfare package is too expensive. Management maintains that labor union demands are extravagant, but workers continue to expand their welfare benefits, and the democratization, if not the revitalization, of industry appears to be advanced with each concession.

## Scientific Knowledge

A profession bases its practice upon a scientific body of knowledge. Education simply does not have a substantial scientific body of knowledge—i.e., principles to guide teachers' actions in the classroom. Many characteristics of a profession such as autonomy, training period, socialization, licensure, legislation, income, power, and prestige are derived largely because of the esoteric body of knowledge that is unknown to laymen. The development of a scientific body of knowledge can come about only through research.

Historically, there has been a disjunction between the practitioner and the theorist in education. The charge that professors are in ivory towers is not restricted to schools of education, but the idea seems to enjoy more widespread support in education than in other fields. This attitude prompts one author to state,

Anti-intellectualism of teachers can no longer be condoned. The reform of teacher education must be to further scholarship. Teachers must become avid readers consumed by history and by language, conversant with scientific principles, and at home with mathematical manipulations.[4]

Some teachers maintain that the research emanating from professors in schools of education leaves much to be desired. On this point, teachers would have the support of professors in practically every other department of a university. It is another argument, however, for teachers to maintain that research and practice are irreconcilable or incompatible. Improved practice is impossible without improved theory. On this point, the university community is virtually unanimous.

Research must be expanded and improved if education is to become more professionalized. Few persons who receive a doctor's degree in education undertake a systematic research study. Many more researchers are needed if scientific principles are to be developed in the field.

Teachers need to use their political power to gain increased funds for research from funding agencies in the government. But gaining funds will be difficult.

Greater investments in research and training will be made only if people feel that important negative consequences follow from the lack of a great knowledge base in the work of, say, typists, nurses, chauffeurs, or teachers.[5]

Another possibility that will doubtless evoke considerable reservation on the part of some teachers is for teacher associations to subsidize directly promising teachers who enter research careers. This support could continue after the teacher finished his professional training and entered a research organization or university. Most important of all, the senseless and erroneous conflict between theory and practice must be put to rest.

### Community Control

Citizens seek to enlarge their control of schools. This movement comes at the same time that teachers seek increased autonomy from lay control. Thus, laymen and teachers are on a collision course, the final determination of which is uncertain.

Gittell notes that administrators and teachers are strongly resisting increased community control of the schools, viewing this as a threat to their status. Historically, the system has been insulated and thus reliant on professional decision making. Since all groups tend to protect their interest and preserve their power and prestige, they understandably resist citizen control and seek to maintain the existing system.[6]

The gains in autonomy by teachers during the past ten years have been discussed previously and are fairly well known to teachers. But citizens have made gains as well in areas such as state legislation mandating district decentralization, Upward Bound, Head Start, performance contracting, the many programs of OEO Community Action Programs, and the policies of some local boards of education to permit citizens to vote for specific sections of a school budget.

The factors involved in the struggle for control of the schools are complex, but they appear to include at least the growing strength of blacks, citizen alienation in the face of strikes and sanctions, an inadequate educational system, inadequate structure for financing education, and the democratization of institutions.

Blacks are often in conflict with teacher organizations for many reasons, but their principal desire is to control the allocation of jobs, especially those of principals, and to promote a distinct set of values—a black subculture.

The minority groups in large cities resist teacher unionization because unions tend to seek the maintenance of a centralized school system while citizens support increasingly a decentralized system to allow them increased power and control. The goal of the UFT strike in New York City in 1969 was to cripple the decentralized experiment, which it feared might lead to a lessening of its bargaining power by giving local communities control of the hiring and firing of principals, teachers, and teacher aides. Stephen Zeluck, former president of the New Rochelle (New York) Federation of Teachers, supports this position, *"The real issue for the UFT was how to destroy community control."*[7] Zeluck argues that both the ghetto residents and teachers have the same goal, wresting power and authority from the same establishment boards of education. He maintains, however, that unless the two groups cooperate for social regeneration and educational progress, the union will be weakened and the students shortchanged.

Teachers and other public employees (firemen, policemen, welfare workers, sanitation workers, etc.) are struggling through collective action to gain higher salaries, improved working conditions, and a measure of control of the policy governing their jobs. By and large, these groups resist inroads by blacks and members of other minority groups. Thus, while the white-dominated public employees gain more and more of a share of the limited wealth in municipalities, blacks gain less and less. An increasing number of blacks view city employees (including teachers) as their oppressors because they gain jobs and increased welfare benefits at the expense of blacks.[8]

It is apparent that whites and blacks are fighting for the benefits attached to public employment. This will bring the victor higher benefits and more political power in dealing with municipal governments. "Teacher militancy seems to be on a collision course with the civil rights movement in the big cities as lower-class parents begin to assert their authority."[9] Corwin speaks of those in the lower levels of the social structure rather than blacks solely, although he would doubtless acknowledge that blacks dominate this group.[10]

Many citizens have little understanding of the rationale in support of increased teacher autonomy. However, many teachers also have little understanding of citizens' need to collaborate with public servants in their local communities. Klein, [11] an advocate of community participation, reviews the traditional arguments against citizen participation: lack of expertise, insufficient time, too personal and biased perspective, lack of technical competence. In addition, he notes that change can be blocked entirely if agreements cannot be reached among local factions.

Professional decision making (authoritative change) is more quick, more rational, scientifically based, and less distorted by local biases and individual prejudice. "In short, it offers the security of authority and expertise."[12]

In spite of the advantages of professional decision making, Klein supports citizen participation. He argues that "top down" change contributes to the weakening of the community because it tends to contribute to insecurity by taking the control of events outside the citizen's sphere of influence.

The conflict between teachers and citizens is usually inevitable when teachers engage in strikes or sanctions. The fact that some parents become alienated does not suggest that strikes should be discontinued. There are many communities where striking teachers have had the overwhelming support of citizens. But, it would be erroneous to assume that strikes or sanctions do not create ill will. Erickson believes there is a danger that teacher negotiations will help produce an educational backlash, particularly in depressed areas. Negotiations reinforce the sameness of urban schools, negate the efforts of principals, and delay much needed educational reform.

Citizens have voiced concern about the inadequacies of schools for the last twenty years, reaching an apogee shortly after Sputnik. Few occupations are free of citizen criticism. The medical profession, for example, is being subjected currently to considerable criticism. Reformers contend that those who control schools have not produced results. The schools have failed to educate adequately large numbers of students. The extent of this concern is evidenced by the formation of parent groups designed to improve the schools for students from low-income families.

Citizens are concerned about the increasing cost of operating a school district. Citizens would be less concerned if they were not faced with a local tax referendum each year. In some school districts with a growing student enrollment, bond referendum is almost a yearly occurrence. With inflation, citizens become more sensitive about the services they receive for their tax dollar. The movement toward funding at the state level would reduce this problem.

The democratization of institutions is a factor in citizen unrest. Revel, a controversial and contemporary French writer, maintains that the United States is in the midst of a revolution affirming individual freedom and equality, and the rejection of authoritarian control. The specific manifestations include: a new approach to moral values, the revolt of blacks, the female attack on masculine domination, the rejection by young persons of exclusively economic-and technical social goals, non-coercive types in education, acceptance of the guilt for poverty, the demand for equality, the rejection of a culture based on authority, a rejection of American foreign policy, commitment to the natural environment.[13]

This movement is also evident in the investigations of Ralph Nader and his associates, administrative training programs, reform within political parties, the Supreme Court's decision to apportion state legislatures based on population, and the landmark California Supreme Court's decision (*Serrano* vs. *Priest*) challenging local property tax as an equitable basis for funding schools. All of these movements tend to democratize the nation. They are based on the assumption that a free and democratic nation requires active citizen participation.

What is likely to occur during the coming decade? Will teachers or citizens succeed in wresting authority from the establishment board? Etzioni points out that school systems (like other corporate bodies) prefer to consult the public in ways which allow parents and taxpayers to see things the school's way. He cautions, however, that until teachers recognize the public's new potency, it will not re-legitimate the schools. School personnel must be willing to learn the reasons why the public has withdrawn legitimacy or be hampered in accomplishing its mission.[14]

It appears that educators will lose some of the trust of citizens, especially in urban areas, and that persons outside the educational establishment will become increasingly a part of the formal structure.

This conflict need not be an unwholesome development. Gittell, for example, does not view citizen involvement as a threat to teacher participation and authority but as an effort to achieve a more appropriate balance between professionals and public participation in policy development. She notes, however, that a redistribution of power within the educational system is taking place, directed toward fulfilling the demands of a democratic system. In her view, this will create an environment in which more meaningful policies are developed and more alternative solutions proposed.[15]

Citizen involvement may have salutary effects on students and not infringe upon teacher autonomy. But, in which areas are citizens to be involved—instruction, staff selection, curriculum?

If parents know how to teach reading, when to impose discipline, which activities to include in social studies, how to create enthusiasm and intellectual curiosity in students, how to write a short play or verse; then there is no need for teachers, professors of education, or departments of education.

Perhaps, then, parents are to be involved in the selection of staff. Staff selection is presently being taken out of the hands of administrators because teachers consider administrators' judgment inferior to theirs. If teachers resist administrators selecting teachers, they will surely resist laymen selecting teachers.

Perhaps citizens are to be involved in the curriculum. Curriculum has a variety of meanings, but to parents it usually means courses of study. While teachers have not been as responsive to local needs as they should be, especially in urban areas, there is no reason to believe that citizens would do a better job. Indeed, a case can be made for teachers listening too closely to the wishes of the citizens and not standing up for the type of educational program they believe most desirable for students.[16]

Teacher associations believe their membership more capable than citizens of making wise decisions concerning the educational program. They resist community control because it passes control from the teacher to pressure groups. What the teacher is confronted with in the Bundy Plan (which would decentralize the school district and afford citizens considerably more authority), and other community formulas, is the audacity of the uninformed.[17]

Citizens should be listened to more seriously than they have been in the past, but a profession does not form its practice on the desires of the clients, much less the desires of the parents or neighbors of its clients. Teachers should resist assiduously all efforts by citizens to reduce their autonomy. The proposition that schools are so bad that nothing can be done to make them worse is decidedly false.

It is apparent that the power struggle between teachers and citizens is not a simple phenomenon. No teacher wishes to establish a school completely autonomous from lay control. Nor do teachers wish to advance their well-being and that of their profession over the diminution of the well-being of citizens. Teachers are not so insensitive and uninformed. Citizens should ponder whether their involvement will come at the expense of teacher autonomy. Clearly, both groups need to decide who should make what decisions in the schools.

### Public Relations

At the local school and district level, a public relations program is needed to concentrate on educating parents concerning the desirability and necessity for teacher governance of their profession. At the national level, such a program is needed to concentrate on critical issues and the citizens' overall image of teachers.

## District Level

Teachers at the district level who seek to be viewed as professionals will avoid asking parents for their appraisal of a given educational program. If laymen are asked their opinions, they quite naturally believe that their opinions will be taken into account in the adoption, discontinuance, or revising of these practices. If not, what reason is there for seeking their opinions? Educational personnel should feel obligated to keep parents and citizens informed about new and established educational programs being offered students, but teachers should keep the final decision making for themselves.

This does not suggest that parents should be seen and not heard. Parents have an important voice in the schools, but if teachers are to become professionals, this voice should be mainly in the form of questions and concerns expressed to teachers or on a ballot on election day. When parents have complaints or concerns about the educational program, they should feel obligated to visit with school officials. School officials should alter educational programs that are not defensible. But, in word and action, professional teachers should make it clear that laymen should not interfere with the autonomy of teachers.

## National Level

The public must grant an occupation professional status. Increased support for teachers as a profession will come when teachers improve in many of the characteristics of a profession, but a concerted and vigorous public relations campaign is necessary to augment and facilitate these improvements.

The NEA has a national public relations program. Their program includes both national television commercials and magazine advertisements.

One significant advantage of a national public relations campaign is the impression it makes on prospective teachers. It is not only the thought of low salaries and inane duty assignments that discourages prospective students—it is the thought that teachers are not actively striving to change the situation. Young persons wish to enter an occupation that is composed of persons willing to fight for what they believe, regardless of the odds.

## Control of Pre-service and In-service Education

Teachers need to govern pre-service and in-service education of teachers. They should be accountable, but they can hardly be expected to clean a house they don't own.

## Pre-service Education

The Teacher Standards and Licensure Act, which will be discussed in the final chapter, seeks to accredit institutions of higher education which prepare teachers, determine certification requirements, adopt and enforce standards of practice, and adopt and enforce a code of ethics. The enactment of such legislation is a priority for teacher associations.

A local association, however, need not wait until the state legislature passes such an act. Hottleman suggests each local association appoint a person or small committee to meet with the president of the nearest state college and indicate its desire for closer cooperation between the association and the college toward the improvement of the college.[18] He also suggests encouraging expert teachers on public school staffs to offer their services to local state colleges as visiting lecturers or panel members.

In addition, Hottleman suggests, along with three other options, a Minimum Standards Committee that would establish minimum standards for the training of all incoming teachers; examine the practices and programs of those colleges and universities which it deems necessary to examine and, where necessary, to meet the established minimum standards; establish a timetable within which suggested changes must be made; determine whether the changes have been made; and in the event of non-compliance with the suggested changes within the timetable, to notify the board of that fact. The standards would be established by natural groupings of teachers such as by subject area, specialist area, and educational level deemed appropriate by the executive committee of the association. Subsequent to the establishment of minimum educational standards, the board would agree not to employ any teachers who do not meet the established standards.[19]

### In-service Education

Goodlad observes that "Public schooling probably is the only large-scale enterprise in this country that does not provide for systematic updating of the skills and abilities of its employees and for payment of the costs involved."[20] Teachers are no different than members of any occupation in the sense that they vary in ability and need to update their practices on a regular basis.

Where in-service education exists, it has been too long on service and too short on education. It has been too fragmented, lacking in integrated activities based upon assessed priority needs, supported insufficiently by budget, and too insignificant to leave a marked and continuing impact upon teachers and the educational programs.[21]

The exact solution is not known, but enough is known to rule out several popular but weak approaches: isolated speeches by "authorities," often designed to shock by drawing dramatic attention to some revolutionary practice such as individualized reading, modular scheduling, or team teaching; classes at colleges and universities that are more often than not unrelated to the teachers' daily problems in the classroom; "professional" leave days where one or two days are set aside for increased knowledge.

Jackson points out that he sees no hope for the future of in-service education unless persons are willing to pay for it. This involves having teachers with one-half the contact hours they have with students at the present time, and the increased use of para-professionals. He notes also that teachers need more than this.

They require an institutional climate that supports and encourages their efforts to learn more about what they are doing. . . . The kind of professional inquiry we are talking about here has been absent for so long in most school systems that the seeds of it no longer exist, even in a dormant state, in the soil. . . . In short, thousands of teachers all over the country are badly in need of leadership, not just leadership of the kind that helps them get higher salaries or better janitorial services (although those things are needed, too), but the kind that will excite their intellectual curiosity, that will inspire . . . them to do their work better.[22]

Robert D. Bhaerman, director of research, American Federation of Teachers, proposes that in-service education be individualized to meet the peculiar needs of each teacher. He proposes a Continuous Progress Alternative that entails the following: meaningful in-service programs contractually provided for, personalized and individualized in-service education, independent study, travel, purchase of professional books and materials, meaningful workshops and institutes, regularly established sabbaticals, research into instructional problems, staff development laboratories for analyzing and solving instructional problems, self-development, self-evaluation, self-improvement, mutual agreement on teaching assignment, mutual agreement on the direction of self-development programs, renewed concentration on recruitment, cooperation among teachers, teachers and teaching as part of a coordinated effort.[23]

The AFT contract in Philadelphia has perhaps the most effective clause to date:

The Board shall negotiate with local area colleges for an extension of inservice training in cooperation with the colleges whereby such course work will be recognized for purpose of teacher certification and advanced degrees. A sum of $600,000 shall be appropriated for the summer of 1967 and a like sum for the summer of 1968 for teacher fellowships for study in accredited colleges and universities under the criteria hereinafter set forth. The intent is to provide a grant of a sum equal to 70 percent of summer-school teacher's salary.[24]

Contracts similar to this need to be established throughout America. Their strength lies in the fact that teachers obtain them through their own efforts; they assess their own strengths and weaknesses; and they develop a program appropriate for correcting their deficiencies.

It would be inaccurate to maintain that teachers have not been able to gain any degree of control over in-service education because administrators and boards have resisted stubbornly. In truth, everyone is responsible for an intolerable in-service program. Teachers have not always taken the initiative to update their practice. Teacher associations have only recently included in-service education provisions in contracts; administrators have not established a structure suitable for in-service education; boards of education have been unwilling to provide time off or funds to support in-service education activities. Schools of education have not been responsive sufficiently to needed changes.

Teacher centers are proposed in the last chapter as an alternative to the existing structure for in-service education. It is apparent to most persons that the present structure is in need of substantial alteration.

## Weaknesses of Collective Bargaining and Contracts

Collective bargaining leads to formal contracts between boards of education and teacher associations. Formal contracts are a natural outgrowth of formal deliberations. No one recommends a handshake and a gentleman's agreement after a six-week bargaining session. Not surprisingly, however, collective bargaining and its resulting contracts have weaknesses.

Perhaps the most valid criticism advanced against contracts is that they reduce the already limited flexibility of the local school and school district by imposing uniform policies and procedures that apply to all or many schools, thus reducing teacher autonomy. They result in elaborate and precise rules and regulations often no less restrictive than those that school administrators employ, thus inhibiting change and innovation.

The provisions of a contract bind all parties—administrators and teachers. No provision in a contract meets with the universal support of all workers. A teacher association may include a provision in a contract concerning student-teacher ratio. All teachers may not support such a provision, but once it becomes a part of a contract, all teachers must comply with it.

A contract can encourage a legalistic structure in what may otherwise have been an innovative organization. As Anderson notes, "collective bargaining may reinforce the centralization of control, which more completely circumscribes the teacher's behavior than before with even less authority invested in individual teachers."[25] A contract may make an already rigid structure more rigid.

Contracts, then, can inhibit innovation by demanding conformity to centralized rules and procedures. Centralized rules and procedures establishing minimums and maximums for certain grades or subjects reduce the flexibility of individual teachers and groups of teachers to use other methods. An innovative principal or teacher would be unable in some instances to introduce many potentially useful programs.

Advocates of collective bargaining are not unmindful of these potential weaknesses. New York City, for example, has an experimentation and demonstration clause in all contracts. The clause does not eliminate, but it does reduce the problem of rigidity as a result of rules and procedures.

The fact that the New York City contract has several hundred items is evidence of the union's attempt to provide for individual needs rather than imposing policies district wide. Thus, the more items in a contract, it could be argued, the more flexible and innovative the contract. However, it is apparent that many items in contracts restrict individual teachers and faculties and create a set of policies and rules that must be obeyed. The significant difference, of course, between rules and procedures that grow out of a teacher association contract and those that come from policies and procedures of the district administration is that the former are established in large measure by fellow teachers. This is a significant advance so far as professionalization of teachers is concerned.

Seniority is cited frequently as a weakness in formal contracts. Seniority affords one status that is attained through length of service with an organization. Seniority is not embraced because of the belief that there is a direct relationship between length of service and competence. Seniority is advanced because workers seek to avoid management making personnel judgments. The power to promote, demote, and transfer is the power to control.

It is often asserted that inexperienced teachers are assigned to schools in ghetto neighborhoods and difficult classes because they lack seniority. These teachers often leave teaching because the assignment overwhelms them. Those who survive usually criticize the practice of assigning inexperienced teachers to difficult schools. These same teachers, however, often are the first to submit their names on the list to seek a transfer to a more comfortable school, one where they can "really teach and not be concerned constantly with discipline."

The most promising practice from an educational standpoint would be to assign a few beginning teachers to difficult schools to work with a larger number of veteran teachers, or to arrange the inexperienced teacher to have certain advantages that veterans do not enjoy—such as three rather than five classes the first couple of years, or a class size not in excess of twenty the first year, or a para-professional in each classroom the first year. Such provisions have been written into several contracts. What is essential on personnel issues such as employment, promotion, and transfer is not that seniority be applied, but that these decisions be made by fellow teachers rather than administrators.

Teachers need to be certain that contracts do not deprive them of their natural motivation to serve students even under adverse circumstances. Collective bargaining has the potential for creating an environment that decreases teachers' service orientation.

The history of unionism in private industry points to the possibility that eventually teachers will be discouraged from voluntarily staying in the school after a specified hour, or that the operation of certain machines or equipment in the school will be limited to a specified few.[26]

This possible criticism should not be dismissed as improbable or unimportant. Teachers have a high service orientation. Efforts should be made to retain this characteristic of a professional. Regardless of the reduction in class size, the increases in salary, and the number of teacher aides, teachers will always be confronted "on their time" with a student who is having difficulty with a word, a sentence, a mathematics problem, or a personal problem. While the established professions may have less of a service orientation than teachers, there is good reason for teachers not to follow their lead. One could argue that the degree of professionalization that teachers now enjoy can be attributed in large part to their high service orientation.

The ultimate practical test of collective bargaining and its threat of strike is whether they succeed. The intent of a strike is to make management and/or the citizens so uncomfortable that they accede to teachers' demands. It is becoming apparent to citizens, however, that students can remain out of school for weeks with no noticeable effect on them. This reduces the power of teacher strikes. In addition, many parents begin to teach their children when strikes begin. In Sweden, students held classes without teachers when the teachers went on strike.[27]

Collective bargaining is a means of obtaining occupational goals. Thus, it can advance or ignore the educational program and the professionalization of teachers. Teachers need to be alert to the disadvantages as well as the advantages of collective bargaining and contracts. The most important question that must be asked is, Will this clause improve the welfare of teachers, preserve their service orientation, contribute to their sense of power and autonomy, contribute to the improvement of education of students, and advance the profession?

### Unified Professional Organizations

Teachers need a unified teacher organization to be maximally effective in asserting their power. A unified organization would have more political power by virtue of increased membership, the elimination of the practice of playing one group against the other, the elimination of bitterness in school faculties where two organizations are represented. In addition, a unified organization serves to demonstrate strong teacher solidarity to the school board and to the public.

The arguments against merger are not compelling. It is true that the American Federation of Teachers sparked the National Education Association to modify its program significantly. Differences in the two organizations are increasingly difficult to detect, but they still need to be worked out. These include the NEA's backing of a labor affiliation with the AFL-CIO, and the AFT's unwillingness to merge with a teacher association controlled or composed in any way by administrators. Minor problems concern deciding the amount of dues allocated to state associations, and finding satisfactory positions for all persons in the united organization.

Lieberman believes that merger between the AFT and NEA will take place in the near future.[28] Evidence of merger can be found in the intermingling and shifting of personnel from one teacher organization to the other. Both teacher organizations have representatives working together as was the case during the strike in Los Angeles in 1970. In addition, the NEA has shifted away from a negotiations no strike position. Finally, there is the realization on the part of many persons in the AFT that the NEA is not a company union.

Most significant has been the development in New York State, where the NEA affiliated New York State Teachers Association and the United Federation of Teachers merged into one teacher association in the summer of 1972. Similar efforts are underway in Michigan, and it appears as if merger is clearly in the wind.

### Framing Legislation Concerning the Profession

Teachers have learned that local boards of education do not often have the power to grant their demands, thus they seek increasingly to influence the state legislature. Frymier notes that the financial demands by teachers cannot be met by local boards. Eventually, only state legislatures, which are empowered to levy taxes, will be able to cope with teachers' demands.[29]

No occupation is or should be permitted to operate independently of legislative control, but any occupation that poses as a profession must have maximum latitude to frame and effect the legislation concerning its occupation. Educators have limited control over legislation affecting schools. While the education lobby is seen as formidable in many states, it lacks the power it would have if the occupation had professional status. The power that results from professional status is probably more significant than any economic or political pressure that teachers as a collective body can exert on legislators.

There are instances where the legislature will wish to express its will over the objection of a profession. There are times when this is both necessary and desirable. Medicare and Medicaid, for example, were passed over the strenuous objection of the American Medical Association.

There is no agreement on the extent of influence that educators should have on legislation. Bowles offers a strong counter thesis. He maintains that in the past, educators operated on a consensus pattern of state educational policy formulation and saw conflicts resolved within the monolithic structure of the educational interest groups. That is, eventually a program or policy was proposed that had the support of the educational establishment. He argues, however, that educational policy should be the result of political policy brought about through an accommodation of conflicting public interests, not the narrower goals of the professionals. This would shift the locus of accommodation from educators to the public.[30]

Bowles proposed this point of view while serving as a special consultant in education to the Republican Assembly Minority in the California Legislature. While California's legislature has not been distinguished by its support of education during the last five years, Bowles' remarks may be more representative of legislators' views than most educators care to admit.

The position that Bowles describes must be resisted if teachers are to become professionals. The governing of education should be left to teachers. The control of education should be left to the legislature. But legislators should seek the advice of teachers on all legislation concerned with control or governance.

### Supply and Demand [31]

The supply and demand of teachers need not be as unpredictable as the interest rate or the Dow-Jones average. Deliberate efforts should be made to control them by teacher associations. Teachers should be wary of adopting wholesale the belief that the more "workers," the more power. There are comparatively few physicians compared to teachers, but physicians have considerable power. Bush maintains, for example, that teachers will not gain status with a labor force of two million. He suggests that one promising alternative is to increase the number of para-professionals and reduce the number of teachers, thus advancing the status of career teachers.[32]

When the demand for teachers exceeds the supply, there are classrooms without teachers or with uncertified teachers; the overall level of competence of teachers is decreased; the standards of schools of education and for admission into schools of education are reduced; there is an increase in salaries and working conditions; there is a tendency toward a reduced commitment on the part of persons entering the field; the ratio of males to females remains approximately the same as before.

With the exception of the increase in salaries and working conditions, there seem to be more advantages when the supply of teachers outweighs the demand. There is a higher percentage of classrooms with certified teachers. The overall level of competence of teachers is increased. The standards of schools of education and for admission into schools of education are increased. There is a tendency toward an increased commitment on the part of persons entering the field. The ratio of males tends to increase.

Conversely, however, it is undesirable to have hundreds and perhaps thousands of certified teachers seeking teaching positions in each state. Prospective students, even capable ones, are not likely to be enthusiastic about entering a field where employment is difficult to acquire. This situation plays into the hands of management, since unemployed teachers can provide a source for superintendents seeking replacements for teachers who are on strike.

The relationship between the supply and demand of teachers and the standards of training required in educational institutions is not clear. Corwin maintains that it is possible that colleges of education could raise their intellectual standards without reducing seriously the existing supply of trained teachers, since lengthy training periods generally mean that persons will remain in the profession.[33]

Teachers should look with favor on educational innovations that reduce the number of teachers and increase the number of para-professionals. Teacher associations should seek to determine the approximate number of teachers needed in each state and to recruit as close to that number as possible.

### Use of Para-Professionals

There is no universally agreed upon definition of para-professional. The para-professional's function varies depending upon the state, school district, principal, and ultimately, the teacher. It is not clear whether a para-professional is a teacher or "sub-teacher." His duties range from teaching mathematics and giving a science demonstration to taking off boots and helping with toilet activities. Bhaerman maintains that tasks that relate to or involve students in any way are instructional, be it grading tests, maintaining order, or supervising students.[34] In these instances, the so-called para-professional is a teacher of students. Many para-professionals do "teach," but if one applies a similar logic to other occupations, nurses would be seen as practicing medicine and perhaps legal secretaries practicing law.

Para-professionals can be justified because they reduce the student-teacher ratio and make teaching less onerous and more appealing to newcomers. But, they are also needed to do *nonprofessional* tasks that could and should be done by clerks. These tasks include supervising the lunchrooms, monitoring restrooms (if required), secretarial duties, grading objective tests, taking off snow boots, supervising clean-up, etc.

There is a need to distinguish more clearly between the various kinds of tasks performed in schools by para-professionals and professionals. Teacher professionalization requires that professional teachers and para-professionals have different tasks and that these tasks be determined by the professional teacher.

### Class Size

Perhaps no issue in education, except reading, has been discussed by teachers or investigated by researchers as frequently as class size. After all the discussion and research, uncertainty still exists. Stevens' study of the research on class size led him to conclude that it is unrelated to achievement of students. "At all levels above the first few grades and in almost all subjects, the size of the class seems completely unrelated to the achievement of the pupils. If there is any advantage, it is in favor of large classes."[35]

Recently, however, Olson and his associates at the Institute of Administrative Research, found that smaller classes produce higher scores than large ones at both the elementary and secondary level. He points out, however, that for certain styles of activity and for certain subjects taught, varying numbers of students in the classroom produced little variation in criterion scores. "What seems clear is that emphasis should be placed on adapting class size to fit the unique needs of particular subjects and the realistic purposes of the various types of educational activities."[36]

Do smaller classes enhance the professionalization of teachers? Smaller classes are easier to manage, and they make the occupation more attractive to persons considering entering the field. Conversely, however, smaller classes increase the number of teachers needed, thus lowering standards. They reduce the possibility of funds being spent for teacher aides, which would free teachers from doing nonprofessional duties. In addition, they reduce the possibility that funds will be used to increase teachers' salaries. All of these latter possibilities are harmful to the professionalization of teachers.

It is unlikely that teachers will gain decreased class size, increased salaries, and professionalization in the immediate future. They are not irreconcilable, but they are unattainable considering the economic situation in most local and state governments. While teacher power is increasing, it is not so strong as to gain all three objectives. If teachers will accept larger classes to gain higher salaries, they will encounter little opposition. The difficulty is in gaining higher salaries, smaller classes, and the aid of para-professionals.

Teachers must begin to face some fundamental facts regarding the entire organization of the school which may make class size an anachronism. In the years ahead, teachers are going to make gains in a variety of areas. One can envision teachers with class sizes of eighteen to twenty, but with no specialist teachers, no assistant teachers, no para-professionals, no instructional materials, no programed materials, and no computer-aided instructional devices. By contrast, one can also envision teachers with class sizes of forty. They would be a member of a professional team with specialist teachers (selected by teachers) who provide in-service education, assistant teachers to help the teacher in planning lessons, and para-professionals to do nonprofessional duties. They might have the latest in instructional materials, programed learning devices, and computer-aided instruction. Under such conditions, the issue of class size becomes far less significant.

It is easy to argue that class size should be eighteen students and that the teacher should also have all the other tools and advantages mentioned above, but such is not the reality of America today, nor will it be in 1990. Education is not the only service vying for the tax dollar. Citizens also want improved highways, child day care centers, a national health plan, improved hospitals, non-polluted streams and cities, the abolition of poverty, an adequate national defense, increased social security benefits, not to mention more efficient snow removal, garbage collection, and sewage disposal. Teachers must make a selection between alternatives. The alternatives they select will make a difference so far as their professionalization is concerned.

## Differentiated Staffing

The most frequently cited definition for differentiated staffing used during the past five years has been, a division and extension of the role of the teacher through the creation of a hierarchy with responsibilities that are commensurate with the range of pay.[37] This definition has been modified and expanded greatly as different models have emerged.

Differentiated staffing has multiple objectives. It purports to make better use of teachers' abilities, talents, and interests; provide great flexibility in the use of time; provide a more systematic evaluation of teachers; provide a wider variety of career patterns; pay on the basis of responsibilities and training; retain good teachers in the classroom; and involve teachers in decision making. The following ranking is illustrative of the roles in differentiated staffing: master teacher, senior teacher, staff teacher, associate teacher, interns, tutors/student teacher/pre-service interns, para-professionals, and community volunteers.

Differentiated staffing has been resisted by many teachers. The American Federation of Teachers has actively resisted the scheme for a variety of reasons.

First, the movement toward levels of responsibility (verticalism) may result in divisiveness within the teaching staff and tends to destroy the cooperative and communal effort necessary for a successful teaching effort.

Second, only a limited number of positions are available for teacher promotion. Thus, if teachers in upper levels remain in their positions, teachers below them hierarchically despite interest and qualifications cannot be promoted.

Third, differentiated staffing increases the status of the specialist while reducing the status of the generalist teacher who remains with students all day.

Fourth, differentiated staffing will destroy the single salary schedule and substitute merit pay in disguise with positions and salaries determined by administrators.

Fifth, teachers may be forced into the position where the most effective bootlickers will be promoted and political skullduggery by teachers will be rewarded.

Sixth, differentiated staffing may be a facade for administrators to ease the administrator's problems of attracting and keeping good teachers rather than improving existing teachers with in-service programs.[38]

The AFT's proposal is for differentiated roles and responsibilities on a horizontal basis with salaries based on experience and education. There would be only one category of professional personnel and that would be professional teacher.

Professional teachers include media specialists; specialists in diagnosing; specialists in instructional techniques; good old-fashioned "generalists," renaissance types, the kind we need more of; etc.[39]

Horizontal differentiation implies the use of such practices as flexible staff assignments, individualized in-service programs, cooperative team approaches, interdisciplinary curriculum, cross-age grouping and the like. Such horizontal plans are in operation.[40]

The AFT would likely endorse the plan of differentiation devised by Joyce.[41] He suggests a direct-instruction team and support center. The instructional team would include a team of teachers with a leader to coordinate, an assistant team leader responsible for orchestrating resources, and classroom teachers. In addition, it would include para-professionals, interns, and teacher aides. The support center would include instructional materials, computers, self-instructional devices, human relations centers, inquiry centers, and guidance and evaluation centers.

The intent of this section is not to describe the strengths or weaknesses of differentiated staffing, but to investigate its effect on teacher professionalization. It would appear to advance professionalization in the sense that master teachers might impress laymen and thus make them more willing to convey professional status. Citizens might also feel more secure in the realization that less competent teachers are being "supervised." Conversely, however, the fact that a master teacher earns $20,000 may serve only to reinforce the layman's view that a majority of teachers are not capable of reaching a high level of responsibility and thus deserve the low salary and status they receive. Citizens may be prone to convey professional status on master teachers only and not on those the master teacher supervises.

Thus, it appears that differentiated staffing, a concept in search of a definition, may both enhance and retard teacher professionalization. One fact is abundantly clear—any plan of differentiated staffing where teachers do not control the determination and tenure of their superiors is a step away from teacher professionalization. So far as advancing the profession, if a district adopts differentiated staffing, teachers rather than administrators should develop the job descriptions, interview candidates, make the final determination of who receives a position, and have the power to terminate the services of all persons serving in supervisory positions.

### Performance Contracting

Performance contracting in education began in Texarkana, Arkansas, as part of a program to prevent dropouts. In performance contracting, the contracting agent receives money depending upon the increase in student performance in the areas designated, normally reading and mathematics. In the 1970–71 school year, the Office of Economic Opportunity spent nearly $6 million on six private companies and eighteen school districts engaged in performance contracting.

Performance contracting is designed to ensure accountability.

Accountability is the product of a process. At its most basic level, it means that an agent, public or private, entering into contractual agreement to perform a service will be held answerable for performing according to agreed-upon terms, within an established time period, and with a stipulated use of resources and performance standards.[42]

It is presumptuous for one author to make any statement about performance contracting after the numerous studies that have been undertaken the past year; most notably, the sixteen-month $300,000 Rand Corporation study of twenty contracts. The Rand Corporation study revealed that performance contracting programs were more rather than less expensive than regular educational programs, and that "no consistent level of improvement in reading and mathematics has emerged."[43]

Objections to performance contracting are varied: (1) too much reliance on hardware, (2) the same program in a new package, (3) performance objectives may encourage teachers to neglect other important areas of study for which monetary compensation is not given, (4) teachers teaching to the test, (5) teaching only limited and measurable aspects of a skill, (6) a disguised form of merit pay, (7) taking governance of education from educators.

What is the relationship between performance contracting and professionalization? By and large, the criticisms of performance contracting are not related directly to teacher professionalization. There are two exceptions: the employment of staff, and the determination of objectives to be sought.

First, some contractors have gained the right to employ whomever they wish at whatever salary they desire. Consequently, some teachers are employed who are not certified and are usually not selected by teachers. Any plan that takes the control for the employment of personnel from the hands of teachers and places it into the hands of business executives who are not responsible to the profession should be resisted strongly by that profession.

Second, the issue of who decides what objectives are to be sought is critical. Do students need a performance contract in reading and mathematics? Why not in self-concept or in gaining a feeling of independence? The AFT, for example, suggests a management-by-objectives approach which includes objectives which are not so narrow as to turn children into machines.[44]

Teachers do not work in a vacuum, a controlled environment with all random factors controlled. So it is impossible to develop a design that will tell you what the teacher should be doing, or which practices are good and which bad, without considering those random factors, or outside influences, that limit the performance of even the best of teachers. The individual student, his family, his socioeconomic background, and the school system itself must all be held accountable in degrees yet to be determined for everyone involved.[45]

The weaknesses of these early contracts will doubtless be eliminated or reduced, but teacher associations should stand firm when it involves the selection of objectives and personnel.

### Summary

The preceding issues are intended to include only the more serious problems facing teachers in their quest for further professionalization. They become insurmountable only if teachers seek to ignore them.

Much of what has been said in this book might cause teachers to believe that teaching will never become a profession. Indeed, it would almost seem that it will become less professionalized rather than more professionalized. This need not be the case. Authorities on occupations have cautioned that no occupation becomes a profession without a struggle. Education will not be an exception.

What is encouraging is that teachers have already begun this struggle. They have begun to see that they possess sufficient power to alter conditions that seemed unalterable a short time ago. Clearly, the actions and programs of the AFT and the NEA are moves in the right direction. If teachers, through their associations, cannot fight for what they believe is right for education, it is certain that no one else will. Teachers are not interested in the professionalization of physicians, lawyers, librarians, social workers, nurses, or their next door neighbors. It follows that these persons are not interested in promoting the professionalization of teachers.

Teachers can become professionals, but it will often require sheer courage of teachers at the level of the local school district; adaptability and accommodation on the part of administrators; and consistent, vigorous, and creative leadership on the part of the AFT and the NEA. Ultimately, it will require citizens who will enthusiastically accord professional status to teaching and who will see in teachers a service orientation toward their clients (their children) that they find lacking in many of the more established professions.

# TEN
# CONCLUSIONS

*"Nobody is going to bestow anything upon the teachers, national crisis or no national crisis. The teachers will have to fight for their place in the sun, and they will have to be much better fighters than they have been in the past. It is doubtful, to say the least, that a suddenly aroused public is going to cut down on its liquor, cigarettes, and television sets in order to pay its teachers more."** *

*"The society generally, will concede autonomy to the profession only if its members are able and willing to police themselves; will grant higher fees or prestige only when both its competence and its area of competence seem to merit them; or will grant an effective monopoly to the profession through licensure boards only when it has persuasively shown that it is the sole master of its special craft, and that its decisions are not to be reviewed by other professions."***

*"Unless the profession can put its own house in order, clarify its own sense of direction, and establish its own policies and procedures, it will be ineffective in working with the public and its own members. Furthermore, feelings of self-esteem and commitment to the profession will be enhanced as teachers come to feel that the profession controls itself and is imbued with a sense of mission."** ***

*"In many areas of our national life the issue is not whether to have administration, bureaucracies and professionals, but whether it is possible to create bureaucracies and professions that are humane and responsible to clients."** ****

It was suggested in the introduction that teachers use collective bargaining to improve their personal welfare, gain a better educational program for students, and enhance their professionalization. It was also suggested that a proper "balance" be sought among these three areas. In addition, it was stressed that collective bargaining, while contributing to teacher professionalization, would not itself ensure teacher professionalization. Thus, there is a need for a two-pronged attack: collective bargaining and professionalization activities at the national, state, and local levels.

Suggesting that teachers be concerned with welfare issues, the educational program for students, and enhancing their profession does not imply that teachers have been negligent to date. Collective bargaining must first demonstrate to teachers that it can deal with their personal needs, such as wages and fringe benefits; then it can be used to assist students and to advance the teaching profession. In this respect, collective bargaining can be likened to Maslow's hierarchy of needs where satisfying physical needs precedes concern for self-actualizing needs.

## Collective Bargaining

In bargaining, teachers have focused primarily on clauses concerned with personal welfare. This is understandable and defensible considering teacher salaries, welfare benefits, and working conditions. Teachers have not, however, ignored the educational program. The trend seems to be toward negotiating more educational clauses into contracts. The fact that teachers are not concentrating solely on welfare issues is not surprising in view of their high service orientation.

The strike of the United Teachers of Los Angeles in 1970, is illustrative. Teachers returned to work after a four and one-half week strike with a loss of pay of approximately $1,000. They offered to forego an increase in salary if the board would spend the funds to reduce class size and restore remedial reading. This is not an isolated case. Teachers belonging to the Apollo-Ridge Elementary Education Association, for example, swapped a $200 pay raise ($45,000) for a local kindergarten program.[1]

The AFT and the NEA are beginning to negotiate education clauses into contracts. Bhaerman, one of the most articulate spokesmen for the AFT, stated in a memorandum on April 7, 1971, that the AFT-QuEST program seeks ultimately to have as many "educational" clauses as "welfare" clauses.[2]

An indication of teachers' interest in the educational program is the fact that 46.1 percent of the 978 comprehensive agreements effective during the 1968–69 school year in school systems with a pupil enrollment of 1,000 or more, contained one or more provisions directly or indirectly affecting the curriculum decision-making process.[3] At this stage, some of the provisions are not significant, but there is reason to believe that matters relating to curriculum and instruction will be subject more often to negotiations.

The AFT has three programs to improve the educational program. The first is through collective bargaining per se, negotiating educational clauses such as the counselor-student ratio, curriculum materials, and para-professional personnel.

The second is QuEST (Quality Educational Standards for Teachers), a program that seeks to encourage classroom teachers to identify and investigate major educational problems in their particular teaching situation and school district, and then formulate teacher-instructed approaches and potential solutions to these educational programs. Several national and regional conferences have been held, more than a dozen QuEST papers have been written, and hundreds of local QuEST groups are in operation at the local district level.

The third is the AFT's More Effective Schools Program.[4] These programs exist in many cities in America. Designed originally for students in ghetto areas, the program has been expanded greatly and includes a wide cross-section of students. While MES programs differ depending upon local needs, most provide for a low student-teacher ratio; secretarial services; psychological, health, speech, and guidance personnel; teacher aides; a special contingency fund; funds for teacher orientation; an in-service component; and special funds for additional supplies.

The NEA, like the AFT, uses collective bargaining to gain educational clauses in contracts. In addition, some state associations have established teacher councils. Teacher councils have been used before; however, they were often controlled by administrators who established them, appointed the members, and had the right to accept or reject their recommendations.

Considering the efforts of the AFT and the NEA, it appears that efforts to improve the educational program will continue. Programs will undoubtedly change, but it seems apparent that collective bargaining will continue to be used as a means for improving the educational program for students. At the same time, it is becoming apparent that collective bargaining will probably decrease gradually at the local level. Selden states that:

collective bargaining as we have known it at the local level cannot meet the needs of our times. . . . We are not ready to abandon local collective bargaining by any means, but much more is needed. The fight for money, increasingly, is in the state legislatures and in Congress, as well as at the local level.[5]

### Professionalization

Teacher professionalization can be advanced through collective bargaining. Gaining higher salaries and duty-free lunches for teachers through collective bargaining is a step in the direction of teacher professionalization. The formation of teacher councils or QuEST programs is a step in the direction of teacher professionalization. An "educational" clause requiring an in-service education program designed by teachers is a step in the direction of teacher professionalization. Thus, collective bargaining can be used as a vehicle for advancing the professionalization of teachers.

Professionalization, however, will not be achieved through collective bargaining per se. Thousands of individual contracts with local boards of education will not ensure the professionalization of teachers. Instead, professionalization must come from and be directed by national teacher associations working with the executive and legislative branches of government at the national and state level. This is not to suggest that collective bargaining is not an essential factor in advancing teacher professionalization. Without the power resulting from collective bargaining, legislators and citizens would ignore teachers' demands to govern their profession.

Teacher professionalization can be advanced by developing a responsive and alert organizational structure at the national, state, regional, and local association levels. In this respect, it is like a powerful political party with insightful leadership in Washington, D.C., and a strong and vigorous organization at the precinct level. Specifically, professionalization can be advanced by the passage of the NEA's Teacher Standards and Licensure Act at the state level, the establishment of Teacher Centers, strong local teacher associations, and vigorous local school faculties.

### Teacher Standards and Licensure Commission

The NEA Teacher Standards and Licensure Act would establish a commission at the state level. The NEA has made governance (autonomy) of the profession by teachers a major priority, arguing that teachers cannot be held accountable until teachers have the responsibility for making decisions about how reading teachers, mathematics teachers, and other teachers should be trained, in what institutions they should study, who should be licensed to teach, and how teachers' skills can be kept up to date. It draws a sharp distinction between control and governance, noting that citizens should decide on the goals and financing of schools, but professionals should decide on how the goals can best be accomplished.

The NEA has tentatively decided to concentrate on pilot states: Iowa, Kansas, Massachusetts, Minnesota, New Jersey, New Mexico, and Wyoming. The model bill would have thirteen members appointed by the governor from a panel of names submitted by groups of certificated professionals.

The model provides for the granting of four types of licenses and states that "it is the intent of the Legislature that the Commission not engage merely in the prescription of certain courses of study and unit counting in developing minimum licensing requirements." The bill also includes a provision for removing or suspending teacher licenses.

Under the bill, teacher preparation institutions would be subject to study and accreditation by the Commission. The statute provides for reciprocal agreements with other states in respect to accreditation and licensing. It also declares that any person who directs or permits an unlicensed person to practice teaching or perform educational duties without Commission authorization is guilty of a misdemeanor.[6]

Darland reports that sixteen states have enacted legislation creating independent professional practices acts. He reports that "all states now have some form of advisory body (usually called a council) on teacher education and certification. . . . In 30 states these bodies are voluntary and extralegal; in 14 states they are created law."[7] More important, perhaps, is his citing of a survey of NEA members reporting that 90 percent responded "yes" to the question, Should a state board composed of educators establish standards for teacher preparation?


### Teacher Centers

The Teacher Standards and Licensure Act would provide teachers governance over pre-service education and licensure. It would not, however, be concerned with in-service education, teacher evaluation and tenure, student training, and collective bargaining. Teacher centers are needed to assist in the performance of these functions. Most local teacher associations are too small to provide the necessary resources and leadership, while state teacher associations are too centralized to know local needs, although several structures designed to decentralize teacher associations have been instituted the past two years.

Local teacher associations have vastly different needs. In addition, the sheer area of most states makes statewide communication difficult. Therefore, teacher centers would *not* be decentralized national or state associations but centralized local associations using appropriate resources of the national and state teacher associations. There is no desired size for a teacher center, but it should represent enough teachers so that there is sufficient talent available to provide the services desired by teachers.

Teacher centers would provide a facility relatively close to home where teachers could meet with colleagues and attempt to understand many of the problems facing the schools and the profession. As the yearly teacher contract becomes more common, some teachers might spend two or three months in the center serving on various committees or attending workshops and seminars.

When will teachers find the time to attend a teacher center? Some persons propose a four-day week for teachers with a fifth day spent at the center. This is a promising plan, but the loss of 20 percent of instruction from certified teachers could be detrimental to students, especially those from "deprived" environments. A four-day week for teachers with para-professionals being responsible for students the fifth day is questionable as it seems to be based on the assumption that para-professionals are as capable as professionals. This idea is somewhat comparable to a lawyer asking his secretary to handle every fifth day in court, or a physician asking his nurse to perform every fifth operation.

**In-service education.**  Teacher centers would provide workshops and seminars for teachers and other auxiliary personnel; a resource center of consultants (usually fellow teachers who have demonstrated considerable competence in a given area); sample instructional materials and courses of study; a professional library, films, filmstrips, and a variety of technological equipment.

**Teacher evaluation and tenure.**  Teacher evaluation and tenure committees are proposed at the local school and local teacher association level in the following section. The intent of such groups is to improve the quality of instruction and to ensure that only qualified persons gain tenure. Such a structure would serve to further rationalize the process of teacher evaluation and tenure. It would not, however, be sufficiently independent of the local teacher association to satisfy citizens that an impartial review had been made by persons who were not involved personally with the teacher.

Professors at universities vote for fellow staff members to gain tenure, but such judgments are sometimes made on personal rather than objective grounds. It is for this reason that the judgment of the faculty members in a particular department, such as reading, is reviewed by a school-wide committee of professors, such as a school of education, and a university-wide committee of professors representing various disciplines.

The teacher center tenure review committee would serve not only to screen out teachers whose teaching was inferior, but also serve to protect teachers who had not been supported enthusiastically by their local faculties for reasons that were not valid.

This final review by an elected and representative committee of teachers at the teacher center is an added safeguard. It is needed at the present time because teachers need to gain control over the issuance of tenure. It is also needed because many citizens lack confidence in teachers' ability to police their own ranks. This lack of confidence is legitimate in many instances and should not be ignored. The structure proposed would tend to assure citizens that a careful and systematic review is being made of all teachers.

Thus far concern has been with evaluation related to tenure, but evaluation is not something that is discontinued after being granted tenure. Evaluation is lifelong. Teacher centers would provide local teacher associations with criteria upon which to make evaluations, but they would not be involved directly in evaluation.

The AFT's Staff Evaluation and Development Program (SED) of the Washington Teachers Union, American Federation of Teachers, [8] could be viewed as a prototype to the teacher evaluation component of teacher centers. SED provides that all teachers—permanent, probationary, and temporary—shall be evaluated both by peer evaluation (primarily) and self-evaluation (secondarily). The DC-SED committee shall be composed of six permanent teachers, two probationary teachers, two temporary teachers, two central administrators in addition to a lay advisory board. No less than three or no more than five peer visitations will be conducted each semester, and no more than two visitations shall be unannounced. The assumptions underlying the SED program are that evaluation shall be diagnostic and constructive in nature, and that it shall be concentrated upon the assessment of needs and the overcoming of weaknesses. Second, staff development shall be viewed as a continuous process.[9] The teacher centers proposed here would not include lay advisory boards, parents, or administrators except as non-voting members.

It should be noted that the Washington, D.C., SED program could become a teacher center by simply assuming the additional functions of a teacher center. Every local association could not become a teacher center, however, because some have such a limited membership that the resources are not available for a full program. In this case, several teacher associations need to be brought together.

**Student training.**   The teacher center would be responsible for the training of prospective teachers. This is clearly differentiated from the theoretical knowledge gained at colleges and universities. Student teaching as it exists presently with a student in a classroom (with a supervising teacher) for varying lengths of time, with a university sponsor who visits once or twice during that period would come to a long overdue end. Student teaching as it presently exists in most states, may do more harm than good as prospective teachers are placed with teachers, some of whom are not worthy models, and almost all of whom are allowed no extra time to adequately supervise the teacher. While student teaching is considered by many students to be the most useful part of their program in education, it is worth noting that they are comparing it to classes in education that are quite often less than compelling.

Students would spend a period of time in the training center working with a small group of children or sometimes adults under supervision of a competent trainer. Trainers would be teachers who would be granted released time to serve in this capacity. Trainers could also come from colleges and universities. Every university has some professors capable of training teachers. Mr. Allan Muskopf, University of Rochester, for example, has a teacher center located in the basement of the Lincoln Park School No. 44, of the Rochester City School District. He has university classes in the center, and workshops for which teachers pay a small sum of money (unfortunately, sometimes their own money rather than the school district's). The center is full of items such as instructional materials, supplies, paints, various constructions, aquariums, cages. It is an excellent example of the in-service education and student-training function of a teacher center.

It might be wise to strive to improve existing university student-teacher programs rather than abandon them, perhaps using models similar to the one established by Mr. Muskopf of the University of Rochester. There may be merit in retaining the university's sponsorship, but the prospects of changing the existing university structure are not promising. Colleges and universities, on the average, are notoriously reluctant to change, regardless of how unsuccessful and inefficient a program. Teacher centers would establish a new structure that would be more amenable to change, using those professors considered competent to train teachers. In the past, trainees had to grin-and-bear-it when assigned to an ineffective teacher or burdened with an ineffective supervisor at a university. Teacher centers would place the control of the program in the hands of teachers. Trainers considered ineffective would not be used again.

There is one additional advantage to a prospective teacher training at a teacher center. It would serve to introduce him to the center itself—where veteran teachers would be engaged in in-service activities; committees of teachers would be at work preparing courses of study; committees of teachers would be evaluating fellow teachers; teachers would be preparing clauses for contracts; teachers would be free to browse, talk, relax, and feel proud of being a member of a worthwhile and vibrant profession.

**Collective bargaining.** The fourth function of teacher centers would be in the area of collective bargaining. In this capacity, they would work closely with the state teacher associations, as many negotiations in the future will be at the state level. The teacher center would serve as a communication link between the local and state teacher association, suggesting issues that are considered important by local associations.

**Teacher Centers and Other Programs.** Teacher centers are not antithetical to the AFT's QuEST program and the NEA's UniServ groups. QuEST programs are designed to:

Anticipate some of the emerging problems resulting from the rapid social changes in our society;
Meet on a regular basis;
Stimulate and initiate confrontations between teachers and these problems at state, local, and national levels;

Organize and coordinate regional and national conferences;
Prepare tentative positions for action by AFT legislative bodies; and
Suggest action programs to implement their findings.[10]

UniServ groups help teachers "win and maintain good contracts, develop political action, strengthen classroom programs, and build strong local associations."[11] UniServ, then, is a structure designed largely to provide state and national support to the local association program.

While there are differences between teacher centers and QuEST and UniServ programs, the principal difference is in the breadth of their operations. Teacher centers incorporate the functions of both groups and include several others. UniServ groups seem to provide the collective bargaining function of teacher centers. If this is so, they could be incorporated within teacher centers. Too many quasi-independent units serve to reduce the power of teachers. There is value to having one teacher center that serves several functions than several organizations each serving a special function. A single organization would have a larger facility, include more teachers, have more capable leadership, and enhance coordination between collective bargaining, teacher training, and in-service education.

Teacher centers should not be confused with or thought to be similar to U.S. Office of Education funded renewal sites, 1,000 of which are projected. They differ in many significant ways. Renewal sites would be located only in financially poor school districts, final authority would be vested in the local board of education, and the membership of the governing council would have equitable representation. The renewal sites would likely impede the professionalization of teachers by strengthening the authority of the citizens and the local board of education and thereby decreasing the authority of teachers to govern their own affairs.

Teacher centers are for teachers, not citizens, parents, administrators, state department officials, or professors. They are not designed to bring these persons and their agencies together nor to provide communication between them. This does not mean that the community and other institutions interested in education would be excluded from participation. But, their participation would be at the pleasure of teachers and their suggestions advisory to teachers.

The membership of teacher centers would be composed of members of local teacher associations and be selected by the membership of the local association. The center would be administered by an executive board composed of the presidents of local teacher associations, unless so many districts were represented that terms would rotate. In urban areas, representative school faculties would need to select a representative. The members of the executive board would select an executive officer to administer the center. The state teacher association might be asked to supply funds for the facilities and maintenance costs; and the local association would assume other costs, although financial arrangements could be handled in a variety of ways. The teacher center, however, would be advisory to local associations but be granted wide latitude to carry out a variety of programs.

Teacher centers could embrace *as a collective*, "control" over the curriculum as the Schools' Council does in Britain. This is considered heresy in America because of the anachronistic idea that citizens determine what to teach and teachers decide how to teach it. State legislatures should have control of the global aims of education, but teachers should establish the curriculum designed to attain those aims. Thus, in reality, teachers would have control of the curriculum.

The leadership of teacher associations should not spend time striving to resist a new organization because it incorporates the functions of an existing organization. It does not matter, for example, whether QuEST or UniServ groups incorporate the functions of teacher centers, or teacher centers incorporate the functions of these groups. What matters is that all significant functions are identified and structures created to perform them.

### Local Teacher Association

Collective bargaining, the Teacher Standards and Licensure Act, and teacher centers, while of sizable value to teacher professionalization, are not sufficient to ensure teacher professionalization. Once achieved, such structures can become as distant to the typical teacher as is the president of the board of education. To vitalize teachers and schools, strong local teacher associations must be prepared to assist teachers in their classrooms, not so much through collective bargaining as by gaining control over the selection, promotion, transfer, in-service education, evaluation, and dismissal of fellow teachers. If teachers want self-governance, they are going to have to be strong enough to help weed out those teachers who are not contributing.[12]

Local teacher associations need clauses in a variety of areas. UniServ groups should assist in this process. In addition, three permanent committees need to be established to advance professionalization: faculty recruitment and selection; assignment, scheduling, transferring, and promotion; and in-service education and tenure.

**Faculty Recruitment and Selection.** A committee elected by and composed wholly of teachers as voting members (citizens, administrators, and students could and hopefully would participate as advisors) would recruit and select teachers and para-professionals using resources and procedures developed by their teacher center. This corresponds closely with Hottleman's recruitment committee except that administrators would not have a vote in the proposed plan. Hottleman also suggests that a balance provision be written into contracts, obviously to eliminate the possibility of the board employing only inexperienced and consequently low-salaried personnel. He suggests that at least one-third of the teachers have at least ten years of experience, two-thirds must have at least five years or more experience, and no more than one-third have fewer than five years experience.[13]

**Assignment, Scheduling, Transferring, and Promotion.** Depending upon the size of the teacher association, this could be another committee. Its membership would be elected by and composed wholly of teachers as voting members. This structure combines scheduling of staff and assignment review committee into one, as well as a proposed committee designated to deliberate on teachers' requests to modify items such as scheduling and grouping policies.

**In-service Education and Tenure.**   The philosophy inherent in Bhaerman's Continuous Progress Alternative (p. 128) is endorsed enthusiastically, as well as in-service clauses in contracts such as in Philadelphia and the SED Program in Washington, D.C. But in-service, tenure, and dismissal for incompetence are two sides of the same coin. It serves no useful purpose to pretend that every teacher is sufficiently talented or motivated to gain tenure. A committee concerned with individualized in-service education is in the best position to determine if a teacher should be granted tenure or be dismissed. In the future, however, tenure should be granted upon issuance of a license.

## Local School Faculty

It is not enough for a Teacher Standards and Licensure Act to be instituted in each state. Every school faculty must be organized. The Teacher Standards and Licensure Act, for example, will certify teachers; but, like teacher centers and local teacher associations, it will neither assign nor evaluate teachers in individual schools. If the teachers in a school are not organized for making such decisions, the principal will surely do so.

The significance of the local school faculty is often underestimated. The fundamental aim of enlarging the professional role of teachers can be realized only through the organized school faculty. The teachers in a school know each other and the students better than anyone else and are, therefore, the most appropriate persons to understand the problems in their schools.

Each school would have an educational council composed of teachers elected by fellow teachers in the school. The principal would be a non-voting member. These councils would not be advisory to the principal except in areas of school management. They would have the authority to make decisions provided they were not inconsistent with policies and procedures entered into by the board of education and the teacher association. This does not mean that teachers would ignore the opinions of the principal, only that his opinions would be advisory.

The functions of the educational council would vary depending upon local needs. Common areas of concern would be grading, grouping, discipline, instructional materials, staff assignment, student grouping, etc.

Educational councils could divide into committees to fulfill some of their functions. Williams, [14] for example, favors a faculty selection committee for new personnel and a teacher review committee for tenure. The faculty selection committee would be elected by the faculty to serve as a personnel screening committee. The screening committee would advise the principal in the hiring of new teachers. Although the role of the committee would be advisory, no teacher would be recommended for employment who was not approved by a majority of this committee. The final hiring decision would remain, as it is now, with the school board.

The tenure review committee would be assigned to each new teacher in the school. Each new teacher would appear before his review committee several times a year, as determined by the local faculty. The teacher would explain his overall goals for the class, describe teaching activities that he thought to be successful, and discuss his shortcomings. At the conclusion of each evaluation session, and at the end of the year, the committee would submit a report to the administration. Such reports would outline the content of the evaluation sessions, present an opinion of the teacher's strengths and weaknesses, list suggestions for improvement, and indicate progress. These reports might well be supplemented by classroom visitations by the administration or committee members. The emphasis in these sessions would likely change during the course of the three-year, pre-tenure period. With especially talented teachers, the sessions might be discontinued after the evaluation committee is satisfied that the new teacher meets acceptable standards. The less competent teacher may receive more assistance in an attempt to raise his performance to an acceptable standard. At the end of three years of such evaluation, the administration and board would have an extensive and carefully considered collegial assessment of each new teacher. Upon such evidence a more fair and legitimate tenure decision should be made.

Williams wisely sees the need for decentralizing evaluation and tenure recommendations. He parts company with most teacher association advocates when he includes principals as voting members in any of these deliberations. In addition, there is a need for a systematic in-service program for all teachers, not merely for those who are beginning.

Concerning tenure, an elaborate mechanism needs to be established that would include the final tenure determination made not by the local faculty or local teacher association, but by the teacher center. In this one area, teacher centers would have considerable power; in other areas, they would be advisory to teacher associations or provide resources.

### Need for Conceptual Scheme and Action

While both the AFT and the NEA have programs designed to improve the educational program and advance teacher professionalization, neither has a comprehensive scheme designed to guide its actions although task forces have been formed, and talented individuals in both organizations have some well-developed schemes of their own. A conceptual scheme would identify relationships among complex interacting phenomena. These phenomena include factors such as teachers' attitudes and knowledge of professionalization and collective bargaining; teachers' attitudes concerning autonomy, peer evaluation, and administrative control; the nature of the conflict, if any, between bureaucratic rules and professionalization; advantages and dysfunctions of strikes or sanctions; the role of the governor, state legislature, state department of education, and teacher associations in licensure, tenure, and revocation of licenses.

During the next decade, teacher associations will need to continue to reorganize their staff so that a portion of the staff is assigned the responsibility for developing conceptual schema. The potential for this exists at the present time in the NEA's new Division of Instruction and Professional Development. Conceivably, an AFT QuEST group could assume this function. The membership for the group should be flexible to allow for the introduction of new persons with fresh ideas. This group should operate somewhat independently of the organization, yet be responsible to it. It should include persons within and outside of the organization. While the group would operate "independently," its success would depend upon the degree to which all members of the organization and, theoretically, all teachers contributed to and understood the theoretical conceptual scheme being advanced.

Aside from the need for the development of a conceptual scheme to guide the actions of teacher associations, there is perhaps a more serious need. It is two-fold. First, there are hundreds of thousands of teachers who are not members of the AFT or the NEA. It can be stated quite positively that teachers who are not members of a teacher association are hindering their fellow teachers in their struggle for teacher professionalization. Second, there is the problem of apathy on the part of some members and nonmembers. Many teachers have not become involved meaningfully in the struggle for collective bargaining and increased teacher professionalization. They need to be reminded that they perpetuate the existing structure of authority by submitting to it.

No occupation becomes a profession without a concerted and continuing program designed specifically toward that end.

The experience of the established professions clearly indicates that occupational groups do not achieve professional status until the members of the groups concerned participate en masse in the movement to achieve professional status. This they cannot do unless they understand the significance of professional status and the problems of professionalization confronting their occupational group.[15]

The major obstacle for teachers is not external (laymen, state legislatures, administrators), but internal—teachers themselves. Many teachers do not have an interest in influencing legislation, identifying and assisting colleagues, or improving the caliber of persons entering the field. Teacher involvement in educational policy making is limited because of the "unwillingness of many classroom teachers either to spend time on mastering the elements of educational policy making, or failing that, to give their leaders authority to speak out on vital issues like curriculum reform."[16]

The teacher who envisions teachers as professionals must be a member of a teacher association; he must support collective bargaining and be willing and even proud to strike; he must support legislation that will grant teachers the right to govern their profession; he must be willing to work with and assist fellow teachers. In addition, he must be alert constantly to national issues as well as to what is happening in his own school. This will require close surveillance of state legislatures, local boards of education, and administrators. Some teachers will contend that such close surveillance will create ill-will, frustration, and antagonism. Indeed it will, and that is one of the reasons the path to teacher professionalization is hard work.

In the years ahead, vigorous leadership will be needed throughout the educational community, particularly at the national and local teacher association level. There will be a temptation for teachers to accept the status quo once some reforms are realized. To counter this, leaders of local and especially state and national teacher associations need to envision the end goal of teacher professionalization and inspire teachers to work vigorously and unrelentlessly in that direction. If they are to be effective leaders, they need to pace the struggle so that laymen do not become disenchanted, and recalcitrant teachers are not taunted or ignored by more zealous colleagues, but are accorded the respect that any minority group deserves in a free society. In any event, teachers must demonstrate through their actions that the struggle cannot be carried on working from 9:00 A.M. to 3:30 P.M. The majority of occupations will not make much progress toward achieving professional status, but those that do will need to change themselves.

### Recommendations

This book has been concerned principally with understanding teachers, the structure in which they work, the process of collective bargaining, and professionalization. Hopefully, teachers and prospective teachers have gained a more accurate view of their occupation and the world outside of their classroom. I have sought to understand rather than advocate by engaging in polemics of which I believe teachers are painfully tired. I have sought to be objective, but I do not wish to conclude without stating what I believe are necessary steps to advance teacher professionalization. Some of the following recommendations are more important than others, but taken together they would greatly advance teacher professionalization and improve significantly the educational program for students.

1. All teachers should be active members of a teacher association.
2. The AFT-AFL/CIO and the NEA should merge into one teacher association.
3. Teachers elected to offices of the executive committee of boards of directors should be given considerably more authority in the association and be eligible for re-election for three additional terms.
4. Teachers should embrace collective bargaining and strikes as a useful and democratic process to use in gaining welfare objectives, improving the educational program, and enhancing teacher professionalization. Legislation should be sought at the state and national level.
5. The AFT and the NEA should continue the trend to increase negotiations at the state level.
6. A Teacher Standards and Licensure Commission similar to the model proposed by the NEA should be instituted in each state. It would be concerned with licensure and the revoking and suspending of licenses, as well as the accreditation of teacher preparation institutions. The AFT should endorse and support the NEA in its efforts to have this act adopted at the state level.

7. Teachers should reject any method of differentiated staffing that permits administrators to appoint supervisors with authority over teachers.

8. All supervisors, team chairmen, and department chairmen should be elected for a specific term of office by tenured teachers within each school and be subject to removal by teachers at the end of each term. Principals who wish to serve in the capacity of instructional leader rather than hospital administrator should be similarly selected.

9. Teacher centers should be formed by local teacher associations composed wholly of teachers to (1) develop procedures for in-service education, teacher evaluation, and tenure; (2) develop prototype in-service education programs; (3) provide teachers a resource center for consultants; (4) provide sample instructional materials, equipment, and professional books; (5) assist in developing curriculum materials and courses of study; (6) provide a place for teachers to meet and discuss problems and issues of mutual concern; (7) provide sample clauses for contracts in areas designed as important by teachers; (8) review all tenure recommendations of local associations. The AFT and the NEA should cooperate in assisting local associations establish these centers. The AFT and the NEA should consider the possibility of incorporating the existing function of QuEST and UniServ into Teacher Centers.

10. A minimum five-year training program for teachers should be instituted in all states.

11. The AFT and the NEA should oppose the implementation of the voucher plan because it could lead to racial and economic isolation.

12. The AFT and the NEA should offer financial, legal, and moral support to those persons who seek the abolition of the inequitable local property tax as a source of revenue to finance schools. The New York State Fleischmann Commission agreed with the California Supreme Court that it is repugnant to the idea of equal educational opportunity, that the quality of a child's education, insofar as that education is provided through public funds, is determined by accidents of birth, wealth, or geography.

13. Teachers should object strongly to all administrators who, in their legitimate role as public relations agents, approach citizens and citizen groups in a way that suggests parents have a vote on educational programs (such as modern or traditional mathematics), or a choice in educational practices (such as letting parents decide whether their children are placed in a team set-up or a self-contained classroom).

14. A national public relations campaign should be continued and expanded, designed to upgrade the status of teachers; focus on significant welfare issues, e.g., low salaries and poor working conditions; and concentrate on educational issues, e.g., the need to provide pre-school programs and adequate libraries and instructional facilities.

15. The AFT's More Effective Schools should be continued, expanded, and endorsed enthusiastically by the NEA.

16. Teacher organizations should seek to expand greatly funds allocated for educational research so that a more rigorous scientific base of knowledge might be realized. Efforts should be made to increase the number of researchers (not necessarily professors).

17. Teacher hostility toward theory needs to be reduced greatly because research is needed to provide sound principles upon which to teach.

18. The AFT and the NEA should put the full force of their political power (including the use of such tactics as a one-day national strike and protest marches on Washington, D.C.) to gain the passage of legislation deemed critical for children; such as the federal child day care bill which would provide educational, nutritional, and health services for all pre-school children.

19. The AFT and the NEA should seek to have enacted legislation that would outlaw the use of injunctions in teacher strikes.

20. Beginning teachers should serve a one-year internship where they would work under the close supervision of a team of teachers. Their class loads should be reduced, and they should be exposed to a wide variety of subjects, teachers, and students.

21. Local teacher associations should retain considerable power in framing their own contracts, faculty recruitments, selection, in-service education, and teacher evaluation. This can be done by having a structure such as Faculty Recruitment and Selection Committee; Assignment, Scheduling, Transferring, and Promotion Committee; and In-service Education and Tenure Committee.

22. The vitality of the local school faculty is essential. The faculty should select teachers for "their" school, evaluate teachers in "their" school, and make initial recommendations for tenure. Also, unique educational programs should be encouraged by the local teacher association.

23. Performance contracts should be opposed strongly that: (1) provide external contractors the power to make educational decisions; (2) permit external contractors to select non-certified teachers for employment; (3) permit external contractors the right to select, evaluate, and dismiss teachers and para-professionals.

24. The AFT and the NEA should continue to stress the need for a continuous management-supported (on management time) in-service education program for all teachers. This in-service program should normally take place at Teacher Centers rather than colleges and universities.

25. The AFT and the NEA should continue to support legislation at the state and national levels that would permit teachers to move across state lines without losing retirement benefits.

26. The AFT and the NEA should oppose the operation of "block schools" (established by neighborhoods or self-interest groups) unless staffed by certified teachers, and their program approved as substantially equivalent to public schools by the chief school officer in the school district.

27. The AFT and the NEA should seek supportive staff to free teachers from performing nonprofessional duties.

28. Teacher associations should oppose non-certified teachers serving as substitutes when teachers are absent from the classroom due to illness, professional, or personal leave.

153   CONCLUSIONS

# APPENDIXES

## Appendix A  Highest Degree Held by Public-School Teachers, 1961 to 1970

| | No degree | 2-year diploma | Bachelor's degree | Master's ` degree | Education specialist* | Doctor's degree |
|---|---|---|---|---|---|---|
| **ALL TEACHERS** | | | | | | |
| 1961 . . . . . . . | 2.1% | 10.2% | 61.7% | 25.8% | . . . | 0.2% |
| 1962 . . . . . . . | 3.1 | 10.6 | 62.5 | 23.7 | . . . | 0.1 |
| 1963 . . . . . . . | 2.9 | 8.0 | 64.5 | 22.5 | 1.9% | 0.2 |
| 1964 . . . . . . . | 2.3 | 6.8 | 64.8 | 24.3 | 1.5 | 0.3 |
| 1965 . . . . . . . | 2.5 | 6.1 | 67.3 | 22.5 | 1.5 | 0.1 |
| 1966 . . . . . . . | 2.3 | 4.3 | 67.2 | 25.1 | 1.1 | . . . |
| 1967 . . . . . . . | 1.6 | 4.5 | 68.2 | 24.4 | 1.2 | 0.1 |
| 1968 . . . . . . . | 1.3 | 3.4 | 67.4 | 26.5 | 1.2 | 0.2 |
| 1969 . . . . . . . | 1.3 | 3.2 | 65.2 | 28.3 | 2.0 | 0.1 |
| 1970 . . . . . . . | 0.8 | 2.8 | 65.8 | 28.6 | 1.7 | 0.3 |
| **ELEMENTARY** | | | | | | |
| 1961 . . . . . . . | 3.4 | 16.9 | 62.8 | 16.7 | . . . | 0.2 |
| 1962 . . . . . . . | 4.5 | 18.6 | 62.9 | 14.0 | . . . | 0.2 |
| 1963 . . . . . . . | 4.1 | 13.5 | 65.0 | 15.7 | 1.5 | 0.1 |
| 1964 . . . . . . . | 3.8 | 12.1 | 66.7 | 16.6 | 0.7 | 0.1 |
| 1965 . . . . . . . | 3.9 | 11.2 | 70.8 | 13.3 | 0.8 | . . . |
| 1966 . . . . . . . | 3.7 | 7.2 | 70.9 | 17.9 | 0.4 | . . . |
| 1967 . . . . . . . | 2.4 | 7.9 | 72.9 | 15.7 | 1.1 | . . . |
| 1968 . . . . . . . | 1.5 | 6.4 | 73.2 | 18.1 | 0.8 | . . . |
| 1969 . . . . . . . | 1.8 | 6.0 | 71.1 | 19.9 | 1.2 | . . . |
| 1970 . . . . . . . | 0.9 | 5.0 | 72.0 | 20.5 | 1.4 | 0.2 |
| **SECONDARY** | | | | | | |
| 1961 . . . . . . . | 0.3 | 1.2 | 60.2 | 38.1 | . . . | 0.2 |
| 1962 . . . . . . . | 1.3 | 0.8 | 62.0 | 35.7 | . . . | 0.2 |
| 1963 . . . . . . . | 1.3 | 0.6 | 63.9 | 31.4 | 2.4 | 0.3 |
| 1964 . . . . . . . | 0.4 | 0.6 | 62.6 | 33.5 | 2.4 | 0.4 |
| 1965 . . . . . . . | 1.0 | 0.7 | 63.5 | 32.5 | 2.2 | 0.1 |
| 1966 . . . . . . . | 0.9 | 1.2 | 63.2 | 32.9 | 1.8 | . . . |
| 1967 . . . . . . . | 0.8 | 0.7 | 63.0 | 34.1 | 1.3 | 0.1 |
| 1968 . . . . . . . | 1.1 | 0.3 | 61.4 | 35.1 | 1.7 | 0.4 |
| 1969 . . . . . . . | 0.7 | 0.4 | 59.1 | 36.9 | 2.8 | 0.1 |
| 1970 . . . . . . . | 0.7 | 0.5 | 59.2 | 37.2 | 2.1 | 0.3 |

Source: *NEA Research Bulletin*, XLIX (Washington, D.C.: Research Division, National Education Association, May, 1971), p. 56.

*Education specialist or professional diploma based on six years of college was not included in the question asked in 1961 and 1962.

# Appendix B  Minimum Requirements for Lowest Regular Teaching Certificates*

| State | Elementary School | | | Secondary School | | |
|---|---|---|---|---|---|---|
| | Degree or Number of Semester Hours Required | Professional Education Required, Semester Hours (Total) | Directed Teaching Required, Semester Hours (Included in Column 3) | Degree or Number of Semester Hours Required | Professional Education Required, Semester Hours (Total) | Directed Teaching Required, Semester Hours (Included in Column 6) |
| 1 | 2 | 3 | 4 | 5 | 6 | 7 |
| Alabama | B | 27 | 6 | B | 21 | 6 |
| Alaska | B | 24 | C | B | 18 | C |
| Arizona | 5[a] | 24 | 6 | 5[a] | 22 | 6 |
| Arkansas | B | 18 | 6 | B | 18 | 6 |
| California | B[b] | AC[b] | AC[b] | B[b] | AC[b] | AC[b] |
| Colorado | B | AC | AC | B | AC | AC |
| Connecticut | B | 30 | 6 | B | 18 | 6 |
| Delaware | B | 30 | 6 | B | 18 | 6 |
| District of Col. | B[c] | 15 | C | 5[c] | 15 | C |
| Florida | B | 20 | 6 | B | 20 | 6 |
| Georgia | B | 18 | 6 | B | 18 | 6 |
| Hawaii | B | 18 | AC[d] | B | 18 | AC[d] |
| Idaho | B | 24 | 6 | B | 20 | 6 |
| Illinois | B | 16 | 5 | B | 16 | 5 |
| Indiana | B | 27 | 8 | B | 18 | 6 |
| Iowa | B | 20 | 5 | B | 20 | 5 |
| Kansas | B | 24 | 5 | B | 20 | 5 |
| Kentucky | B | 24 | 8[e] | B | 17 | 8[e] |
| Louisiana | B | 24 | 4 | B | 18 | 4 |
| Maine | B | 30 | 6 | B | 18 | 6 |
| Maryland | B[f] | 26 | 8 | B[f] | 18 | 6 |
| Massachusetts | B[f] | 18 | 2 | B[f] | 12 | 2 |
| Michigan | B | 20 | 5[g] | B | 20 | 5[g] |

| State | | | | | | |
|---|---|---|---|---|---|---|
| Minnesota | B | 30 | 6 | B | 18 | 4 |
| Mississippi | B | 36 | 6 | B | 18 | 6 |
| Missouri | B | 18 | 5 | B | 18 | 5 |
| Montana | B | AC | AC | B | 16 | AC |
| Nebraska | 60[h] | 8 | 3 | B | AC | AC |
| Nevada | B[i] | 18[j] | 6 | B | 20 | 6 |
| New Hampshire | B | 30 | 6 | B | 18 | 6 |
| New Jersey | B | 30 | 6[k] | B | 21 | 6[k] |
| New Mexico | B | 24 | 6 | B | 18 | 6 |
| New York | B | 24 | C[l] | B | 12 | C[l] |
| North Carolina | B | 24 | 6 | B | 18 | 6 |
| North Dakota | B | 16 | 3 | B | 16 | 3 |
| Ohio | B | 28 | 6 | B | 17 | 6 |
| Oklahoma | B | 21[m] | 6 | B | 21[m] | 6 |
| Oregon | B | 20 | _[n] | B[o] | 14 | _[n] |
| Pennsylvania | B | AC | 6-12[p] | B | AC | 6-12[p] |
| Puerto Rico | 68[q] | 53[q] | 6[q] | B[q] | 29[q] | 5[q] |
| Rhode Island | B | 30 | 6 | B | 18 | 6 |
| South Carolina | B | 21 | 6 | B | 18 | 6 |
| South Dakota | 60[r] | 15 | 3 | B | 20 | 6 |
| Tennessee | B | 24 | 4 | B | 24 | 4 |
| Texas | B | 18 | 6 | B | 18 | 6 |
| Utah | B | 26 | 8 | B | 21 | 8 |
| Vermont | 90 | 18 | 6 | B | 18 | 6 |
| Virginia | B | 18 | 6 | B | 15 | 6 |
| Washington | B[s] | AC | AC | B[s] | AC | AC |
| West Virginia | B | 20 | 6 | B | 20 | 6 |
| Wisconsin | 64[t] | 26 | 5 | B | 18 | 5 |
| Wyoming | B | 23 | C | B | 20 | C |

Source: *A Manual on Certification Requirements for School Personnel in the United States, 1970 Edition,* by T. M. Stinnett, with the assistance of Geraldine E. Pershing (Washington, D.C.: National Commission on Teacher Education and Professional Standards, National Education Association, 1970), p. 48.

*Professional requirements listed are the basic requirements for degree or lowest regular certificates. Some variations from the professional requirements as stated in this table may be found in the requirements for specific certificates listed for the respective states in chapter three.

### Appendix C  Average Salaries Paid Instructional Staff, School Years in 1929–30 Through 1970–71, in Current Dollars and in Terms of 1969–70 and 1959–60 Purchasing Power

| School year 1 | Average annual salary In current dollars 2 | Purchasing power In 1969–70 prices 3 | Purchasing power In 1959–60 prices 4 | Purchasing power of $1 In 1969–70 prices 5 | Purchasing power of $1 In 1959–60 prices 6 |
|---|---|---|---|---|---|
| 1929–30 . . . . . . . . | $1,420 | $3,181 | $2,471 | $2.24 | $1.74 |
| 1930–31 . . . . . . . . | 1,440 | 3,485 | 2,707 | 2.42 | 1.88 |
| 1931–32 . . . . . . . . | 1,417 | 3,826 | 2,962 | 2.70 | 2.09 |
| 1932–33 . . . . . . . . | 1,316 | 3,869 | 3,000 | 2.94 | 2.28 |
| 1933–34 . . . . . . . . | 1,227 | 3,521 | 2,724 | 2.87 | 2.22 |
| 1934–35 . . . . . . . . | 1,244 | 3,483 | 2,699 | 2.80 | 2.17 |
| 1935–36 . . . . . . . . | 1,283 | 3,554 | 2,758 | 2.77 | 2.15 |
| 1936–37 . . . . . . . . | 1,327 | 3,556 | 2,760 | 2.68 | 2.08 |
| 1937–38 . . . . . . . . | 1,374 | 3,669 | 2,844 | 2.67 | 2.07 |
| 1938–39 . . . . . . . . | 1,408 | 3,858 | 2,985 | 2.74 | 2.12 |
| 1939–40 . . . . . . . . | 1,441 | 3,920 | 3,041 | 2.72 | 2.11 |
| 1940–41 . . . . . . . . | 1,470 | 3,925 | 3,043 | 2.67 | 2.07 |
| 1941–42 . . . . . . . . | 1,507 | 3,632 | 2,818 | 2.41 | 1.87 |
| 1942–43 . . . . . . . . | 1,599 | 3,566 | 2,766 | 2.23 | 1.73 |
| 1943–44 . . . . . . . . | 1,728 | 3,767 | 2,920 | 2.18 | 1.69 |
| 1944–45 . . . . . . . . | 1,846 | 3,932 | 3,046 | 2.13 | 1.65 |
| 1945–46 . . . . . . . . | 1,995 | 4,110 | 3,192 | 2.06 | 1.60 |
| 1946–47 . . . . . . . . | 2,254 | 3,967 | 3,065 | 1.76 | 1.36 |
| 1947–48 . . . . . . . . | 2,639 | 4,249 | 3,299 | 1.61 | 1.25 |
| 1948–49 . . . . . . . . | 2,846 | 4,525 | 3,501 | 1.59 | 1.23 |
| 1949–50 . . . . . . . . | 3,010 | 4,816 | 3,732 | 1.60 | 1.24 |
| 1950–51 . . . . . . . . | 3,126 | 4,689 | 3,626 | 1.50 | 1.16 |
| 1951–52 . . . . . . . . | 3,450 | 4,968 | 3,864 | 1.44 | 1.12 |
| 1952–53 . . . . . . . . | 3,554 | 5,082 | 3,945 | 1.43 | 1.11 |
| 1953–54 . . . . . . . . | 3,825 | 5,432 | 4,208 | 1.42 | 1.10 |
| 1954–55 . . . . . . . . | 3,950 | 5,609 | 4,345 | 1.42 | 1.10 |
| 1955–56 . . . . . . . . | 4,156 | 5,860 | 4,530 | 1.41 | 1.09 |
| 1956–57 . . . . . . . . | 4,350 | 5,960 | 4,611 | 1.37 | 1.06 |
| 1957–58 . . . . . . . . | 4,720 | 6,278 | 4,862 | 1.33 | 1.03 |
| 1958–59 . . . . . . . . | 4,939 | 6,470 | 5,038 | 1.31 | 1.02 |
| 1959–60 . . . . . . . . | 5,159 | 6,655 | 5,159 | 1.29 | 1.00 |
| 1960–61 . . . . . . . . | 5,449 | 6,975 | 5,395 | 1.28 | .99 |
| 1961–62 . . . . . . . . | 5,700 | 7,239 | 5,586 | 1.27 | .98 |
| 1962–63 . . . . . . . . | 5,921 | 7,401 | 5,743 | 1.25 | .97 |
| 1963–64 . . . . . . . . | 6,240 | 7,675 | 5,928 | 1.23 | .95 |
| 1964–65 . . . . . . . . | 6,465 | 7,887 | 6,142 | 1.22 | .95 |
| 1965–66 . . . . . . . . | 6,935 | 8,253 | 6,380 | 1.19 | .92 |
| 1966–67 . . . . . . . . | 7,129 | 8,198 | 6,345 | 1.15 | .89 |
| 1967–68 . . . . . . . . | 7,709 | 8,557 | 6,630 | 1.11 | .86 |
| 1968–69 . . . . . . . . | 8,272 | 8,768 | 6,783 | 1.06 | .82 |
| 1969–70 . . . . . . . . | 9,047 | 9,047 | 7,057 | 1.00 | .78 |
| 1970–71 . . . . . . . . | 9,689* | 9,398** | . . . | . . . | . . . |

Source: *Economic Status of the Teaching Profession, 1970–71, Research Report 1971–R4* (Washington, D.C.: Research Division, National Education Association, 1971), p. 29.
*Preliminary estimate.
**Based on prices as of September 1970.

Appendix D  Average Annual Earnings of Public School
Teachers and Nonsupervisory Employees in Selected
Industries, 1960–1969 (Calendar Years)

| Industry 1 | 1960 2 | 1961 3 | 1962 4 | 1963 5 | 1964 6 | 1965 7 | 1966 8 | 1967 9 | 1968 10 | 1969 11 | Percentage increase, 1969 over 1968 12 |
|---|---|---|---|---|---|---|---|---|---|---|---|
| Public-school teachers | $5,088 | $5,355 | $5,587 | $5,820 | $6,062 | $6,292 | $6,600 | $7,028 | $7,599 | $8,180 | 7.6% |
| All industries, total | 4,707 | 4,843 | 5,065 | 5,243 | 5,499 | 5,705 | 5,974 | 6,231 | 6,638 | 7,061 | 6.4 |
| Agriculture, forestry, and fisheries | 1,738 | 1,776 | 1,728 | 1,771 | 1,893 | 2,030 | 2,260 | 2,434 | 2,666 | 2,894 | 8.6 |
| Mining | 5,685 | 5,835 | 6,017 | 6,240 | 6,521 | 6,783 | 7,134 | 7,556 | 7,964 | 8,587 | 7.8 |
| Contract construction | 5,488 | 5,660 | 5,846 | 6,018 | 6,332 | 6,593 | 7,033 | 7,417 | 7,941 | 8,628 | 8.7 |
| Manufacturing—total | 5,342 | 5,509 | 5,730 | 5,920 | 6,196 | 6,386 | 6,643 | 6,880 | 7,347 | 7,768 | 5.7 |
| Nondurable goods—total | ... | ... | 5,137 | 5,284 | 5,526 | 5,689 | 5,920 | 6,180 | 6,586 | 6,977 | 5.9 |
| Printing and publishing | 5,610 | 5,770 | 5,909 | 6,076 | 6,317 | 6,497 | 6,767 | 6,993 | 7,362 | 7,832 | 6.4 |
| Chemicals and allied products | 6,321 | 6,544 | 6,852 | 7,065 | 7,361 | 7,553 | 7,849 | 8,136 | 8,600 | 9,137 | 6.2 |
| Petroleum refining and related industries | ... | ... | 7,490 | 7,812 | 7,984 | 8,266 | 8,598 | 8,967 | 9,468 | 10,184 | 7.6 |
| Durable goods—total | ... | ... | 6,191 | 6,407 | 6,703 | 6,898 | 7,149 | 7,369 | 7,880 | 8,319 | 5.6 |
| Primary metal products | 6,341 | 6,551 | 6,824 | 7,008 | 7,317 | 7,556 | 7,833 | 7,873 | 8,464 | 8,999 | 6.3 |
| Machinery, except electrical | 6,025 | 6,194 | 6,515 | 6,703 | 7,069 | 7,280 | 7,635 | 7,830 | 8,304 | 8,863 | 6.7 |
| Transportation equipment[a] | 6,625 | 6,974 | 7,204 | 7,521 | 7,831 | 8,045 | 8,303 | 8,477 | 8,861 | 9,420 | 6.3 |
| Motor vehicles and equipment | 6,558 | 6,507 | 7,144 | 7,528 | 7,866 | 8,152 | 8,328 | 8,475 | 9,595 | 9,759 | 1.7 |
| Transportation | 5,928 | 6,085 | 6,638 | 6,852 | 7,161 | 7,473 | 7,785 | 8,129 | 8,674 | 9,293 | 7.1 |
| Communication | 5,642 | 5,886 | 5,895 | 6,128 | 6,435 | 6,618 | 6,864 | 7,041 | 7,500 | 8,032 | 7.1 |
| Finance, insurance and real estate | 4,840 | 5,035 | 5,410 | 5,595 | 5,851 | 6,070 | 6,347 | 6,717 | 7,220 | 7,596 | 5.2 |
| Banking | 4,689 | 4,826 | 5,053 | 5,207 | 5,400 | 5,608 | 5,784 | 6,044 | 6,401 | 6,808 | 6.4 |
| Security and commodity brokers | 8,358 | 9,607 | 9,355 | 9,758 | 10,549 | 11,548 | 12,807 | 14,698 | 16,122 | 15,055 | 6.6 |
| Government and government enterprises | 4,683 | 4,870 | 4,993 | 5,205 | 5,474 | 5,701 | 5,938 | 6,222 | 6,717 | 7,188 | 7.0 |
| Federal civilian | 5,946 | 6,285 | 6,450 | 6,792 | 7,267 | 7,614 | 7,841 | 7,985 | 8,746 | 9,445 | 8.0 |
| State and local | 4,827 | 4,952 | 5,017 | 5,180 | 5,370 | 5,592 | 5,906 | 6,324 | 6,796 | 7,232 | 6.4 |

Source: *Economic Status of the Teaching Profession, 1970–71, Research Report 1971–R4* (Washington, D.C.: Research Division, National Education Association, 1971), p. 49.
[a]Except motor vehicles.

## Appendix E  Comparison of Traditional Approach to School Personnel Administration with Collective Bargaining Approach

*Traditional Approach*                                  *Collective Bargaining*

### Spirit of Bargaining

| Traditional Approach | Collective Bargaining |
|---|---|
| 1. Board could act unilaterally without consultation with its employees. | Consultation with employees required under the good faith assumption. |
| 2. Mutuality of interests and interdependency assumed. | Mutuality of interests and interdependency, plus divergency of interest and needs, are assumed. |
| 3. Grievances and other personnel matters sometimes overlooked. | Grievances and other personnel concerns are considered important, and provisions are made in writing to handle them. |
| 4. Much taken for granted. | Nothing taken for granted. |
| 5. A day's work in teaching often puzzling to determine. | A day's work in teaching and responsibilities specifically defined. |

### Procedures

| Traditional Approach | Collective Bargaining |
|---|---|
| 6. One-way communications. | Two-way communications. |
| 7. Narrow sphere of bargaining, often confined to economic matters only. | Parties may elect to bargain on a broad scale. |
| 8. Superintendent represented teachers to the board and the board to teachers. | Both parties represented by expert representatives of their own choosing. |
| 9. Board always had last word. | Impasse procedures provided; neither party can be allowed to paralyze the bargaining process. |
| 10. Courts finally resolved disputes; losers paid costs. | Third parties called in to intervene in resolution of disputes; costs shared equally. |
| 11. Good faith not mandated. | Good faith bargaining mandated and assured legislatively and by written agreement. |
| 12. Written personnel policies sometimes lacking. | Written agreements set terms and conditions of personnel administration. |
| 13. Divergencies between policy and practice often went unexplained. | Constant dialogue permits discussion of divergencies between policy and practice. |

### Power Relationships

| Traditional Approach | Collective Bargaining |
|---|---|
| 14. Unilateral. | Bilateral. |
| 15. Paternalistic. | Cooperative sharing of decision making. |
| 16. Authoritarian. | Democratic. |
| 17. Management stronger. | Egalitarian. |
| 18. Board more powerful. | Parties equal in power to require performance from other party. |
| 19. Counteroffer not required. | Quid pro quo. |
| 20. Parties not required to meet. | Confrontation mandated. |

From: Chester M. Nolte, *Status and Scope of Collective Bargaining in Education* (Eugene, Oregon: ERIC Clearinghouse on Educational Administration, University of Oregon, 1970), pp. 13–14.

**Appendix F  Summary of Teacher Strikes, Work
Stoppages, and Interruptions of Service, by Type of
Organization Involved, January 1940 Through June 1971**

| *Type of organization*<br>*1* | *Number of strikes,<br>work stoppages, and<br>interruptions of<br>service* | | *Estimated number<br>of personnel<br>involved* | | *Estimated number<br>of man-days<br>involved* | |
|---|---|---|---|---|---|---|
| | *Number*<br>*2* | *Percentage<br>of total[a]*<br>*3* | *Number*<br>*4* | *Percentage<br>of total[a]*<br>*5* | *Number*<br>*6* | *Percentage<br>of total[a]*<br>*7* |
| Professional association . . . . . | 460 | 62.4% | 320,735 | 51.4% | 1,397,952 | 22.6% |
| Teacher union . . . . . . . . . . . . | 205 | 27.8 | 281,138 | 45.0 | 4,447,263 | 71.9 · |
| Independent organization . . . | 17 | 2.3 | 3,103 | 0.5 | 9,158 | 0.2 |
| No organization. . . . . . . . . . | 46 | 6.2 | 2,479 | 0.4 | 21,400 | 0.4 |
| Joint union/association . . . . . | 9 | 1.2 | 16,731 | 2.7 | 310,741 | 5.0 |
| Total | 737 | 99.9% | 624,187 | 100.0% | 6,186,514 | 100.1% |

Source: *NEA Research Memo*, Research Division, National Education Association, December, 1971, Research
Memo 1971–28, p. 5.

[a]Percentages may not add to 100.0% owing to rounding.

**Appendix G  Summary of Teacher Strikes, Work
Stoppages, and Interruptions of Service, by School Year,
by Organization, by Month, July 1960 Through June
1971**

| School year, type of organization, and month | Number of strikes, work stoppages, and interruptions of service | | Estimated number of personnel involved | | Estimated number of man-days involved | |
|---|---|---|---|---|---|---|
| | Number | Percentage of total[a] | Number | Percentage of total[a] | Number | Percentage of total[a] |
| 1 | 2 | 3 | 4 | 5 | 6 | 7 |
| SCHOOL YEAR | | | | | | |
| 1960–61 . . . . . . . . . . . . . . | 3 | 0.5% | 5,080 | 0.9% | 5,080 | 0.1% |
| 1961–62 . . . . . . . . . . . . . . | 1 | 0.2 | 22,000 | 3.7 | 22,000 | 0.4 |
| 1962–63 . . . . . . . . . . . . . . | 2 | 0.3 | 2,200 | 0.4 | 3,000 | 0.1 |
| 1963–64 . . . . . . . . . . . . . . | 5 | 0.8 | 11,980 | 2.0 | 24,020 | 0.4 |
| 1964–65 . . . . . . . . . . . . . . | 12 | 1.9 | 15,083 | 2.5 | 27,453 | 0.5 |
| 1965–66 . . . . . . . . . . . . . . | 18 | 2.9 | 33,620 | 5.6 | 49,220 | 0.8 |
| 1966–67 . . . . . . . . . . . . . . | 34 | 5.4 | 10,633 | 1.8 | 29,079 | 0.5 |
| 1967–68 . . . . . . . . . . . . . . | 114 | 18.1 | 162,604 | 27.1 | 1,433,786 | 24.1 |
| 1968–69 . . . . . . . . . . . . . . | 131 | 20.8 | 128,888 | 21.5 | 2,733,802 | 45.9 |
| 1969–70 . . . . . . . . . . . . . . | 181 | 28.7 | 118,636 | 19.7 | 911,032 | 15.3 |
| 1970–71 . . . . . . . . . . . . . . | 130 | 20.6 | 89,651 | 14.9 | 717,217 | 12.0 |
| | 631 | 100.2% | 600,375 | 100.1% | 5,955,689 | 100.1% |
| TYPE OF ORGANIZATION | | | | | | |
| Professional association . . . | 439 | 69.6% | 316,005 | 52.6% | 1,373,812 | 23.1% |
| Teacher union . . . . . . . . . . | 156 | 24.7 | 264,272 | 44.0 | 4,263,238 | 71.6 |
| Independent organization . . | 8 | 1.3 | 2,178 | 0.4 | 5,018 | 0.1 |
| No organization . . . . . . . . | 19 | 3.0 | 1,189 | 0.2 | 2,880 | 0.1 |
| Joint union/association  . . . | 9 | 1.4 | 16,731 | 2.8 | 310,741 | 5.2 |
| | 631 | 100.0% | 600,375 | 100.0% | 5,955,689 | 100.1% |

Source: *NEA Research Memo*, Research Division, National Education Association, December, 1971, Research
Memo 1971–28, p. 5.

[a]The three groups of figures may not add to this total because of rounding.

# NOTES

## Notes to Chapter 1

*Benjamin Solomon, "A Profession Taken for Granted," *The School Review*, LXIX (August, 1961), 298.

**Albert Shanker, President, United Federation of Teachers, in "Teacher-Supervisory Relationships: A Symposium," *Changing Education*, I (Spring, 1966), 23.

***T. M. Stinnett, *Turmoil in Teaching* (New York: The Macmillan Company, 1968), p. 34.

****James W. Becker, Assistant Executive Secretary for Instruction and Professional Development, National Education Association, as reported in New York State Teachers Association Newspaper, *The Challenger*, I (December 3, 1971), 9.

*****Philip W. Jackson, "Old Dogs and New Tricks: Observations on the Continuing Education of Teachers," *Improving In-Service Education: Proposals and Procedures for Change*, ed. Louis J. Rubin (Boston: Allyn and Bacon, Inc., 1971), p. 29.

1. This concept was first advanced by Chester I. Barnard, *The Functions of an Executive* (Cambridge, Mass.: Harvard University Press, 1938). See chapter XII, "The Theory of Authority," pp. 161–84. See also, Edwin M. Bridges, "Administrative Man: Origin or Pawn in Decision Making?", *Educational Administration Quarterly*, VI (Winter, 1970), 7–25.

2. Gertrude Bertrand Ujhely, "Servant? No! Service Professional? Yes!", *RN*, XXVII (February, 1964), 56–60.

3. Dan C. Lortie, "The Balance of Control and Autonomy in Elementary School Teaching," *The Semi-Professions and Their Organization: Teachers, Nurses, Social Workers*, ed. Amitai Etzioni (New York: © 1969 by The Free Press, A Division of the Macmillan Company), p. 4.

4. Adapted from James G. Anderson, "The Authority Structure of the School: System of Social Exchange," *Educational Administration Quarterly*, III (Spring, 1967), 130–48.

5. *Ibid.*, 144.

6. Margaret Lindsey, "Decision-Making and the Teacher," reprinted by permission of the publisher from A. Harry Passow, *Curriculum Crossroads* (New York: Teachers College Press, copyright 1962 by Teachers College, Columbia University), p. 38.

7. *Ibid.*

8. Gerald H. Moeller and W. W. Charters, "Relation of Bureaucratization to Sense of Power Among Teachers," *Administrative Science Quarterly*, X (March, 1966), 446.

9. Lortie, *op. cit.*, p. 9.

10. *Ibid.*

11. Rose Altmark, "Teacher and Decision-Making," Unpublished paper submitted to meet the requirements for a course at the University of California Extension, Los Angeles, July 10, 1970.

12. David W. Johnson, "Influence on Teachers' Acceptance of Change," *The Elementary School Journal*, LXX (December, 1969), 147.

Notes to Chapter 2

*William J. Cirone, former sixth-grade teacher, Public School No. 125, New York City, as quoted in *Those Who Teach Children* (Atlanta: Westab Educational Services, n.d.), n.p.

**F. J. C. Seymour, "What is Professionalism?", *The ATA Magazine* (June, 1963), Alberta Teachers' Association, 23.

***Stenographic report of a talk by John Dewey at a meeting of the Parents' Association of the University Elementary School, 1899, somewhat revised. John Dewey, *The School and Society* (Chicago: The University of Chicago Press, 1900), p. 116.

1. John S. Brubacher, "The Evolution of Professional Education," *Education for the Professions*, Sixty-First Yearbook of the National Society for the Study of Education, Part II, ed. Nelson B. Henry (Chicago: The University of Chicago Press, 1962), pp. 47–67.

2. Cogan presents a thorough discussion of the meaning of profession; see, Morris L. Cogan, "Toward a Definition of Profession," *Harvard Educational Review*, XXIII (Winter, 1953), 33–50.

3. Howard M. Vollmer and Donald L. Mills (eds.), *Professionalization* (Englewood Cliffs, New Jersey: Prentice-Hall, Inc., 1966), pp. vii–viii.

4. "Teachers' Professional and Welfare Status," *What Teachers Think: A Summary of Teacher Opinion Poll Findings, 1960–1965, Research Report 1965-R13* (Washington, D.C.: Research Division, National Education Association, 1965), p. 44.

5. Ronald G. Corwin, "The Anatomy of Militant Professionalization," *Above the Salt: Militancy in Education; Proceedings of Mont Chateau Conference on Collective Negotiations in Education*, ed. Harold I. Goodwin and Patrick W. Carlton (Morgantown, West Virginia: College of Human Resources and Education, West Virginia Education Association, West Virginia University, 1968), pp. 55–61.

6. Bernard Barber, "Some Problems in the Sociology of the Professions," *Daedalus*, Journal of the American Academy of Arts and Sciences, Boston, Mass., Fall 1963, *The Professions*, p. 671.

7. Abraham Flexner, "Is Social Work a Profession?" *Proceedings of the National Conference of Charities and Correction* (Chicago: Hildmann Printing Co., 1915), pp. 578–81; as reported in Howard S. Becker, "The Nature of a Profession," *Education for the Professions*, Sixty-First Yearbook of the National Society for the Study of Education, Part II, *op. cit.*, pp. 27–28.

8. Goode views 1 and 2 as core characteristics, with 4 through 13 as features which are derived from the core characteristics; see William J. Goode, "Encroachment, Charlatanism, and the Emerging Professions: Psychology, Sociology, and Medicine," *American Sociological Review*, XXV (December, 1960), 903. Function, #3, is discussed the most thoroughly by Myron Lieberman, *Education as a Profession* (Englewood Cliffs, New Jersey: Prentice-Hall, Inc., 1956), pp. 19–48.

9. Hall argues that the characteristics of a profession are of two basic types: structural and attitudinal. The structural attributes are: (1) creation of a full-time occupation, (2) establishment of a training school, (3) formulation of professional associations, (4) formulation of a code of ethics. The attitudinal

attributes are: (1) the use of the professional organization as a major reference, (2) a belief in service to the public, (3) belief in self-regulation, (4) sense of calling to the field, (5) autonomy; see, Richard H. Hall, "Professionalization and Bureaucratization," *American Sociological Review*, XXXIII (February, 1968), 92–104.

10. F. J. C. Seymour, "What is Professionalism," *A.T.A Magazine*, XLIII (June, 1963), 20; Alberta Teachers' Association.

11. Ernest Greenwood, "The Elements of Professionalization: (Social Work)," Reprinted with the permission of the National Association of Social Workers, from *Social Work*, II (July, 1957), p. 54.

12. Everett, C. Hughes, "Professions," *Daedalus*, Journal of the American Academy of Arts and Sciences, Boston, Mass., Fall 1963, *The Professions*, p. 656.

13. Greenwood, *op. cit.*, p. 46.

14. William Goode, "The Librarian: From Occupation to Profession," *The Library Quarterly*, XXXI (October, 1961), p. 315.

15. Greenwood, *op. cit.*, p. 15.

16. Lieberman, *op. cit.*, p. 20.

17. G. Lester Anderson and Merton W. Ertell, "Extra-institutional Forces Affecting Professional Education," *Education for the Professions*, Sixty-First Yearbook of the National Society for the Study of Education, Part II, *op. cit.*, pp. 238–39.

18. Warren G. Bennis, "Post-Bureaucratic Leadership," *Trans-Action*, VI (November, 1969).

19. Katz makes this point on page 435 of his insightful and thorough article concerning authority in complex social organizations; see, Fred E. Katz, "The School as a Complex Social Organization," *Harvard Educational Review*, XXXIV (Summer, 1964), 428–55.

20. Greenwood, *op. cit.*, p. 47–48.

21. *Ibid.*, p. 13.

22. Ronald G. Corwin, *A Sociology of Education: Emerging Patterns of Class, Status, and Power in Public Schools* (New York: Appleton-Century-Crofts, Education Division, Meredith Corporation, 1965).

23. Richard H. Hall, "Professionalization and Bureaucratization," *American Sociological Review*, XXXIII (February, 1968), 93.

24. William J. Goode, "Community Within a Community: The Professions," *American Sociological Review*, XXII (April, 1957), 194–200. For a detailed analysis of the professional culture, see Greenwood, *op. cit.*, pp. 16–17.

### Notes for Chapter 3

*Harold I. Goodwin and Patrick W. Carlton (eds.), *Above the Salt: Militancy in Education, Proceedings of Mont Chateau Conference on Collective Negotiations in Education* (Morgantown, West Va.: College of Human Resources, West Virginia University, and West Virginia Education Association, March, 1968), Foreword.

**Ronald G. Corwin, "Professional Persons in Public Organizations," *Educational Administration Quarterly*, I (Autumn, 1965), 4.

***Alan Rosenthal, *Pedagogues and Power: Teacher Groups in School Politics* (Syracuse, New York: Syracuse University Press, 1969), pp. 1–2.

1. Dan C. Lortie, "The Balance of Control and Autonomy in Elementary School Teaching," *The Semi-Professions and Their Organization: Teachers, Nurses, Social Workers*, ed. Amitai Etzioni (New York: © 1969 by The Free Press, A Division of The Macmillan Company), p. 24.

2. Amitai Etzioni, "Schools as a 'Guidable' System," *Freedom, Bureaucracy, & Schooling*, 1971 Yearbook of the Association for Supervision and Curriculum Development, ed. Vernon F. Haubrich (Washington, D.C.: The Association, 1971), pp. 34–39.

3. *Ibid.*, p. 35.

4. James D. Koerner, *The Miseducation of American Teachers* (Boston, Mass.: Houghton Mifflin Company, 1963), p. 50.

5. *Ibid.*, p. 56.

6. James Bryant Conant, *The Education of American Teachers* (New York: McGraw-Hill Book Company, Inc., 1963), p. 141.

7. Philip W. Jackson, *Life in Classrooms* (New York: Holt, Rinehart and Winston, Inc., 1968), pp. 143–55.

8. See, Emil J. Haller, "Technical Socialization: Pupil Influences on Teachers' Speech," Ph.D. dissertation, Department of Education, University of Chicago, 1966; as reported in Lortie, *op. cit.*, p. 52.

9. B. Othanel Smith in collaboration with Saul B. Cohen and Arthur Pearl, *Teachers for the Real World* (Washington, D.C.: American Association of Colleges for Teacher Education, 1969), p. 45.

10. Frederick B. Davis (ed.), *The Literature of Research in Reading with Emphasis on Models* (New Brunswick, New Jersey: Graduate School of Education, Rutgers–The State University, 1971).

11. Richard C. Williams, "Teacher Militancy: Implications for the Schools," *Social and Technological Change: Implications for Education*, ed. Philip K. Piele and Terry L. Eidell, with Stuart C. Smith (Eugene, Oregon: The Center for the Advanced Study of Educational Administration, University of Oregon, 1970), pp. 105–106.

12. Personal correspondence with D. D. Darland, former executive secretary, Commission on Teacher Education and Professional Standards, National Education Association.

13. Richard H. Hall, "Professionalization and Bureaucratization," *American Sociological Review*, XXXIII (February, 1968), 97.

14. William Goode, " 'Professions' and 'Non-Professions' (Librarianship)," *Professionalization*, ed. Howard M. Vollmer and Donald L. Mills (Englewood Cliffs, New Jersey: Prentice-Hall, Inc., 1966), p. 37.

15. Myron Lieberman, *Education as a Profession* (Englewood Cliffs, New Jersey: Prentice-Hall, Inc., 1956), p. 47.

16. Lortie, *op. cit.*, p. 10.

17. To gain an historical perspective, see, T. M. Stinnett, "Accreditation and the Professionalization of Teaching," *Journal of Teacher Education*, III (March, 1952), 30–39; or Lucien B. Kinney, *Certification in Education* (Englewood Cliffs, New Jersey: Prentice-Hall, Inc., 1964).

18. Lieberman, *op. cit.*, p. 126.

19. Conant, *op cit.*, p. 43.

20. "Facts on American Education," *NEA Research Bulletin*, XLIX (May, 1971), 48.

21. James G. Anderson, "The Authority Structure of the School: System of Social Exchange," *Educational Administration Quarterly*, III (Spring, 1967), 142.

22. Alvin P. Lierheimer, "Changing the Palace Guard," *Phi Delta Kappan*, LII (September, 1970), 21–22.

23. Conant, *op. cit.*, pp. 54–55.

24. T. M. Stinnett, with the assistance of Geraldine E. Pershing, *A Manual on Certification Requirements for School Personnel in the United States, 1970 Edition* (Washington, D.C.: National Commission on Teacher Education and Professional Standards, National Education Association, 1970), pp. 23–24.

25. Myron Lieberman, *The Future of Public Education* (Chicago: The University of Chicago Press, 1960), p. 105.

26. "Number of States in Which All or a Majority of the Board Members of the Occupation Licensed Must be Practitioners of the Occupation Licensed," *Occupational Licensing in the States* (Chicago: The Council of State Governments, 1952), pp. 84–87; and information received from the American Medical Association and the American Dental Association.

27. Anderson, *op. cit.*, 143.

28. "Table 23—Average Salaries Paid Instructional Staff, *School Years* 1929–30 through 1970–71, in Current Dollars and in Terms of 1969–70 and 1959–60 Purchasing Power," *Economic Status of the Teaching Profession, 1970–71* (Washington, D.C.: Research Division, National Education Association, 1971), p. 29.

29. *Estimates of School Statistics, 1971–72, Research Report 1971-R-13* (Washington, D.C.: Research Division, National Education Association, 1971), p. 15.

30. Erick L. Lindman, "Are Teachers' Salaries IMPROVING?", *Phi Delta Kappan*, LI (April, 1970), 420–22.

31. John Oliver, "Can Teachers Beat the Cost of Living?", *American Teacher*, LV (February, 1971), 7.

32. John Oliver, "First Time in 20 Years, Average Teacher's Spendable Pay Down," *American Teacher*, LVI (March, 1972), 19.

33. *Economic Status of the Teaching Profession*, 1970–71, *op. cit.*, p. 5.

34. *Ibid.*, p. 49.

35. Stanley M. Elam, "What are the Lessons of Florida?", *Phi Delta Kappan*, XLIX (June, 1968), 553.

36. "Some of the Highest Scheduled Salaries for Teachers, 1970–71," *NEA Research Bulletin*, XLVIII (December, 1970), 99–103.

37. Ronald D. Michman, "The Moonlighters," *American Teacher*, LVI (December, 1971), 18.

38. Harold Guthrie, "Who Moonlights and Why," *Illinois Business Review* (March, 1965); as reported in Michman, *Ibid.*

39. Joel E. Gerstl, "Education and the Sociology of Work," *On Education—Sociological Perspective*, ed. Donald A. Hansen and Joel E. Gerstl (New York: John Wiley & Sons, Inc., 1967), p. 233.

40. Robert W. Hodge, Paul M. Siegel, and Peter H. Rossi, "Occupational Prestige in the U.S. 1925–63," *The American Journal of Sociology*, LXX (November, 1964), 290.

41. Lortie, *op. cit.*, p. 20.

42. Gerstl, *op. cit.*, p. 235.

43. Lieberman, *Education As a Profession, op. cit.*, p. 467.

44. James A. Davis, *Great Aspirations* (Chicago: Aldine Publishing Co., 1964), as reported in Gerstl, *op. cit.*, p. 237.

45. Gerstl, *op. cit.*, p. 237.

46. *Ibid.*, p. 249.

47. Alma S. Wittlin, "The Teacher," *Daedalus: The Professions*, XCII (Fall, 1963), 753.

48. Oswald Hall, "The Social Structure of the Teaching Profession," *Struggle for Power in Education*, ed. Frank W. Lutz and Joseph Azzarelli (New York: The Center for Applied Research in Education, Inc., 1966), pp. 35–48.

49. Arthur F. Corey, "Overview of Factors Affecting the Holding Power of the Teaching Profession," *The Teacher Dropout*, ed. T. M. Stinnett (Bloomington, Indiana: Phi Delta Kappa, Incorporated, 1970), p. 1.

50. *The American Public School Teacher, 1965–66, Research Report 1967-R-4* (Washington, D.C.: Research Division, National Education Association, 1967), p. 50.

51. *Ibid.*, p. 15.

52. Theodore Caplow, *The Sociology of Work* (Minneapolis: University of Minnesota Press, 1954), p. 106; as quoted in Gerstl, *op. cit.*, p. 229.

53. *Teacher Supply and Demand in Public Schools, 1970, Research Report 1970-R-14* (Washington, D.C.: Research Division, National Education Association), p. 8.

54. Smith, *op. cit.*, p. 24.

55. Morton R. Godine, "Collective Negotiations and Public Policy, with Special Reference to Public Education," *Readings on Collective Negotiations in Public Education*, ed. Stanley M. Elam et. al. (Chicago: Rand McNally & Company, 1967), p. 33.

56. Lester S. Vander Werf, "Militancy and the Profession of Teaching," *School and Society*, XCVIII (March, 1970), 171.

57. Sol M. Elkin, "Another Look at Collective Negotiations for Professions," *School and Society*, XCVIII (March, 1970), 173.

58. Howard S. Becker, "The Nature of a Profession," *Education for the Professions*, Sixty-First Yearbook of the National Society for the Study of Education, Part II, ed. Nelson B. Henry (Chicago: The Society, 1962), pp. 27–46.

59. *Ibid.*, p. 46.

### Notes for Chapter 4

*Teacher, Institute for Development of Educational Activities (IDEA), Research Division, Teachers' Seminar, Los Angeles, 1968.

**Charles Robbin, *The School as a Social Institution* (Norwood, Mass.: Norwood Press, 1918), p. 448.

***Urie Bronfenbrenner, with the assistance of John C. Condry, Jr., *Two Worlds of Childhood: U.S. and U.S.S.R.* (New York: Russell Sage Foundation, 1970), p. 154.

****From the book, *Up the Down Staircase* by Bel Kaufman, p. 44. © 1964 by Bel Kaufman. Reprinted with permission of the publisher, Prentice-Hall, Inc., Englewood Cliffs, New Jersey.

1. Sloan R. Wayland, "The Teacher as a Decision-Maker," *Curriculum Crossroads*, ed. A. Harry Passow (New York: Bureau of Publications, Teachers College, Columbia University, 1962), pp. 45–46.

2. David W. Johnson, "Influence on Teachers' Acceptance of Change," *The Elementary School Journal*, LXX (December, 1969), 146.

3. Amitai Etzioni, "Schools as a 'Guidable' System," *Freedom, Bureaucracy, & Schooling*, 1971 Yearbook of the Association for Supervision and Curriculum Development, ed. Vernon F. Haubrich (Washington, D.C.: The Association, 1971), pp. 40–41.

4. Sam Leles, "Teacher Power—What's It All About?", *Theory Into Practice*, The Ohio State University, VII (April, 1968), 60–61.

5. For an analysis of the factors contributing to this high withdrawal rate, read "The Teacher as a Dropout," *Teachers for the Real World*, B. Othanel Smith in collaboration with Saul B. Cohen and Arthur Pearl (Washington, D.C.: The American Association of Colleges for Teacher Education, 1969), pp. 21–30.

6. Lloyd K. Bishop, "The Teacher: Developing a Climate for Professional Behavior, *ISR Journal*, I (Summer, 1969), 174–76.

7. Roald F. Campbell, Luvern L. Cunningham, and Roderick F. McPhee, *The Organization and Control of American Schools* (Columbus, Ohio: Chàrles E. Merrill Books, Inc., 1965), p. 46.

8. Wayland, *op. cit.*

9. See also Ward Sherman Mason, *The Beginning Teacher: A Survey of New Teachers in the Public Schools* (Washington, D.C.: U.S. Department of Health, Education, and Welfare, Office of Education, 1961); as reported in Joel E. Gerstl, "Education and the Sociology of Work," *On Education—Sociological Perspectives*, ed. Donald A. Hansen and Joel E. Gerstl (New York: John Wiley & Sons, Inc., 1967), p. 244.

10. Cremin makes a similar point. See, Lawrence A. Cremin, *The Genius of American Education* (New York: Random House, Inc., 1966), pp. 98–99.

11. Wayland, *op. cit.*, pp. 49–50.

12. James D. Koerner, *Who Controls American Education? A Guide for Laymen* (Boston: Beacon Press, 1968), pp. 46–78.

### Notes to Chapter 5

*Amitai Etzioni (ed.), *The Semi-Professions and Their Organization: Teachers, Nurses, Social Workers* (New York: The Free Press, 1969), p. vii. © 1969 by The Free Press, A Division of The Macmillan Company.

**John Martin Rich, *Education and Human Values* (Reading, Mass.: Addison-Wesley Publishing Company, 1968), p. 57.

***Myron Lieberman, *Education as a Profession*, p. 15. © 1956. Reprinted by permission of Prentice-Hall, Inc., Englewood Cliffs, New Jersey.

****Alma S. Wittlin, "The Teacher," *Daedalus*, 761. Reprinted by permission of Daedalus, Journal of the American Academy of Arts and Sciences, Boston, Mass., Fall 1963, *The Professions*.

*****Alan Rosenthal, *Pedagogues and Power: Teacher Groups and School Politics* (Syracuse, New York: Syracuse University Press, 1969), p. 5.

1. Much of the material included in this chapter was gleaned from an informative book edited by Amitai Etzioni entitled *The Semi-Professions and Their Organization: Teachers, Nurses, Social Workers* (New York: © 1969 by The Free Press, A Division of The Macmillan Company.

2. Adapted from Sir Alexander Morris Carr-Saunders, "Metropolitan Conditions and Traditional Professional Relationships," *The Metropolis in Modern Life*, ed. Robert Moore Fisher (Garden City, New York: Doubleday & Company, Inc., 1955), 279–88.

3. Leila Sussmann with Marie O'Brien, *Innovation in Education – United States* (Paris: Organisation for Economic Cooperation and Development, 1971), p. 49.

4. Etzioni, *op. cit.*

5. By and large, these categories came from the preface by Etzioni, and from Simpson and Simpson's chapter entitled, "Women and Bureaucracy in the Semi-Professions," Etzioni, *op. cit.*

6. Etzioni, *op. cit.*

7. Dan C. Lortie, "The Balance of Control and Autonomy in Elementary Teaching," Etzioni, *op. cit.*, p. 24.

8. 1970–71 data from the *NEA Research Bulletin*, XLIX (May, 1971), 47.

9. "Estimated Number of Full-time Public-school Professional Employees, by Sex, 1970–71," *NEA Research Bulletin*, XLIX (October, 1971), 68.

10. Arthur L. Stinchcombe, "Social Structure and Organizations," *Handbook of Organizations*, ed. James G. March (Chicago: Rand McNally & Company, 1965), pp. 153–68.

11. Richard H. Hall, "Professionalization and Bureaucratization," *American Sociological Review*, XXXIII (February, 1968), 92–104.

12. Etzioni, *op. cit.*, p. xv.

13. *Ibid.*

14. Simpson and Simpson, "Women and Bureaucracy in the Semi-Professions," Etzioni, *op. cit.*, pp. 196–265.

15. *NEA Research Bulletin*, XLIX (May, 1971), 47.

16. Simpson and Simpson, "Women and Bureaucracy in the Semi-Professions," Etzioni, *op. cit.*, pp. 206–207.

17. Lortie, "The Balance of Control and Autonomy in Elementary Teaching," Etzioni, *op. cit.*, pp. 21–22.

18. Simpson and Simpson, *op. cit.*, pp. 198–99.

19. "Estimated National Distribution of Public-School Teachers by Their Highest Level of Academic Preparation, 1970," *NEA Research Bulletin*, XLIX (May, 1971), 56.

20. Etzioni, *op. cit.*, p. vi.

21. *Ibid.*, pp. vi–vii.


## Notes to Chapter 6

*Richard Nixon, Speech to the Nation on Welfare and Domestic Matters, August 8, 1969.

**David Selden, President, American Federation of Teachers, "From the President," *American Teacher*, LVI (May, 1972), 2A.

***George W. Taylor, "The Public Interest in Collective Negotiations in Education," *Phi Delta Kappan*, XLVIII (September, 1966), 19.

****James G. Anderson, "The Authority Structure of the School: System of Social Exchange," *Educational Administration Quarterly*, III (Spring, 1967), 145.

*****Peter M. Blau, *Bureaucracy in Modern Society* (New York: Random House, Inc., 1956), p. 23.

1. Charles E. Bidwell, "The School as a Formal Organization," *Handbook of Organizations*, ed. James G. March (Chicago: Rand McNally & Company, 1965), p. 994.

2. Some educators establish private schools to escape the restraints of the general public. They soon discover that the parents who enroll their children are often as vociferous in their demands for a particular method of education as is the public at large.

3. Roald F. Campbell, Luvern L. Cunningham, and Roderick F. McPhee, *The Organization and Control of American Schools* (Columbus, Ohio: Charles E. Merrill Books, Inc., 1965), pp. 64–65.

4. Roy L. Cox, "Elective Courses: Gaining State Approval," *Educational Leadership*, XXII (December, 1964), 77–79, 195.

5. William H. Roe, "State Regulation of Education," *Encyclopedia of Educational Research*, ed. Robert L. Ebel (4th ed.; London: The Macmillan Company, Collier-Macmillan Limited, 1969), p. 1301.

6. Campbell, Cunningham, and McPhee, *op. cit.*, p. 56.

7. *Ibid.*, p. 59.

8. *Ibid.*

9. In 1931–32, there were 127,422 school districts and in 1961–62, 35,676; see, *Estimates of School Statistics, 1971–72, Research Report 1971–R13*, Research Division, National Education Association, 1971, 6.

10. "Who Makes the Buying Decisions for Schools? Boardmen, that's Who," *American School Board Journal*, CLVII (October, 1969), 19.

11. Campbell, Cunningham, and McPhee, *op. cit.*, p. 226.

12. For an insightful analysis of various scholars' attempts to define bureaucracy, see, Keith F. Punch, "Bureaucratic Structure in Schools: Towards Redefinition and Measurement," *Educational Administration Quarterly*, V (Spring, 1969), 44–45.

13. Peter M. Blau and W. Richard Scott, *Formal Organizations: A Comparative Approach* (San Francisco: Chandler Publishing Company, 1962), pp. 32–36. Another excellent source is H. H. Gerth and C. Wright Mills (eds.) *From Max Weber: Essays in Sociology* (New York: A Galaxy Book, Oxford University Press, 1958). See especially pp. 196–244.

14. Robert K. Merton, *Social Theory and Social Structure* (Rev. and enlarged ed.; Glencoe, Ill.: The Free Press, 1957), p. 198.

15. Bidwell, *op. cit.*, p. 974.

16. Benjamin Solomon, "A Profession Taken for Granted," *The School Review*, LXIX (Autumn, 1961), 288.

17. Bidwell, *op. cit.*, p. 976.

18. See, for example, Amitai Etzioni, *Modern Organizations* (Englewood Cliffs, New Jersey: Prentice-Hall, 1964); William Kornhauser, with the assistance of Warren O. Hagstrom, *Scientists in Industry* (Berkeley and Los Angeles, Calif.: University of California Press, 1962); and Victor A. Thompson, *Modern Organization* (New York: Alfred A. Knopf, 1961).

19. Ronald G. Corwin, "Professional Persons in Public Organizations," *Educational Administration Quarterly*, I (Autumn, 1965), 1–22.

20. See James G. Anderson, "The Authority Structure of the School: System of Social Exchange," *Educational Administration Quarterly*, III (Spring,

1967), 130–48; and James G. Anderson, "The Teacher: Bureaucrat or Professional?", *Educational Administration Quarterly*, III (Autumn, 1967), 291–300.

21. Thompson, *op. cit.*

22. Ronald G. Corwin, *A Sociology of Education: Emerging Patterns of Class, Status, and Power in the Public Schools* (New York: Appleton-Century-Crofts, Educational Division, Meredith Corporation, 1965), p. 238.

23. W. Richard Scott, "Professionals in Bureaucracies–Areas of Conflict," *Professionalization*, ed. Howard M. Vollmer and Donald L. Mills (Englewood Cliffs, New Jersey: Prentice-Hall, Inc., 1966), p. 274.

24. *Ibid.*

25. *Ibid.*

26. H. S. Becker, "The Teacher in the Authority System of the Public School," *Journal of Educational Sociology*, XXVII (November, 1953), 137; as reported in Scott, *op. cit.*, p. 274.

27. Hughes suggests that the independent, fee-practicing professional's autonomy may be a myth. "The man who practices privately may, in fact, be the choreboy of his clients, doing only those things which they want in a hurry and which do not warrant the seeking out of a better known or more specialized practitioner, firm or other organization. He may thus have little or no choice of what kinds of work he will do. The man in the larger organization may apply himself to some line of work and become so proficient in it that he need not accept any work not to his taste." Everett C. Hughes, "Professions," *Daedalus: The Professions*, XCII Journal of the American Academy of Arts and Sciences, Boston, Mass. (Fall, 1963), 665–66.

28. Blau and Scott, *op. cit.*, p. 63

29. Luvern L. Cunningham, "Collective Negotiations and the Principalship," *Theory Into Practice*, VII (April, 1968), 68.

### Notes to Chapter 7 *et al,*

*T. M. Stinnett, Jack H. Kleinmann, Martha L. Ware, *Professional Negotiation in Public Education* (New York: The Macmillan Company, 1966), p. 18.

**Kenneth Melley, "The State Education Association as an Instrument for Change–Emphasis on Negotiations," *Above the Salt: Militancy in Education, Proceedings of the Mont Chateau Conference on Collective Negotiations in Education*, ed. Harold I. Goodwin and Patrick W. Carlton (Morgantown, W. Va.: College of Human Resources and Education, West Virginia University, and West Virginia Education Association, March, 1968), p. 17.

***Jack R. Frymier, "Teacher Power, Negotiations, and the Roads Ahead," *Theory Into Practice*, VII, The Ohio State University (April, 1968), 104.

****National Council of Churches, as quoted in *In the Public Interest* (Washington, D.C.: Citizens Committee for Equal Justice for Public Employees, n.d.), p. 17.

1. Section 8 (d) *Labor Management Relations Act, 1947.*

2. Another definition that applies more directly to education is "A set of procedures to provide an orderly method for teachers associations and school boards through professional channels to negotiate on matters of common concern, to reach mutually satisfactory agreement on these matters, and to establish educational channels for mediation and appeal in the event of impasse." *Profes-*

sional *Negotiations with School Boards, A Legal Analysis and Review: School Law Series, Research Report 1965–R3* (Washington, D.C.: Research Division, National Education Association, 1965), p. 15.

3. Chester M. Nolte, *Status and Scope of Collective Bargaining in Education* (Eugene, Oregon: ERIC Clearinghouse on Educational Administration, University of Oregon, 1970), pp. 13–14.

4. John J. Horvat, "The Nature of Teacher Power and Teacher Attitudes Toward Certain Aspects of This Power," *Theory Into Practice*, The Ohio State University, VII (April, 1968), 51.

5. Myron Lieberman, *The Future of Public Education* (Chicago: The University of Chicago Press, 1960), p. 179.

6. Marilyn Gittell and T. Edward Hollander, *Six Urban School Systems: A Comparative Study of Instructional Response* (New York: Frederick A. Praeger Publishers, 1968).

7. "The index is based on the perceptions of teacher leaders. In each policy domain, each of the six participants has been assigned a score of two for every attribution of 'much' power and one for every attribution of 'some' power. Scores have been added, giving a total power attribution figure for each city." See Alan Rosenthal, *Pedagogues and Power: Teacher Groups in School Politics* (Syracuse, New York: Syracuse University Press, 1969), p. 130.

8. *Ibid.*, p. 175.

9. Myron Lieberman, "Power and Policy in Teaching," Bulletin of the School of Education, XL, Indiana University (September, 1964), 28.

10. *NEA Research Memo*, Research Memo 1971–18, Research Division, National Education Association (December, 1971), p. 5.

11. Nolte, *op. cit.*

12. "Classroom Teacher Negotiation Agreement: Three Years' Experience," *Negotiation Research Digest*, III, Research Division, National Education Association (June, 1970), 22.

13. *Ibid.*

14. *Ibid.*, p. 24.

15. "1970–71 Survey of Written Negotiation Agreements," *Negotiation Research Digest*, IV, Research Division, National Education Association (June, 1971), 19.

16. "Chief Negotiator for the Administrator–Board Team," *ERS Information Aid*, No. 3; Operated jointly by the American Association of School Administrators and the Research Division, National Education Association (February, 1970), 2.

17. Michael H. Moskow, *Teachers and Unions* (Philadelphia, Pa.: University of Pennsylvania, Wharton School of Finance and Commerce, Industrial Research Unit, 1966), pp. 196–208.

18. The following sections of this chapter draw heavily upon the insightful analysis of teacher militancy by Richard C. Williams, "Teacher Militancy: Implications for the School," *Social and Technological Change: Implications for Education*, ed. Philip K. Piele and Terry L. Eidell (Eugene, Oregon: The Center for the Advanced Study of Educational Administration, University of Oregon, 1970), pp. 69–118.

19. Adapted from Williams, *Ibid.*, pp. 78–85.

20. *Time*, October 31, 1969, p. 68.

21. Rosenthal, *op. cit.*, p. 15.

22. John Kenneth Galbraith, *American Capitalism: The Concept of Countervailing Power* (Boston: Houghton Mifflin Company, 1952).

23. Harold I. Goodwin and Gerald W. Thompson, "Teacher Militancy and Countervailing Power," *The Collective Dilemma: Negotiations in Education*, ed. Patrick W. Carlton and Harold I. Goodwin (Worthington, Ohio: Charles A. Jones Publishing Company, 1969), p. 275.

24. Cyrus F. Smythe, *Introduction to Teacher-Administrator-School Board Relationships* (Minneapolis, Minn.: University of Minnesota, 1967); as summarized in Williams, *op. cit.*, pp. 76–77.

25. National Education Association, Research Division, "Teacher Opinion Poll," July, 1971.

26. National Education Association, *Addresses and Proceedings*, 100th Annual Meeting of NEA, Denver (Washington, D.C.: The Association, 1962), p. 175.

27. National Education Association, Research Division, "Teacher Opinion Poll," July, 1971.

28. James Cass, "Politics and Education in the Sunshine State—The Florida Story," *Theory Into Practice*, VII (April, 1968), 95.

29. Patrick W. Carlton, "Educator Attitudes and Value Differences in Collective Negotiations," *The Collective Dilemma: Negotiations in Education*, ed. Patrick W. Carlton and Harold I. Goodwin (Worthington, Ohio: Charles A. Jones Publishing Company, 1969), p. 25. Used by permission of *The High School Journal*.

30. W. Willard Wirtz, "Public Employment and Public Policy," *Readings on Collective Negotiations in Public Education*, ed. Stanley M. Elam et al. (Chicago: Rand McNally & Company, 1967), p. 8.

31. Citizens Committee for Equal Justice for Public Employees, *In the Public Interest* (Washington, D.C.: The Committee, n.d.).

32. Williams, *op. cit.*, pp. 86–103; Williams acknowledges that much of the content of this section is based on that of Joseph Garbarino, "Professional Negotiations in Education," *Industrial Relations* (February, 1968), 93–106.

33. Ronald G. Corwin, "Professional Persons in Public Organizations," *Educational Administration Quarterly*, I (Autumn, 1965), 1–22.

34. Richard C. Williams, "An Academic Alternative to Collective Negotiations," *Phi Delta Kappan*, LXIX (June, 1968), 573.

35. *Ibid.*

36. Patrick W. Carlton, "Social and Attitudinal Correlates of Collective Negotiations in Education," *ISR Journal* (Winter, 1969), 33–35.

37. *Ibid.*

### Notes to Chapter 8

*Teachers and School Committees: Negotiations in Good Faith* (Cambridge, Mass.: The New England Development Council, September, 1967), reprinted in *The Collective Dilemma: Negotiations in Education*, eds., Patrick W. Carlton and Harold I. Goodwin (Worthington, Ohio: Charles A. Jones Publishing Company, 1969), p. 78. Used by permission of Albert Shanker.

**Luvern L. Cunningham, "Collective Negotiations and the Principalship," *Theory Into Practice*, VII (April, 1968), 63.

***John G. Sperling, *QuEST Paper on Collective Bargaining and the*

*Teaching-Learning Process, 11* (Washington, D.C.: Department of Research, American Federation of Teachers, August, 1970), p. 8.

****Ronald G. Corwin, "Professional Persons in Public Organizations," *Educational Administration Quarterly*, I (Autumn, 1965), 20.

1. Frank W. Lutz, Lou Kleinman, and Sy Evans, *Grievances and Their Resolution: Problems in School Personnel Administration* (Danville, Ill.: The Interstate Printers & Publishers, Inc., 1967), p. 84. The authors divide the principal's loss of power into four categories: bureaucratization and role modification, changing employment relationships and principal leadership, staff leadership and grievance resolution, principal-staff relations.

2. *Ibid.*, p. 82.

3. William R. Beck, "The Teachers and the Principal," *Perspectives on the Changing Role of the Principal*, comp. and ed. Richard W. Saxe (Springfield, Ill.: Charles C. Thomas Publisher, 1968), p. 80.

4. Dan C. Lortie, "The Balance of Control and Autonomy in Elementary School Teaching," *The Semi-Professions and Their Organization: Teachers, Nurses, Social Workers*, ed. Amitai Etzioni (New York: © 1969 by The Free Press, A Division of The Macmillan Company, pp. 7–9.

5. *Ibid.*, p. 8.

6. See William E. Griffiths, "Student Constitutional Rights: The Role of the Principal," *The Bulletin of the National Association of Secondary School Principals*, LII (September, 1968), 30–37; also the American Civil Liberties Union, *Academic Freedom in the Secondary Schools* (New York: The American Civil Liberties Union, 1968).

7. "The Teacher's View of Authority Given Principals," *NEA Research Bulletin*, XLVIII (December, 1970), 125–26.

8. Charles E. Bidwell, "The School as a Formal Organization," *Handbook of Organizations*, ed. James G. March (Chicago: Rand McNally & Company, 1965), p. 1013.

9. Clagett G. Smith and Arnold S. Tannenbaum, "Organizational Control Structure: A Comparative Analysis," *Human Relations*, XVI (November, 1963), 299–316.

10. Personal correspondence with Ellwood Erickson, staff associate, National Education Association.

11. Richard E. Walton and Robert B. McKersie, *A Behavioral Theory of Labor Negotiations:* An Analysis of a Social Interaction System (New York: McGraw-Hill Book Co., 1965).

12. Amitai Etzioni, *Modern Organizations* (Englewood Cliffs, New Jersey: Prentice-Hall, Inc., 1964).

13. Donald C. Klein, *Community Dynamics and Mental Health* (New York: John Wiley & Sons, Inc., 1968), p. 48.

14. Morton R. Godine, "Collective Negotiations and Public Policy, with Special Reference to Public Education," *Readings on Collective Negotiations in Public Education*, ed. Stanley M. Elam et al. (Chicago: Rand McNally & Company, 1967), p. 33.

15. Edwin M. Bridges, "Bureaucratic Role and Socialization: The Influence of Experience on the Elementary Principal," *Educational Administration Quarterly*, I (Spring, 1965), 26–27.

16. Donald A. Myers, "The Principal as a Procedural Administrator," *The National Elementary Principal*, XLVII (February, 1968), 25–29.

17. Richard Schmuck and Jack Nelson, "The Principal as Convener of Organizational Problem Solving," Center for the Advanced Study of Educational Administration, University of Oregon, Mimeographed, p. 2; also, see Arthur Blumberg, William Wayson, and Wilford Weber, "The Elementary School Cabinet: Report of an Experience in Participative Decision Making, *Educational Administration Quarterly*, V (Autumn, 1969), 39–52.

18. John Martin Rich, *Education and Human Values* (Reading, Mass.: Addison-Wesley Publishing Company, 1968), p. 63.

19. Ronald G. Corwin, "Professional Persons in Public Organizations," *Educational Administration Quarterly*, I (Autumn, 1965), 17.

20. Keith Goldhammer and Gerald L. Becker, "What Makes a Good Elementary School Principal?", *American Education*, VI (April, 1970), 11–13.

21. Corwin, *op. cit.*, p. 17.

22. Edwin M. Bridges, "Administrative Man: Origin or Pawn in Decision Making?", *Educational Administration Quarterly*, VI (Winter, 1970), 7–25.

23. Joseph J. Azzarelli, "Coda," *Struggle for Power in Education*, ed. Frank W. Lutz and Joseph J. Azzarelli (New York: The Center for Applied Research in Education, Inc., 1966), p. 112.

24. Luvern L. Cunningham, "Implication of Collective Negotiations for the Role of the Principal," *Readings on Collective Negotiations in Public Education,* ed. Stanley M. Elam et al. (Chicago: Rand McNally & Company, 1967), p. 310.

25. There has been very little theoretical research conducted on the role of the superintendent concerning collective bargaining. Most of the writing have been weak laments ranging from the superintendent as an instructional leader, to "how to do it" articles on collective bargaining; see, for example, Walter W. Scott, "Collective Negotiations: Implications for Preparation of Administrators," (pp. 81–96); and Roy B. Allen, "Implications of Collective Negotiation for the Role of Superintendent," *Collective Negotiations and Educational Administration*, ed. Roy B. Allen and John Schmid (Fayetteville, Arkansas: College of Education, University of Arkansas, and Columbus, Ohio: University Council for Educational Administration, 1966), pp. 115–26.

26. Jack F. Parker, "Let's Abolish the NEA," *Phi Delta Kappan*, XLIX (June, 1968), 569.

27. Bernard E. Donovan, "Negotiations: Ten Years Later," *The Bulletin of the National Association of Secondary School Principals: Collective Negotiations*, LV (December, 1971), 44.

28. *Negotiation Research Digest, op. cit.*

29. Laurence Iannaccone, "The Future of State Politics of Education," *Struggle for Power in Education*, ed. Frank W. Lutz and Joseph Azzarelli (New York: The Center for Applied Research in Education, Inc., 1966), p. 65.


### Notes to Chapter 9

*Richard C. Williams, "Teacher Militancy: Implications for the Schools," *Social and Technological Change: Implications for Education*, ed. Philip K. Piele, Terry L. Eidell, with Stuart C. Smith (Eugene, Oregon: The Center for the Advanced Study of Educational Administration, University of Oregon, 1970), p. 109.

**Kenneth Melley, as quoted in *Above the Salt: Militancy in Education, Proceedings of Mont Chateau Conference on Collective Negotiations in Education,* ed. Harold I. Goodwin and Patrick W. Carlton (Morgantown, West Va.: College of Human Resources and Education, West Virginia University, and West Virginia Education Association, March, 1968), pp. 72–73.

***Amitai Etzioni, "Schools as a 'Guidable' System," *Freedom, Bureaucracy & Schooling*, 1971 Yearbook of the Association for Supervision and Curriculum Development, ed. Vernon F. Haubrich (Washington, D.C.: The Association, 1971), p. 41.

1. James A. Craft, *Professionalism, Unionism, and Collective Negotiation: Teacher Negotiations Experience in California* (Lafayette, Indiana: Institute for Research in the Behavioral, Economic, and Management Sciences, Herman C. Krannert Graduate School of Industrial Administration, 1970), pp. 1–20.

2. James Cass, "Politics and Education in the Sunshine State—The Florida Story," *Theory Into Practice*, VII (April, 1968), 95.

3. A reviewer of the manuscript asked if physicians should do the same. My reply was that they do, but the two occupations are hardly comparable in this respect. The average physician is not asked to support himself and his dependents on less than $10,000 per year.

4. B. Othanel Smith in collaboration with Saul B. Cohen and Arthur· Pearl, *Teachers for the Real World* (Washington, D.C.: American Association of Colleges for Teacher Education, 1969), p. 9.

5. William J. Goode, "The Theoretical Limits of Professionalization," *The Semi-Professions and Their Organization: Teachers, Nurses, Social Workers*, ed. Amitai Etzioni (New York: © 1969 by The Free Press, A Division of The Macmillan Company, p. 288.

6. Marilyn Gittell, "Supervisors and Coordinators: Power in the System," ·*Freedom, Bureaucracy, & Schooling*, 1971 Yearbook of the Association for Supervision and Curriculum Development, ed. Vernon F. Haubrich (Washington, D.C.: The Association, 1971), p. 171.

7. Stephen Zeluck, "The UFT Strike: Will it Destroy the AFT?", *Phi Delta Kappan*, L (January, 1969), 253.

8. Frances Fox Piven, "Militant Civil Servants in New York City," *Trans-Action*, VII (November, 1969).

9. *Ibid.*, p. 55.

10. Ronald G. Corwin, "Teacher Militancy in the United States: Reflections on its Sources and Prospects," *Theory Into Practice*, VII, The Ohio State University (April, 1968), 101.

11: Donald C. Klein, *Community Dynamics and Mental Health* (New York: John Wiley & Sons, Inc., 1968).

12. *Ibid.*, p. 141.

13. Jean-François Revel, "Without Marx or Jesus," *Saturday Review*, LIV (July 24, 1971), 15–17.

14. Amitai Etzioni, "Schools as a 'Guidable' System," *Freedom, Bureaucracy, & Schooling*, 1971 Yearbook of the Association for Supervision and Curriculum Development, ed. Vernon F. Haubrich (Washington, D.C.: The Association, 1971), p. 44.

15. Gittell, *op. cit.*, p. 171.

16. See Raymond E. Callahan, *Education and the Cult of Efficiency* (Chicago: The University of Chicago Press, 1962); and Herbert M. Kliebard, "Bureaucracy and Curriculum Theory," *Freedom, Bureaucracy, & Schooling, op. cit.*, pp. 74–93.

17. Irving A. Yuvish, "Decentralization, Discipline, and the Disadvantaged Teacher," *Phi Delta Kappan*, L (November, 1968), 179.

18. Girard D. Hottleman, *The Place of Negotiations in the Improvement of Curriculum and Instruction*, Massachusetts Teachers Association, n.d., pp. 1–2.

19. Girard D. Hottleman, *Negotiations for the Improvement of Professional Standards and Performance*, Prepared for the National Commission on Teacher Education and Professional Standards (Washington, D.C.: National Education Association, n.d.), pp. 2–4.

20. John I. Goodlad, "The Schools vs. Education," *Saturday Review*, LII (April 19, 1969), 61.

21. Bob Bhaerman, "A Paradigm for Accountability," *QuEST Paper on a Paradigm for Accountability, 12* (Washington, D.C.: Department of Research, American Federation of Teachers, n.d.), p. 3.

22. Philip W. Jackson, "Old Dogs and New Tricks: Observations on the Continuing Education of Teachers," *Improving In-Service Education: Proposals and Procedures for Change*, ed. Louis J. Rubin (Boston: Allyn and Bacon, Inc., 1971), pp. 30–31.

23. Robert D. Bhaerman, "Several Educators' Cure for the Common Cold, Among Other Things," *QuEST Paper 7* (Washington, D.C.: Department of Research, American Federation of Teachers, n.d.), pp. 9–10.

24. As reported in *QuEST Paper 3* (Washington, D.C.: Department of Research, American Federation of Teachers, n.d.), p. 4.

25. James G. Anderson, "The Teacher: Bureaucrat or Professional?", *Educational Administration Quarterly*, III (Autumn, 1967), 298.

26. Richard C. Williams, "Teacher Militancy: Implications for the Schools," *Social and Technological Change: Implications for Education*, ed. Philip K. Piele and Terry L. Eidell (Eugene, Oregon: The Center for the Advanced Study of Educational Administration, University of Oregon, 1970), p. 107.

27. Knut Akerlund, as told to Floyd L. Bergman, *Phi Delta Kappan*, LI (April, 1970), 430–32.

28. Myron Lieberman, "Implications of the Coming NEA-AFT Merger," *Phi Delta Kappan*, L (November, 1968), 139–44.

29. Jack R. Frymier (ed.), "Teacher Power," *Theory Into Practice*, VII (April, 1968), 49.

30. B. Dean Bowles, "The Power Structure in State Education Policies," *Phi Delta Kappan*, XLIX (February, 1968), 339–40.

31. See, *Teacher Supply and Demand in Public Schools, 1970, Research Report 1970-R14* (Washington, D.C.: Research Division, National Education Association, 1970). This is the 23rd annual survey of the supply and demand for public-school teachers.

32. Robert N. Bush, "The Status of the Career Teacher: Its Effect Upon the Teacher Dropout Problem," *The Teacher Dropout*, ed. T. M. Stinnett (Bloomington, Indiana: Phi Delta Kappa, Incorporated, 1970), p. 115.

33. Ronald G. Corwin, *A Sociology of Education: Emerging Patterns of Class, Status, and Power in the Public Schools*, (New York: Appleton-Century-Crofts, Educational Division, Meredith Corporation, 1965), p. 419.

34. Robert D. Bhaerman, "Education's New Dualisms," *QuEST Paper on Paraprofessionals and Professionalism, 8* (Washington: D.C.: Department of Research, American Federation of Teachers, n.d.), pp. 1–8.

35. J. M. Stevens, *The Process of Schooling: A Psychological Examination*

(New York: Holt, Rinehart and Winston, Inc., 1967), p. 75. He points out that against this overwhelming mass of negative results, there are some exceptions.

36. Martin N. Olson, "Classroom Variables that Predict School System Quality," *IAR Research Bulletin*, XI (November, 1970), 8.

37. Fenwick English, *Differentiated Staffing: Giving Teachers a Chance to Improve Learning* (Tallahassee, Fla.: Florida State Department of Education, September, 1968), pp. 5–6.

38. Adapted from *QuEST Papers 2, 7, 8, and 12*; as well as a policy statement entitled *American Federation of Teachers' Statement on Vertical Staffing*, submitted to the Bureau of Educational Personnel Development, U.S. Office of Education (March, 1971), written largely, but not exclusively, by Robert Bhaerman, director of educational research, AFT.

39. Bhaerman, "Several Educators' Cure for the Common Cold, Among Other Things," *QuEST Paper 7, op. cit.*, p. 5.

40. *American Federation of Teachers' Statement on Vertical Staffing*, submitted to the Bureau of Educational Personnel Development, USOE (March, 1971), pp. 3–7.

41. Bruce R. Joyce, *The Teacher and His Staff: Man, Media, and Machines* (Washington, D.C.: National Commission on Teacher Education and Professional Standards and Center for the Study of Instruction, National Education Association, 1967).

42. Leon Lessinger, "Engineering Accountability for Results in Public Education," *Phi Delta Kappan*, LII (December, 1970), 217.

43. As quoted in *American Teacher*, LVI (January, 1972), 17.

44. Robert Bhaerman, "Accountability for Reading," *American Teacher*, LVI (January, 1972), 18.

45. *Ibid.*


## Notes to Chapter 10

*Myron Lieberman, *The Future of Public Education* (Chicago: The University of Chicago Press, 1960), p. 178.

**William J. Goode, "Encroachment, Charlatanism, and the Emerging Profession: Psychology, Sociology, and Medicine," *American Sociological Review*, XXV (December, 1960), 903.

***D. D. Darland, "Preparation in the Governance of the Profession," *Teachers for the Real World* (Washington, D.C.: The American Association of Colleges for Teacher Education, 1969), p. 135.

****Joseph Featherstone, "The British and Us," *The New Republic*, September 11, 1971, p. 25. From *Informal Schools in Britain Today*, An Introduction by Joseph Featherstone, © Schools Council Publications, 1971. Used by permission of Citation Press, a division of Scholastic Magazines, Inc.

1. National Education Association, Research Division, "Pennsylvania: Teachers Trade Pay Raise for Kindergarten Program," *National Research Digest*, IV (September, 1970), 14.

2. Memorandum from Bob Bhaerman to Al Loewenthal, April 7, 1971, mimeographed, p. 1. Used by permission of Bob Bhaerman.

3. "Curriculum Review in Negotiation Agreements," *NEA Research Bulletin*, XLVIII (December, 1970), 106–108.

4. See *Design for an Effective School Program in Urban Centers* (Washington, D.C.: American Federation of Teachers, AFL-CIO, 1965).

5. David Selden, "Giant Step Toward Teacher Unity," *American Teacher*, V (May, 1972), 2B.

6. "Governance of the Profession," *Today's Education*, LX (December, 1971), 21.

7. D. D. Darland, "The Profession's Quest for Responsibility and Accountability," *Phi Delta Kappan*, LII (September, 1970), 42.

8. *Article XVII*—Staff Evaluation and Development Program (SED), Washington Teachers Union, AFT (Rev.; March 28, 1971).

9. *Ibid.*, p. 1.

10. *The QuEST for Educational Change* (Washington, D.C.: American Federation of Teachers, n.d.), p. 3.

11. *NEA Reporter*, II (February, 1972), 1.

12. James W. Becker, Assistant Executive Secretary for Instruction and Professional Development, NEA; interview as reported in *The Challenger*, I, New York State Teachers Association Newspaper (December 3, 1971), 9.

13. See Girard D. Hottleman, "Negotiations for the Improvement of Professional Standards and Performance," Prepared for the National Commission on Teacher Education and Professional Standards, National Education Association, n.d.

14. Richard Williams, "A Proposal for Improving the Selection and Evaluation of Public School Teachers," Paper distributed at Institute for Development of Educational Activities, Research Division, May 4, 1970, pp. 1–7. (Mimeographed.)

15. Myron Lieberman, *Education as a Profession* (Englewood Cliffs, New Jersey: Prentice-Hall, Inc., 1956), p. vii.

16. J. M. Paton, "Trade Union or Professional Association? The Canadian Experience," *Phi Delta Kappan*, XLIX (June, 1968), 565.

# SELECTED BIBLIOGRAPHY

Akerlund, Knut. As told to Floyd L. Bergman. "Schools, Strikes, and Students: Swedish Style." *Phi Delta Kappan*, LI (April, 1970), 430–32.

Allen, Roy B., and Schmid, John (eds.). *Collective Negotiations and Educational Administration*. Fayetteville, Arkansas: College of Education, University of Arkansas, and Columbus, Ohio: University Council for Educational Administration.

American Association of School Administrators. "School Administrators View Professional Negotiations." *Readings on Collective Negotiations in Public Education*. Edited by Stanley M. Elam, Myron Lieberman, and Michael H. Moskow. Chicago: Rand McNally & Company, 1967, pp. 203–18.

American Federation of Teachers. *1971–72 Catalogue of AFT Publications*. Washington, D.C.: American Federation of Teachers.

*American Federation of Teachers' Statement on Vertical Staffing*. A policy statement from the AFT to the Bureau of Educational Personnel Development, U.S. Office of Education, March, 1971.

*American Teacher*. Published monthly except July and August by the American Federation of Teachers, AFL-CIO, 1012 14th Street, N.W., Washington, D.C. $5 to non-members.

Anderson, James G. "The Authority Structure of the School: System of Social Exchange." *Educational Administration Quarterly*, III (Spring, 1967), 130–48.

———. "The Teacher: Bureaucrat or Professional?" *Educational Administration Quarterly*, III (Autumn, 1967), 291–300.

Arnold, Owen G., and Taylor, John Gordon. *Teacher-School Board Negotiations: A Bibliography*. Bloomington, Indiana: Phi Delta Kappa, Inc., 1967. Revised edition in 1968, by Neville L. Robertson. $1.00.

Arnstine, Donald. "Freedom and Bureaucracy in the Schools." *Freedom, Bureaucracy, & Schooling*. Edited by Vernon F. Haubrich. Washington, D.C.: Association for Supervision and Curriculum Development, 1971, pp. 3–28.

Association for Supervision and Curriculum Development. *Freedom, Bureaucracy, & Schooling*. 1971 Yearbook of the Association for Supervision and Curriculum Development. Edited by Vernon F. Haubrich. Washington, D.C.: The Association, 1971.

Bailey, Stephen K. "Teachers' Centers: A British First." *Phi Delta Kappan*, LIII (November, 1971), 146–49.

Barber, Bernard. "Some Problems in the Sociology of the Professions." *Daedalus: The Professions*, XCII (Fall, 1963), 669–88.

Barstow, Robbins. "Connecticut's Teacher Negotiation Law: An Early Analysis," *Phi Delta Kappan*, XLVII (March, 1966), 345–51.

Becker, Howard S. "The Nature of a Profession." *Education for the Professions*. The Sixty-First Yearbook of the National Society for the Study of Education. Part II. Edited by Nelson B. Henry. Chicago: University of Chicago Press, 1962, pp. 27–46.

Bendiner, Robert. *The Politics of Schools: A Crisis in Self-Government*. New York: Harper & Row Publishers, 1969.

Bennis, Warren G. *Changing Organizations*. New York: McGraw-Hill Book Company, 1966.

———. "Post-Bureaucratic Leadership." *Trans-Action*, VI (November, 1969), 44–51, 61.

Benson, Charles S. "Collective Negotiations and the Rule of Seniority." *Readings on Collective Negotiations in Public Education*. Edited by Stanley M. Elam, Myron Lieberman, and Michael H. Moskow. Chicago: Rand McNally & Company, 1967, pp. 433–37.

Bhaerman, Robert. "A Paradigm for Accountability." *QuEST Paper on a Paradigm for Accountability, 12*. Washington, D.C.: Department of Research, American Federation of Teachers.

——. "Needed: A Conceptual Framework for Collective Bargaining in Education." *QuEST Paper on a Conceptual Framework for Collective Bargaining, 9*. Washington, D.C.: Department of Research, American Federation of Teachers.

——. "Several Educators' Cure for the Common Cold, Among Other Things or One Unionist View of Staff Differentiation." *QuEST Paper, 7*. Washington, D.C.: Department of Research, American Federation of Teachers.

——. *QuEST Paper on Paraprofessionals and Professionalism, 8*. Washington, D.C.: Department of Research, American Federation of Teachers.

——. "Which Way for Teacher Certification?" *QuEST Paper, 2*. Washington, D.C.: Department of Research, American Federation of Teachers. (Reprinted from *American Teacher*, February, 1969.)

Bidwell, Charles E. "The School as a Formal Organization." *Handbook of Organizations*. Edited by James G. March. Chicago: Rand McNally & Company, 1965, pp. 972–1022.

Bishop, Leslee J. *Collective Negotiation in Curriculum and Instruction: Questions and Concerns*. Washington, D.C.: Association for Supervision and Curriculum Development, 1967.

Blau, Peter M., and Scott, W. Richard. *Formal Organizations: A Comparative Approach*. San Francisco: Chandler Publishing Company, 1962.

Blumberg, Arthur, Wayson, William, and Weber, Wilford. "The Elementary School Cabinet: Report of an Experience in Participative Decision-Making." *Educational Administration Quarterly*, V (Autumn, 1969), 39–52.

Bowles, B. Dean. "The Power Structure in State Education Politics." *Phi Delta Kappan*, XLIX (February, 1968), 337–40.

Boyan, Norman J. "The Emergent Role of the Teacher and the Authority Structure of the School." *Collective Negotiations and Educational Administration*. Edited by Roy B. Allen and John Schmid. Fayetteville, Arkansas: College of Education, University of Arkansas; and Columbus, Ohio: University Council for Educational Administration, 1966, pp. 1–21.

Bridges, Edwin M. "Administrative Man: Origin or Pawn in Decision Making." *Educational Administration Quarterly*, VI (Winter, 1970), 7–25.

——. "Bureaucratic Role and Socialization: The Influence of Experience on the Elementary Principal." *Educational Administration Quarterly*, I (Spring, 1965), 19–28.

Brubacher, John S. "The Evolution of Professional Education." *Education for the Professions*. The Sixty-First Yearbook of the National Society for the Study of Education. Part II. Edited by Nelson B. Henry. Chicago: The University of Chicago Press, 1962, pp. 47–67.

Callahan, Raymond E. "The History of the Fight to Control Policy in Public Education." *Struggle for Power in Education*. Edited by Frank W. Lutz and Joseph Azzarelli. New York: The Center for Applied Research in Education, Inc., 1966, pp. 16–34.

Campbell, Roald F., Cunningham, Luvern L., and McPhee, Roderick F. *The Organization and Control of American Schools*. Columbus, Ohio: Charles E. Merrill Books, Inc., 1965.

Carlton, Patrick W. "Educator Attitudes and Value Differences in Collective Negotiations." *The High School Journal*, LII (October, 1968), 10–21.

———. "Teacher-Administrator-Board Salary Negotiations in Oregon." *Above the Salt: Militancy in Education. Proceedings of Mont Chateau Conference on Collective Negotiations in Education*. Edited by Harold I. Goodwin and Patrick W. Carlton. Morgantown, West Va.: College of Human Resources and Education, West Virginia University, and West Virginia Education Association, March, 1968, pp. 22–28.

———. and Goodwin, Harold I. (eds.). *The Collective Dilemma: Negotiations in Education*. Worthington, Ohio: Charles A. Jones Publishing Company, 1969.

Carr-Saunders, Alexander Morris, and Wilson, P. A. *The Professions*. Oxford, England: The Clarendon Press, 1933.

Cass, James. "Politics and Education in the Sunshine State–The Florida Story." *Saturday Review*, LI (April 20, 1968), 63–65, 76–79.

Charters, Jr., W. W. "The Social Background of Teaching." *Handbook of Research on Teaching*. Edited by N. L. Gage. Chicago: Rand McNally & Company, 1963, pp. 715–813.

"Chief Negotiator for the Administrator–Board Team." *ERS Information Aid*. No. 3 (February, 1970). Washington, D.C.: Educational Research Service, 18.

Citizens Committee for Equal Justice for Public Employees. *In the Public Interest*. Washington, D.C.: The Committee, P. O. Box 28086, n.d.

Cogan, Charles. "The American Federation of Teachers and Collective Negotiations." *Readings on Collective Negotiations in Public Education*. Edited by Stanley M. Elam, Myron Lieberman, and Michael H. Moskow. Chicago: Rand McNally & Company, 1967, pp. 162–72.

———. "The American Federation of Teachers–Force for Change." *Above the Salt: Militancy in Education. Proceedings of Mont Chateau Conference on Collective Negotiations in Education*. Edited by Harold I. Goodwin and Patrick W. Carlton. Morgantown, West Va.: College of Human Resources and Education, West Virginia University, and West Virginia Education, March, 1968, pp. 37–42.

Cole, Stephen. "The Unionization of Teachers: Determinants of Rank-and-File Support." *Sociology of Education*, XLI (Winter, 1968), 66–87.

Conant, James Bryant. *The Education of American Teachers*. New York: McGraw-Hill Book Company, Inc., 1963.

Conrad, Donald L. "Collective Negotiations and Professionalism." *Readings on Collective Negotiations in Public Education*. Edited by Stanley M. Elam, Myron Lieberman, and Michael H. Moskow. Chicago: Rand McNally & Company, 1967, pp. 405–11.

Corey, Arthur F. "Educational Power and the Teaching Profession." *Phi Delta Kappan*, XLIX (February, 1968), 331–34.

———. *The Responsibility of the Organized Profession for the Improvement of Instruction*. Washington, D.C.: National Education Association, Center for the Study of Instruction, 1966.

Corwin, Ronald G. *A Sociology of Education: Emerging Patterns of Class, Status, and Power in the Public Schools*. New York: Appleton-Century-Crofts, 1965.

Corwin, Ronald G. "Education and the Sociology of Complex Organizations." *On Education—Sociological Perspectives*. Edited by Donald A. Hansen and Joel E. Gerstl. New York: John Wiley & Sons, Inc., 1967, pp. 156–223.

——. "Professional Persons in Public Organizations." *Educational Administration Quarterly*, I (Autumn, 1965), 1–22. Reprinted also in Stanley M. Elam et al. (eds.). *Readings on Collective Negotiations in Public Education*. Chicago: Rand McNally & Company, 1967, pp. 47–67.

——. "Teacher Militancy in the United States: Reflections on Its Sources and Prospects. *Theory Into Practice*, The Ohio State University VII (April, 1968), 96–102.

——. "The Anatomy of Militant Professionalization." *Above the Salt: Militancy in Education. Proceedings of Mont Chateau Conference on Collective Negotiations in Education*. Edited by Harold I. Goodwin and Patrick W. Carlton. Morgantown, West Va.: College of Human Resources and Education, West Virginia University, and West Virginia Education Association, March, 1968, pp. 55–61.

Craft, James A. *Professionalism, Unionism, and Collective Negotiation: Teacher Negotiations Experience in California*. Paper No. 284, July, 1970, Lafayette, Ind.: Institute for Research in the Behavioral, Economic, and Management Sciences, Herman C. Krannert Graduate School of Industrial Administration.

Cronin, Joseph H. "School Boards and Principals—Before and After Negotiations." *Phi Delta Kappan*, XLIX (November, 1967), 123–27.

Cunningham, Luvern L. "Collective Negotiations and the Principalship." *Theory Into Practice*, The Ohio State University VII (April, 1968), 62–70.

——. "Implication of Collective Negotiations for the Role of the Principal." *Readings on Collective Negotiations in Public Education*. Edited by Stanley M. Elam, Myron Lieberman, and Michael H. Moskow. Chicago: Rand McNally & Company, 1967, pp. 298–313.

*Daedalus: The Professions,* XCII (Fall, 1963), 647–865.

Darland, D. D. "The Profession's Quest for Responsibility and Accountability," *Phi Delta Kappan*, LII (September, 1970), 41–44.

Davis, Bertram H. "Unions and Higher Education: Another View." *Educational Record*, XLIX (Spring, 1968), 139–44. A reply to Davis' thesis by Kugler is offered in a subsequent issue (XLIX, Fall, 1968) of the same journal.

Dershimer, Richard A. "Professional Educational Organizations." *Encyclopedia of Educational Research*. Edited by Robert L. Ebel. 4th ed. New York: The Macmillan Company, 1969, pp. 1008–16.

Doherty, Robert E. "Labor Relations Negotiations on Bargaining: Factories vs. the Schools." *The Collective Dilemma: Negotiations in Education*. Edited by Patrick W. Carlton and Harold I. Goodwin. Worthington, Ohio: Charles A. Jones Publishing Company, 1969, pp. 218–28.

——. "Teacher Bargaining: The Relevance of Private Sector Experience." *The Collective Dilemma: Negotiations in Education*. Edited by Patrick W. Carlton and Harold I. Goodwin. Worthington, Ohio: Charles A Jones Publishing Company, 1969, pp. 187–96.

——, and Oberer, Walter E. *Teachers, School Boards, and Collective Bargaining: A Changing of the Guard*. Ithaca, New York: New York State School of Industrial Labor Relations, a Statutory College of the State University, Cornell University, 1967.

Donovan, Bernard E. "Collective Bargaining vs. Professional Negotiations." *School Management,* IX (November, 1965), 69–71.

——. "Negotiations: Ten Years Later." *The Bulletin of the National Association of Secondary School Principals,* entitled "Collective Negotiations," LV (December, 1971), 40–48.

——. "New York City–Workshop for Teacher Militancy." *Above the Salt: Militancy in Education. Proceedings of Mont Chateau Conference on Collective Negotiations in Education.* Edited by Harold I. Goodwin and Patrick W. Carlton. Morgantown, West Va.: College of Human Resources and Education, West Virginia University, and West Virginia Education Association, March, 1968, pp. 29–36.

*Education for the Professions.* The Sixty-First Yearbook of the National Society for the Study of Education, Part II. Edited by Nelson B. Henry. Chicago: The University of Chicago Press, 1962.

Elam, Stanley M. "Prospects for an NEA-AFT Merger." *The Nation,* CCI (October 18, 1965), 247–49.

——, Lieberman, Myron, and Moskow, Michael H. (eds.). *Readings on Collective Negotiations in Public Education.* Chicago: Rand McNally & Company, 1967.

Elkin, Sol M. "Another Look at Collective Negotiations for Professionals." *School and Society,* XCVIII (March, 1970), 173–75.

English, Fenwick. *Differentiated Staffing: Giving Teaching a Chance to Improve Learning.* Tallahassee, Fla.: Florida State Department of Education, Division of Curriculum and Instruction, September, 1968.

——. "Teacher May I? Take Three Giant Steps! The Differentiated Staff." *Phi Delta Kappan,* LI (December, 1969), 211–14.

Erickson, Kai L. "New Management Figures in Michigan School Administration." *Phi Delta Kappan,* LI (April, 1970), 426–27.

Etzioni, Amitai. "Schools as a 'Guidable' System." *Freedom, Bureaucracy, and Schooling.* Edited by Vernon F. Haubrich. Washington, D.C.: Association for Supervision and Curriculum Development, 1971, pp. 29–45.

—— (ed.). *The Semi-Professions and Their Organization: Teachers, Nurses, Social Workers.* New York: The Free Press, 1969.

Evans, Seymour. "Teacher Turnover: The Persistent Problem of Manpower Waste." *ISR Journal,* I (Summer, 1969), 210–11.

Fox, Bernard A. "Bureaucratic Behavior of Principals Under a Union Contract." *The ISR Journal of Education Personnel Relation,* II (Spring, 1970), 154–59.

Frankie, Richard J., and Howe, Ray A. "Faculty Power in the Community College." *Theory Into Practice,* VII The Ohio State University (April, 1968), 83–88.

Frymier, Jack R. "Teacher Power, Negotiations, and the Roads Ahead." *Theory Into Practice,* VII The Ohio State University (April, 1968), 103–104.

Gerstl, Joel E. "Education and the Sociology of Work." *On Education– Sociological Perspectives.* Edited by Donald A. Hansen and Joel E. Gerstl. New York: John Wiley & Sons, Inc. 1967, pp. 224–61.

Gerth, H. H., and Mills, C. Wright (eds.). *From Max Weber: Essays in Sociology.* New York: A Galaxy Book, 1958.

Gittell, Marilyn. "Supervisors and Coordinators: Power in the System."

*Freedom, Bureaucracy, & Schooling.* 1971 Yearbook of the Association for Supervision and Curriculum Development. Edited by Vernon F. Haubrich. Washington, D.C.: The Association, 1971, pp. 161–73.

——. "Teacher Power and Its Implications for Urban Education." *Theory Into Practice*, VII (April, 1968), 80–82.

Godine, Morton R. "Collective Negotiations and Public Policy, with Special Reference to Public Education." *Readings on Collective Negotiations in Public Education.* Edited by Stanley M. Elam et al. Chicago: Rand McNally & Company, 1967, pp. 27–36.

Goldhammer, Keith, and Becker, Gerald L. "What Makes a Good Elementary School Principal?" *American Education*, VI (March, 1970), 11–13.

Goode, William J. "Community Within a Community: The Professions." *American Sociological Review*, XXII (February, 1957), 194–200.

——. "Encroachment, Charlatanism, and the Emerging Profession: Psychology, Sociology, and Medicine." *American Sociological Journal*, XXV (December, 1960), 902–14.

——. "The Librarian: From Occupation to Profession." *The Library Quarterly*, XXXI (October, 1961), 306–18.

——. "The Theoretical Limits of Professionalization." *The Semi-Professions and Their Organization: Teachers, Nurses, Social Workers.* Edited by Amitai Etzioni. New York: The Free Press, 1969, pp. 266–313.

Goodwin, Harold I., and Thompson, Gerald W. "Teacher Militancy and Countervailing Power." *The Collective Dilemma: Negotiations in Education.* Edited by Patrick W. Carlton and Harold I. Goodwin. Worthington, Ohio: Charles A. Jones Publishing Company, 1969, pp. 272–80.

Gould, Sir Ronald. "The Changing Role of Teachers in the Last 100 Years." *Educational Review*, XXIII (November, 1970), 3–18.

Greenwood, Ernest, "Attributes of a Profession." *Social Work*, II (July, 1957).

Griffiths, Daniel E. *Administrative Theory.* New York: Appleton-Century-Crofts, Inc.

Hall, Oswald. "The Social Structure of the Teaching Profession." *Struggle for Power in Education.* Edited by Frank W. Lutz and Joseph Azzarelli. New York: The Center for Applied Research in Education, Inc., 1966, pp. 35–48.

Hall, Richard H. "Professionalization and Bureaucratization." *American Sociological Review*, XXXIII (February, 1968), 92–104,

Hansen, Donald A., and Gerstl, Joel E. (eds.). *On Education–Sociological Perspectives.* New York: John Wiley & Sons, Inc., 1967.

Harnack, Robert S. *The Teacher: Decision Maker and Curriculum Planner.* Scranton, Pennsylvnia: International Textbook Company, 1968.

Haug, Marie R., and Sussman, Marvin B. "Professional Autonomy and the Revolt of the Client." *Social Problems*, XVII (Fall, 1969), 153–61.

Heisel, W. D., and Hallihan, J. D. *Questions & Answers on Public Employee Negotiation.* Chicago: Public Personnel Association, 1967.

Horvat, John J. "The Nature of Teacher Power and Teacher Attitudes Toward Certain Aspects of This Power." *Theory Into Practice*, The Ohio State University VII (April, 1968), 51–56.

Hottleman, Girard D. *Negotiations for the Improvement of Professional*

*Standards and Performance*. Prepared for the National Commission on Teacher Education and Professional Standards. Washington, D.C.: The National Education Association, n.d.

Hottleman, Girard D. *The Place of Negotiations in the Improvement of Curriculum and Instruction*. Boston, Mass.: Massachusetts Teachers Association, n.d.

Hughes, Everett C. "Professions." *Daedalus: The Professions*, XCII (Fall, 1963), 655–68.

Iannaccone, Laurence. "The Future of State Politics of Education." *Struggle for Power in Education*. Edited by Frank W. Lutz and Joseph Azzarelli. New York: The Center for Applied Research in Education, Inc., 1966, pp. 49–66.

——, and Lutz, Frank W. *Politics, Power and Policy: The Governing of Local School Districts*. Columbus, Ohio: Charles E. Merrill Publishing Company, 1970.

Jackson, Philip W. "Old Dogs and New Tricks: Observations on the Continuing Education of Teachers." *Improving In-Service Education: Proposals and Procedures for Change*. Edited by Louis J. Rubin. Boston: Allyn and Bacon, Inc., 1971, pp. 19–35.

Johnson, David W. "Influence on Teachers' Acceptance of Change." *The Elementary School Journal*, LXX (December, 1969), 142–53.

Katz, Fred E. "The School as a Complex Social Organization." *Harvard Educational Review*, XXXIV (Summer, 1964), 428–54.

Kimbrough, Ralph B., and Williams, James O. "An Analysis of Power Bases and Power Uses in Teacher Militancy." *The High School Journal*, LII (October, 1968), 3–9.

Kinney, Lucien B. *Certification in Education*. Englewood Cliffs, New Jersey: Prentice-Hall, Inc., 1964.

Klein, Donald C. *Community Dynamics and Mental Health*. New York: John Wiley & Sons, Inc. 1968.

Kliebard, Herbert M. "Bureaucracy and Curriculum Theory." *Freedom, Bureaucracy & Schooling*. 1971 Yearbook of the Association for Supervision and Curriculum Development, 1971. Edited by Vernon F. Haubrich. Washington, D.C.: The Association, 1971, pp. 74–93.

Knapp, Henry. "A Tribute to the 'Real' Fathers." *Phi Delta Kappan*, XLIX (June, 1968), 575–77.

Koerner, James D. *Who Controls American Education? A Guide for Laymen*. Boston: Beacon Press, 1968.

——. *The Miseducation of American Teachers*. Boston: Houghton Mifflin Company, 1963.

Kramer, Louis I. *Principals and Grievance Procedures*. Washington, D.C.: The National Association of Secondary School Principals, 1969.

Kratzman, Arthur. "The Alberta Teachers Association: A Vision Vindicated." *Phi Delta Kappan*, XLV (March, 1964), 288–92.

Kugler, Israel. "The Union Speaks for Itself." *Educational Record*, XLIX (Fall, 1968), 414–18.

Leles, Sam. "Teacher Power—What's It all About?" *Theory Into Practice*, The Ohio State University VII (April, 1968), 57–61.

Lieberman, Myron. *Education as a Profession*. Englewood Cliffs, New Jersey: Prentice-Hall, Inc., 1956.

Lieberman, Myron. "Implications of the Coming NEA-AFT Merger." *Phi Delta Kappan*, L (November, 1968), 139–44.

——. "Power and Policy in Teaching." *Bulletin of the School of Education.* Indiana University, XL (September, 1964).

——. "NEA-AFT Merger: Breakthrough in New York. *Phi Delta Kappan*, LIII (June, 1972), 622–25.

——. *The Future of Public Education.* Chicago: The University of Chicago Press, 1960.

——. "The Union Merger Movement: Will 3,500,000 Teachers Put it all Together." *Saturday Review*, LV (June 24, 1972), 50–56.

——, and Michael H. Moskow. *Collective Negotiations for Teachers: An Approach to School Administration.* Chicago: Rand McNally & Company, 1966.

Lierheimer, Alvin P. "An Anchor to Windward." *TEPS Write-in Papers on Flexible Staffing Patterns.* Washington, D.C.: National Commission on Teacher Education and Professional Standards, National Education Association, 1969.

——. "Changing the Palace Guard." *Phi Delta Kappan*, LII (September, 1970), pp. 20–25.

——. "Red-Faced Over Red Tape: Progress in Interstate Certification of Teachers." *Compact*, IV (April, 1970), 28–30.

Ligtenberg, John, and Miller, Charles W. *Landmark Cases in the History of the American Federation of Teachers.* Washington, D.C.: American Federation of Teachers.

Lindman, Erick L. "Are Teachers' Salaries IMPROVING?" *Phi Delta Kappan*, LI (April, 1970), 420–22.

Lindsey, Margaret. "Decision-Making and the Teacher." *Curriculum Crossroads.* A Report of a Curriculum Conference Sponsored by the Department of Curriculum and Teaching, Teachers College, Columbia University. Edited by A. Harry Passow. New York: Bureau of Publications, Teachers College, Columbia University, 1962, pp. 27–40.

Linn, John Phillip, and Nolte, M. Chester. "Guide to Collective Bargaining for Teachers." *Compact*, II (August, 1968), pp. 44–54.

Lortie, Dan C. "The Balance of Control and Autonomy in Elementary School Teaching." *The Semi-Professions and Their Organization: Teachers, Nurses, Social Workers.* Edited by Amitai Etzioni. New York: The Free Press, 1969, pp. 1–53.

Lucio, William H., and McNeil, John D. *Supervision: A Synthesis of Thought and Action.* 2d ed. New York: McGraw-Hill Book Company Inc., 1962.

Lutz, Frank W. "Local Power in the Teacher Group–School Board Relationship." *Struggle for Power in Education.* Edited by Frank W. Lutz, and Joseph Azzarelli. New York: The Center for Applied Research in Education, Inc., 1966, pp. 67–85.

——, and Azzarelli, Joseph (eds.). *Struggle for Power in Education.* New York: The Center for Applied Research in Education, Inc., 1966.

——; Kleinman, Lou; and Evans, Sy. *Grievances and Their Resolution: Problems in School Personnel Administration.* Danville, Ill.: The Interstate Printers & Publishers, Inc., 1967;

Marmion, Harry A. "Unions and Higher Education." *Educational Record*, XLIX (Winter, 1968), 41–48. A rebuttal to this article by Bertram H. Davis, is in a subsequent issue of the same journal (XLIX, Spring, 1968).

McGhan, Barry R., and Litz, Charles E. "The Anatomy of a Merger." *Phi Delta Kappan*, LI (June, 1970), 535–39.

McLennan, Kenneth, and Moskow, Michael H. "Resolving Impasses in Negotiations." *The Collective Dilemma: Negotiations in Education*. Edited by Patrick W. Carlton and Harold I. Goodwin. Worthington, Ohio: Charles A. Jones Publishing Company, 1969, pp. 197–204.

Merton, Robert K. "Bureaucratic Structure and Personality." *Social Theory and Social Structure*. Rev. and Enlarged Edition. Glencoe, Ill.: The Free Press, 1957, pp. 195–206.

——, Gray, Ailsa P., Hockey, Barbara, and Selvin, Hanan C. (eds.). *Reader in Bureaucracy*. Glencoe, Ill.: The Free Press, 1952.

Moeller, Gerald H., and Charters, W. W. "Relation of Bureaucratization to Sense of Power Among Teachers." *Administrative Science Quarterly*, X (March, 1966), 444–65.

Muir, J. Douglas. "The Tough New Teacher." *American School Board Journal*, CLVI (November, 1968), 9–14.

Murphy, Joseph S. "The Role of the American Arbitration Association in Public Education." *Readings on Collective Negotiations in Public Education*. Edited by Stanley M. Elam, Myron Lieberman, and Michael H. Moskow. Chicago: Rand McNally & Company, 1967, pp. 314–22.

Myers, Donald A. "Are Curriculum and Instruction Specialists Necessary?" *The California Journal for Instructional Improvement*, XII (March, 1969), 2–11.

——. *Decision Making in Curriculum and Instruction*. Melbourne, Fla.: Institute for Development of Educational Activities, Inc., 1970.

——. "The Principal as a Procedural Administrator." *The National Elementary Principal*, XLVII (February, 1968), 25–29.

National Association of Secondary School Principals. "Collective Negotiations." *The Bulletin*, LV (December, 1971).

National Education Association. *Negotiations for Improvement of the Profession: A Handbook for Local Teachers Associations Negotiators*. Washington, D.C.: The Association, 1971.

——, Research Division. *Grievance Procedures for Teachers in Negotiation Agreements*. Research Report 1969–R8. Washington, D.C.: The Association, 1969.

——. *High Spots in State School Legislation, January 1–August 31, 1969*. School Law Series. Research Report 1969–R12. Washington, D.C.: The Association, 1969.

——. *Paid Leave Provisions for Teachers in Negotiation Agreements*. Research Report 1969–R9. Washington, D.C.: The Association, 1969.

——. *Professional Negotiation with School Boards: A Legal Analysis and Review*. School Law Series. Research Report 1965–R3. Washington, D.C.: The Association, 1965.

——. *NEA Research Bulletin*. Washington, D.C.: The Association.

——. *Negotiation Research Digest*. Washington, D.C.: The Association.

Nimer, Gilda. Professions and Professionalism: A Bibliographic Overview. College Park, Maryland: School of Library and Information Services, University of Maryland, Manpower Research Project, Issue No. 2 (July, 1968).

Nolte, Chester M. *Status and Scope of Collective Bargaining in Public Education*. Eugene, Oregon: The ERIC Clearinghouse on Educational Administration, University of Oregon, 1970.

Norton, Gayle. "The Florida Story." *Phi Delta Kappan*, XLIX (June, 1968), 555–60.

Ohm, Robert E. "Collective Negotiations: Implications for Research." *Collective Negotiations and Educational Administration.* Edited by Roy B. Allen and John Schmid. Fayetteville, Arkansas, College of Education, University of Arkansas, and Columbus, Ohio: University Council for Educational Administration, pp. 97–113.

Oliver, John. *American Federation of Teachers, AFL-CIO, Survey of Teacher's Fringe Benefits and General Working Conditions in School Systems with 6,000 or More Pupils, 1968–69.* Washington, D.C.: American Federation of Teachers, AFL-CIO, 1969.

———. *Survey of Teachers' Salaries in U.S. Public School Systems, Statistical Appendix.* Washington, D.C.: American Federation of Teachers, AFL-CIO, January, 1971.

Olson, Jr., Mancur. *The Logic of Collective Action: Public Goods and the Theory of Groups.* Cambridge, Mass.: Harvard University Press, 1965.

Olson, Martin N. "Classroom Variables that Predict School System Quality." *IAR Research Bulletin*, XI (November, 1970), 1–11.

Owens, Robert G. *Organizational Behavior in Schools.* Englewood Cliffs, New Jersey: Prentice-Hall, Inc., 1970.

Parker, Hyman. "The New Michigan Labor Relations Law and Public School Teachers." *Readings on Collective Negotiations in Public Education.* Edited by Stanley M. Elam, Myron Lieberman, and Michael H. Moskow. Chicago: Rand McNally & Company, 1967, pp. 123–27.

Parker, Jack F. "Let's Abolish the NEA." *Phi Delta Kappan*, XLIX (June, 1968), 567–71.

Parker, Tom. "Collective Negotiations in Canadian Education." *Readings on Collective Negotiations in Public Education.* Edited by Stanley M. Elam, Myron Lieberman, and Michael H. Moskow. Chicago: Rand McNally & Company, 1967, pp. 128–42.

Paton, J. M. "Movements Toward Teacher Autonomy in Canada." *Phi Delta Kappan*, LII (September, 1970), 45–49.

———. "Trade Union or Professional Association? The Canadian Experience." *Phi Delta Kappan*, XLIX (June, 1968), 563–66.

Perry, Charles R., and Wildman, Wesley A. *The Impact of Negotiations in Public Education: The Evidence from the Schools.* Worthington, Ohio: Charles A. Jones Publishing Company, 1970.

*Phi Delta Kappan.* A professional education journal available to members of Phi Delta Kappa professional fraternity or to any interested person.

Pindara, Wally. "Negotiations in Canada, Implications for the American Scene." *Above the Salt: Militancy in Education. Proceedings on Mont Chateau Conference on Collective Negotiations in Education.* Morgantown, West Va.: College of Human Resources and Education, West Virginia University, and West Virginia Education Association, March, 1968, pp. 62–66.

Piven, Frances Fox. "Militant Civil Servants in New York City." *Trans-Action*, VII (November, 1969), 24–28, 55.

Punch, Keith F. "Bureaucratic Structure in Schools: Towards Redefinition and Measurement." Educational Administration Quarterly, V (Spring, 1969), 43–57.

*QuEST Papers*. Published several times each year by the Department of Research, American Federation of Teacher.

*Research Reports*. Publications of the Research Division, National Education Association.

Rice, Arthur H. "Where the Action Is." *California Teachers Association Journal*, LXIV (October, 1968), 31–38.

Roe, William H. "State Regulation of Education." *Encyclopedia of Educational Research*. Edited by Robert L. Ebel. 4th Edition. New York: The Macmillan Company, 1969, pp. 1299–1307.

Rosenthal, Alan (ed.). *Governing Education: A Reader on Politics, Power, and Public School Policy*. Garden City, New York: Doubleday & Company, Inc., 1969.

——. *Pedagogues and Power: Teacher Groups in School Politics*. Syracuse, New York: Syracuse University Press, 1969.

Rubin, Louis J. (ed.). *Improving In-Service Education: Proposals and Procedures for Change*. Boston: Allyn and Bacon, Inc., 1971.

Ryan, David G. *Characteristics of Teachers: Their Description, Comparison, and Appraisal*. Washington, D.C.: American Council on Education, 1960.

Schmuck, Richard, and Nelson, Jack. "The Principal as Convener of Organizational Problem Solving." Center for the Advanced Study of Educational Administration, University of Oregon. Mimeographed.

Scott, W. Richard. "Professionals in Bureaucracies—Areas of Conflict, (General)." *Professionalization*. Edited by Howard M. Vollmer and Donald L. Mills. Englewood Cliffs, New Jersey: Prentice-Hall, Inc., 1966, 265–75.

Scott, Walter W. "Collective Negotiations: Implications for Preparation of Administrators." *Collective Negotiations and Educational Administration*. Edited by Roy B. Allen and John Schmid. Fayetteville, Arkansas: College of Education, University of Arkansas, and Columbus, Ohio: University Council for Educational Administration, pp. 81–96.

Selden, David. "Evaluate Teachers?" *QuEST Paper 4*. Washington, D.C.: Department of Research, American Federation of Teachers, n.d., 1–5.

——. "Evaluate Teachers?" *The ISR Journal*, I (Spring, 1969), 106–10.

——. "Giant Step Toward Teacher Unity." *American Teacher* (May, 1972), 2B.

——. *QuEST Paper 5*. Washington, D.C.: Department of Research, American Federation of Teachers.

——. "Winning Collective Bargaining." *Readings on Collective Negotiations in Public Education*. Edited by Stanley M. Elam, Myron Lieberman, and Michael H. Moskow. Chicago: Rand McNally & Company, 1967, pp. 333–49.

——, and Bhaerman, Robert. "Instructional Technology and the Teaching Profession." *QuEST Paper 6*. Washington, D.C.: Department of Research, American Federation of Teachers, n.d.

Seymour, F. J. C. "What is Professionalism?" *The ATA Magazine* (June, 1963), 20–23.

Shanker, Albert. "The Future of Teacher Involvement in Educational Decision Making." *The Collective Dilemma: Negotiations in Education*. Edited by Patrick W. Carlton and Harold I. Goodwin. Worthington, Ohio: Charles A. Jones Publishing Company, 1969, pp. 76–83.

Shils, Edward B., and Whittier, C. Taylor. *Teachers, Administrators and Collective Bargaining*. New York: Thomas Y. Crowell Company, 1968.

Sibelman, Larry. "Merger in Los Angeles." *American Teacher*, LVI (October, 1971), 24.

Simpson, Richard L., and Simpson, Ida Harper. "Women and Bureaucracy in the Semi-Professions." *The Semi-Professions and Their Organization: Teachers, Nurses, Social Workers*. Edited by Amitai Etzioni. New York: The Free Press, 1969, pp. 196–265.

Slavney, Morrow. "Impasse Procedures in Public Education." *Readings on Collective Negotiations in Public Education*. Edited by Stanley M. Elam, Myron Lieberman, and Michael H. Moskow. Chicago: Rand McNally & Company, 1967, pp. 426–32.

Smith, B. Othanel, in collaboration with Saul B. Cohen and Arthur Pearl. *Teachers for the Real World*. Washington, D.C.: The American Association of Colleges for Teacher Education, 1969.

Solomon, Benjamin. "A Comment on 'The Authority Structure of the School'." *Educational Administration Quarterly*, III (Autumn, 1967), 281–90.

——. "A Profession Taken for Granted." *The School Review*, LXIX (Autumn, 1961), 286–99.

Sperling, John G. "Collective Bargaining and the Teaching Learning Process." *QuEST Paper 11*. Washington, D.C.: Department of Research, American Federation of Teachers, n.d.

Stanley, William O. "Issues in Teacher Professionalization." *Bulletin of the School of Education*, Indiana University, XXXX (September, 1964), 1–8.

Staudohar, Paul D. "Fact-Finding for Settlement of Teacher Labor Disputes." *Phi Delta Kappan*, LI (April, 1970), 422–25.

Stinnett, T. M. (ed.). *The Teacher Dropout*. Bloomington, Indiana: Phi Delta Kappa, Incorporated, 1970.

——. *Turmoil in Teaching: A History of the Organizational Struggle for America's Teachers*. New York: The Macmillan Company, 1968.

——, and Huggett, Albert J. *Professional Problems of Teachers*. 2d Edition. New York: The Macmillan Company, 1963.

——; Kleinmann, Jack H.; and Ware, Martha L. *Professional Negotiation in Public Education*. New York: The Macmillan Company, 1966.

——, with the assistance of Geraldine E. Pershing. *A Manual on Certification Requirements for School Personnel in the United States, 1970 Edition*. Washington, D.C.: National Education Association, Commission on Teacher Education and Professional Standards, 1970.

Sutherland, Edwin H. *The Professional Thief*. Chicago: The University of Chicago Press, 1937. See especially pp. 197–206, 215–17.

Taylor, George W. "The Public Interest in Collective Negotiations in Education." *Phi Delta Kappan*, XLVIII (September, 1966), 16–22.

*Theory Into Practice*. "Teacher Power." Columbus, Ohio: College of Education, The Ohio State University. VII (April, 1968).

Thompson, Victor A. *Bureaucracy and Innovation*. University, Alabama: University of Alabama Press, 1969.

*Today's Education*. Washington, D.C.: National Education Association. Published monthly except for June, July, and August.

Tyler, Louise L. "A Code of Ethics for Educators." *The Clearing House*, XL (January, 1966), 263–66.

———. "Is Teaching a Profession?" *The Educational Forum*, XXVIII (May, 1964), 413–21.

Vander Werf, Lester S. "Militancy and the Profession of Teaching." *School and Society*, XCVIII (March, 1970), 171–73.

Vollmer, Howard M., and Mills, Donald L. (eds.). *Professionalization*. Englewood Cliffs, New Jersey: Prentice-Hall, Inc., 1966.

Walton, Richard E., and McKersie, Robert B. *A Behavioral Theory of Labor Negotiations:* An Analysis of a Social Interaction System. New York: McGraw-Hill Book Co., 1965.

Warner, Kenneth O. "What Does Public Management Think About Collective Bargaining in the Public Service?" *The Collective Dilemma: Negotiations in Education*. Worthington, Ohio: Charles A. Jones Publishing Company, 1969.

Watson, Bernard C. "The Principal: Forgotten Man in Negotiations." *Administrator's Notebook*, XV (October, 1966).

Wayland, Sloan R. "The Teacher as Decision-Maker." *Curriculum Crossroads*. A Report of a Curriculum Conference Sponsored by the Department of Curriculum and Teaching, Teachers College, Columbia University. Edited by A. Harry Passow. New York: Bureau of Publications, Teachers College, Columbia University, 1962, pp. 41–52.

Webb, Harold. "The National School Boards Association and Collective Negotiations." *Readings on Collective Negotiations in Public Education*. Edited by Stanley M. Elam, Myron Lieberman, and Michael H. Moskow. Chicago: Rand McNally & Company, 1967, pp. 196–202.

Whittier, C. Taylor. "Teacher Power as Viewed by the School Board and Superintendent." *Theory Into Practice*, The Ohio State University VII (April, 1968), 76–79.

Wildman, Wesley A. "What's Negotiable?" *American School Board Journal*, CLV (November, 1967), 7–10.

Williams, James O. "Professionalism and Bureaucracy: Natural Conflict." *The Bulletin of the National Association of Secondary School Principals* entitled "Collective Negotiations," LV (December, 1971, 61–68.

Williams, Richard C. "A Proposal for Improving the Selection and Evaluation of Public School Teachers." Paper distributed and discussed at IDEA, Research Division, Los Angeles, California, May 4, 1970. Mimeographed.

———. "An Academic Alternative to Collective Negotiations." *Phi Delta Kappan*, XLIX (June, 1968), 571–74.

———. "Teacher Militancy: Implications for the Schools." *Social and Technological Changes: Implications for Schools*. Edited by Philip K. Piele and Terry L. Eidell, with Stuart C. Smith. Eugene, Oregon: The Center for the Advanced Study of Educational Administration, University of Oregon, pp. 71–118.

Wirtz, W. Willard. "Public Employment and Public Policy." *Readings on Collective Negotiations in Public Education*. Edited by Stanley M. Elam, Myron Lieberman, and Michael H. Moskow. Chicago: Rand McNally & Company, 1967, pp. 5–10.

Wittlin, Alma S. "The Teacher." *Daedalus: The Professions*, XCII (Fall, 1963), 745–63.

Wollett, Donald H. "The Strategy of Negotiation." *Readings on Collective Negotiations in Public Education*. Edited by Stanley M. Elam, Myron Lieberman, and Michael H. Moskow. Chicago: Rand McNally & Company, 1967, pp. 364–80.

Wynn, Richard. "Collective Bargaining." *Phi Delta Kappan*, LI (April, 1970), 415–19.

Yevish, Irving A. "Decentralization, Discipline, and the Disadvantaged Teacher." *Phi Delta Kappan*, L (November, 1968), 137–38, 178–81.

Young, Charles R. "The Superintendent of Schools in a Collective Bargaining Milieu." *The Collective Dilemma: Negotiations in Education*. Edited by Patrick W. Carlton and Harold I. Goodwin. Worthington, Ohio: Charles A. Jones Publishing Company, 1969, pp. 102–13.

Ziegler, Harmon. *The Political World of the High School Teacher*. Eugene, Oregon: The Center for the Advanced Study of Educational Administration, 1966.

Zeluck, Stephen. "The UFT Strike: Will It Destroy the AFT?" *Phi Delta Kappan*, L (January, 1969), 250–54.

# INDEX

AFL–CIO, 131
Accrediting agencies, 61
Administrators, 59–60, 107–18
American Federation of Teachers, 21, 95, 96,
    128, 131, 135, 136, 138, 140, 141, 144,
    150
American Medical Association, 99, 132
Anderson, James G., 13, 40, 83, 129
Appollo-Ridge Elementary Education Associa-
    tion, 140
Autonomy, 27–28, 49, 66
Azzarelli, Joseph J., 115–16

Beck, William R., 108–9
Becker, Howard S., 51, 87
Becker and Solomon, 51
Bhaerman, Robert D., 128, 133–34
Bidwell, Charles E., 82, 110
Bishop, Lloyd K., 56
Blau, Peter M., and W. Richard, Scott, 80, 87
Boards of education, 78, 116–18
Bowles, Chester A., 132
Bridges, Edwin M., 113, 115
Burden, Joel, xv
Bureaucracy: education and, 82; nature of,
    80–81; school as a, 73–88

Campbell et al., 75–77
Carlton, Patrick W., 105
Carr-Saunders, Sir Alexander Morris, 63–64
Cass, James, 99, 120
Centralization, 9
Certification, 26, 39–41
Citizens' Committee for Equal Justice for
    Public Employees, 100
Civil disobedience, 96–98
Collective bargaining, 3, 89–105, 116–18,
    120–21, 129–31, 140–41, 145
College Entrance Board examinations, 61
Community: control of schools by, 122–25,
    goals of, 55
Competence, 55–56
Conant, James Bryant, 32, 40
Continuity and sequence, need for, 58
Corwin, Ronald G., 82, 83, 102, 115, 123
Cuisenaire Rods, 13–14

Darland, David D., xv, 35, 142
DeCecco, Dominick, xv
Decision-making, 59, 60–62, 86
Dewey, John, 37
Diene's multi-base arithmetic blocks, 13-14

Differentiated staffing, 135–37
Donovan, Bernard E., 116
Duke, Daniel, xv

*Education as a Profession,* xv
Educational Research Service, 94
Elam, Stanley M., 44
Elementary and Secondary Education Act, 75
Erickson, Ellwood R., xv, 111
Etzioni, Amitai, 32, 55, 64–67, 71, 111
Evaluation and tenure, 143–44

Facilities, limitations of, 57
Faculty: local school, 148–49; recruitment
    and   selection, 147
Flexner, Abraham, 21–22
Frymier, Jack R., 132
Functionary, teacher as, 53–62

Galbraith, John Kenneth, 96
Gerstl, Joel E., 45, 48, 82
Gittell, Marilyn, 92, 122, 124–25
Godine, Morton R., 50, 113
Goldhammer, Keith, and Gerald L. Becker,
    114–15
Goode, William, 37
Goodlad, John, xv, 127
Goodman, 54
Greenwood, Ernest, 23, 24
Guba, Egon G., 109, 110
Guthrie, Harold, 44

Hall, Richard H., 35, 49–50
Haller, Emil J., 33
Head Start, 122
Hottleman, Girard, xv, 127, 147
Hruby, Mary, xv

Illich, 54
Income, 27, 43–45
In-service education, 127–29, 143, 148
Institute of Administrative Research, 134

Jackson, Philip W., 33, 127–28
Jacobs, Leland B., 35, 36
Johnson, David W., 17, 54
Joyce, Betsy, xv
Joyce, Bruce, xv, 136

Kennedy, John F., 92
Klein, Donald C., 113, 123
Koerner, James D., 32, 61

# ABOUT THE AUTHOR

**Donald Myers** received the B.A. at the University of Nebraska, Omaha, and the M.A. and Ph.D. in education at the University of Chicago.

He taught for three years at Thornton Township High School and Junior College, Harvey, Illinois; was principal of a junior and senior high school in Nebraska; director of research at Pattonville R-3 School District, St. Louis County, Missouri; assistant superintendent of schools, School District of Riverview Gardens, St. Louis County, Missouri; research specialist in the Center for the Study of Instruction, National Education Association; and research specialist at the Institute for Development of Educational Activities, Inc., Los Angeles.

He has been on the staff at Washington University, California Western University, George Peabody College, and the University of California, Los Angeles. He is presently an associate professor in the department of Curriculum and Instruction, the State University of New York, Albany.

In the past five years, he has authored or coauthored four books and monographs as well as dozens of articles, including an annotated bibliography concerning teacher professionalization and collective bargaining for the American Federation of Teachers.